VerAegis

Spirit:
Live beyond Your Comfort Zone

~~Touch~~ Live a Life

~~Inspire~~ Make a Contribution

~~Ignite~~ Kindle a Spirit

James M. Haden

The Legacy Series

MW01292192

Books by James M. Haden

The Legacy Series:
VerAegis—Relationships
VerAegis—Contribution
VerAegis—Spirit

ISBN-10: **151228792X**
ISBN 13: **978-1512287929**

Dedication

I dedicate *VerAegis* to my wife, Sheri; my daughter, Teagan; and my son, Jimmy, whom I love and cherish deeply.

To all who read *VerAegis*:

In the Legacy Series, I've tried to capture many thoughts and cover some deep topics while keeping it simple and fun. This book series is designed to be an entertaining and informative reference for all aspects of everyday life. I hope that you are stimulated and challenged by *VerAegis—Spirit* and will find something of use and perhaps even life changing between its covers.

If you can't explain it simply, you don't understand it well enough.

Albert Einstein

Words are, of course, the most powerful drug used by mankind.

Rudyard Kipling

Table of Contents

Table of Figures

Introduction

It's all about quality of life and finding a happy balance between work and friends and family.

Sir Philip Green

The greatest obstacle to discovery is not ignorance—it is the illusion of knowledge.

Daniel J. Boorstin

I believe that being successful means having a balance of success stories across the many areas of your life. You can't truly be considered successful in your business life if your home life is in shambles.

Zig Ziglar

It isn't until you come to a spiritual understanding of who you are—not necessarily a religious feeling, but deep down, the spirit within—that you can begin to take control.

Oprah Winfrey

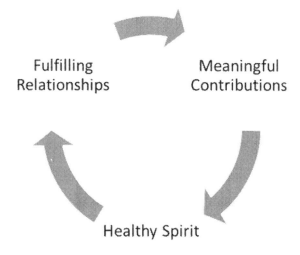

Fulfilling Relationships

Meaningful Contributions

Healthy Spirit

I have learned that age is necessary but not sufficient for gaining wisdom. Throughout my formative years of elementary and high school, many (if not all) of my teachers and coaches stressed that not only should I alone be an optimist but we should all view a partially filled glass as half-full rather than half-empty. At that time in my life, I reasoned that both views were (for all intents and purposes) equivalent and that my paradigm du jour would depend largely on my fondness for the liquid therein contained: was it a struggle to finish the task at hand, or did I savor every last sip, enjoying the challenge and potential reward?

Later in life, I read Jim Collins's book *Good to Great* and learned of the so-called Stockdale paradox. Collins described Admiral Jim Stockdale's tale of imprisonment and torture at the "Hanoi Hilton," a Vietnam prisoner-of-war camp. Stockdale was tortured over twenty times during his eight years of imprisonment from 1965 to 1973. As a prisoner, he had neither rights nor any idea of when he would be released. Yet he survived the horrific ordeal. Stockdale explained to Collins that the optimists didn't make it; they simply died of broken hearts as their expectations (based on unfounded hopes) were repeatedly dashed. They thought, "We'll be out by Christmas...Easter...summer," and each letdown killed part of their hearts until they eventually succumbed to despair. Stockdale went on to explain a profoundly important lesson about those who prevailed: "You must never confuse faith that you will prevail in the end—which you can never afford to lose—with the discipline to confront the most brutal facts of your current reality, whatever they might be (2001)."

I imagine the pessimists died next, as they did not have faith that they would prevail, and without hope, they had nothing to live for. Who was left? I like to refer to the survivors as pragmatic optimists. Jim Collins refers to the survivor phenomenon as the Stockdale paradox. Survivors are those who:

- are willing to face and deal with the reality of their situation, however dismal (pragmatic in attitude and action);

- are confident that they will prevail (retain an optimistic attitude); and

- do not set arbitrary goals based on false hopes (balance optimism with an equally pragmatic attitude).

Brian Dyson, former CEO of Coca-Cola from 1986 to 1991, delivered a memorable and inspirational speech to his many employees. In the speech, Dyson addressed a reality of life: we each have a great deal to balance, but when we approach our opportunities and problems in a healthy manner, we can prevail. To a great extent, I believe this speech is a reflection of Dyson's pragmatic optimism. My daughter, Teagan, was a newborn when a friend e-mailed a copy of Mr. Dyson's speech to me. At the time, I was working twelve to sixteen hours a day and trying to keep up with an increasing workload. Teagan was asleep when I left for work and, more often than not, asleep when I returned home. I read and reread this short, simple, yet powerful speech.

> Imagine life as a game in which you are juggling some five balls in the air. You name them—*work, family, health, friends*, and *spirit*...and you're keeping all of these in the air.

> You will soon understand that *work* is a rubber ball. If you drop it, it will bounce back. But the other four balls—*family, health, friends*, and *spirit*—are made of glass. If you drop one of these, they will be irrevocably scuffed, marked, nicked, damaged, or even shattered. They will never be the same. You must understand that and strive for it...Work efficiently during office hours and leave on time. Give proper time to your family and friends, and have proper rest. Value has a value only if its value is valued.

I lived and worked in Silicon Valley. My twenty-mile commute was so congested that I rode my bike two to four times a week to avoid traffic—and to take advantage of the opportunity to exercise. Riding 80 to 160 miles per week kept me in pretty good physical condition, but I was unable to sit for much more than ninety minutes without suffering shooting pain down my back and the side of my right leg. I walked to the office of a mentor and told him of my predicament. No matter what hours I worked, I could not keep up. "What should I do?" I asked. He smiled wryly and replied that when work becomes overwhelming, the only thing you can do is work more!

There I stood, with two pagers (one for general purposes—the other for emergency response) and a cell phone, feeling like roadkill on the information highway. I was in complete shock; the only advice he gave was to work more. I quietly left his office and mentally fired him as a mentor. On the way back to my office, I noticed a flyer advertising a lunchtime stress-management seminar scheduled for noon the next day. I cleared my calendar.

The next morning at eleven thirty, I snuck into the lunchroom, grabbed my sack lunch, and stealthily made my way into the conference room to await the seminar. Fifteen minutes later, the door opened. The presenter walked in, turned on the light, and was surprised to find me eating in the dark. She was taken aback when I explained that I had to be stealthy in order to avoid being pulled into some sort of crisis-management situation. I paraphrased Brian's speech to her and explained my situation. We spoke for a few minutes longer, until she had to set up for the class. As she prepared, I thought about our conversation in relation to Dyson's simple speech, and a powerful concept emerged: the consequences of stress are varied, but one thing is certain—as long as your actions are not aligned with your beliefs and values, you will remain stressed.

Considering the concept—aligning actions to values and beliefs—in conjunction with Brian Dyson's speech—and assuming that we truly believe that there is more to life than work, we must conclude that we need to allocate ample time to nurture (juggle) the glass balls in order to avoid undue stress. This stress will manifest itself in one or more of many symptoms, including anxiety, anger, aches, pains, and even illnesses. Once stress manifests itself as physical and emotional ailments, it is likely that we have already dropped the health ball, with the family, friends, and spirit balls not far behind.

The seminar concluded, and I left at one o'clock sharp. I called my wife, Sheri, and asked what time she was planned to have dinner. After she picked herself up from the floor (only a slight exaggeration of her surprise), we agreed to begin having family dinners each night at six thirty; I would call in advance if for some reason I could not make it on time. Within two weeks of eating together as a family, my back and leg pains were gone. I was in better spirits. I felt better, both physically and mentally. My family was happy, and (believe it or not) things got better at work—not worse.

In life, we are faced time and again with challenging circumstances, situations, and people who tend to pull us away from our intended paths. Yet we are defined not by these problems but by our responses to them. As Jesus stated over two thousand years ago, "If a house is divided against itself, that house cannot stand" (Mark 3:25 [NIV]). It follows that if our actions are "divided" against our beliefs, we "cannot stand"; the stress will take its toll. The solution is that when negatively (or even positively) motivated, we must choose to respond with an approach in line with our beliefs and values.

Upon further consideration of Brian Dyson's speech, we find that the balls we juggle fall into three primary sectors of our lives:

- Relationships: Family, friends, coworkers, mentors, and so on

- Contribution: Work, or what we give back

- Spirit: Spiritual and physical well-being. Are you in good spirits or ill-tempered and in poor spirits?

Essentially, the key to our effectiveness and ultimately our happiness is responding to life in a manner that balances relationships, contribution, and spirit. Note that spiritual and physical health are combined into the single category of spirit. This was done purposefully, because while physical health may falter and eventually fail, your spirit need not. I believe the combined message is that we need to be pragmatically optimistic that despite living in a chaotic world of information overload, we not only can focus our efforts on—but have the responsibility to focus on that which is important—not only on what is fun or urgent. Furthermore, the ability to focus; to direct the majority of our effort toward our highest priorities, is vital to our effectiveness.

Visualize life as a three-legged stool. One leg represents the health of your relationships, the next the impact of your contributions (negative or positive), and the final the health of your spirit. If one leg is short, the stool (your life) is wobbly and unstable. With two short legs, it is terribly wobbly and will possibly topple or collapse. Only with three solid legs will the stool effectively support the weight of its burden (Figure 1).

Figure 1: Being balanced and effective is possible only with three strong legs. Our relationships, sense of contribution, and spirits all must be healthy in order to achieve lasting effectiveness.

Accordingly, this series is organized into three books. Each book is represented by one leg of the stool:

- Relationships: Live your life. Touch another.
- Contribution: Make a difference. Inspire another.
- Spirit: Kindle your spirit. Ignite another.

A common thread links each of these three books: you *will* leave a legacy. It is within your power and responsibility to leave the legacy you desire.

Why *VerAegis*? Being VerAegis (Vĕr-ā-jis) represents a way of life that leads to balance between our contributions, our relationships, and the manner in which we approach life—our spirt. With balance comes the ability to significantly expand our comfort zones and be the authors of our legacies. Being VerAegis is daring to stretch beyond our current comfort zones.

Book 1 is devoted to relationships. Humans are social beings who rely on one another—not solely for survival but to derive the most from ourselves and from life. We will learn how to better manage our closest relationships while pondering the meanings of maturity, trust, and setting appropriate boundaries based on convictions and principles. We will consider reconciliation and the importance of family. We will dig into the fundamentals of thought and how to best manage change rather than becoming roadkill on the information highway. Most of all, we will enjoy our journey together.

Book 2 is devoted to our contribution—our ability to positively impact others. We often define ourselves by what we do, the impact we create, and the lives we affect. Not many people reach the end of their days lamenting that they should have worked more; in Book 2, we will dig into tools and techniques to help us to work smarter and learn how to better manage our finances and our time. We will learn how to set boundaries that allow us the freedom to think creatively about our contributions while balancing our time so that we do not neglect relationships or ourselves. We will dig more deeply into the applications of the fundamentals of thought and how to apply what we learned in Book 1. We will also expand the concept of change management and show how this simple model can be used to manage both innovation and continuous improvement. Finally we will investigate how to dream of a better us—a better future—and then how to set goals and make better decisions so that we can reach those dreams.

Book 3 is devoted to our spirit—our ability to positively influence others. We are often judged by how we achieve our accomplishments;

how we impact the lives of those with whom we interact. We need to learn to set boundaries on how we relate to others as we manage our relationships and our contribution. Not many people reach the end of their days lamenting that they were loved by too many—or loved too many people. In Book 3, we will dig into how the choices we make affect our spirits and how our spirits influence our closest relationships. We will learn how to recognize and turn away from temptations and how to help others do so as well. We dig more deeply into principles and values and discuss in more detail the need to balance courage with consideration. We will learn about the purpose of anger and how to better manage our frustrations. We will ponder the golden rule, and we will learn of the need to call upon a higher authority to genuinely achieve our full potential. We will learn of parables and true stories of life. We will consider the legacies of well-known public figures whose values became misaligned with principles. Finally we will investigate how to invoke self-discipline and tap into an infinite source of power to better ourselves. We will learn to leverage the nature of our spirits to increase the value of our relationships and our contributions. We will learn to live beyond our comfort zones.

VerAegis Book 3: Spirit Is Vital to Relationships, Success, and the Value of Our Contribution

Be whole in a manner that ignites a spirit. What better way to bestow a legacy?

Great spirits have always encountered violent opposition from mediocre minds.

Albert Einstein

I never considered a difference of opinion in politics, in religion, in philosophy, as cause for withdrawing from a friend.

Thomas Jefferson

Spiritual relationship is far more precious than physical. Physical relationship divorced from spiritual is body without soul.

Mahatma Gandhi

You have to decide what your highest priorities are and have the courage (pleasantly, smilingly, non-apologetically) to say "no" to other things. And the way you do that is to have a bigger "yes" burning inside.

Stephen Covey

Will your burning yes be the drive to leave a legacy by freeing your good spirit to ignite the spirit of others?

What is it that makes some people more likable than others? Why do some of us have great résumés and work-lives but a succession of failed marriages and broken relationships? Why do others have great friendships but cannot hold a decent job? Perhaps even more perplexing…why do some people seem to have it altogether?

Spirit. People who strive to have great spirits have made a conscious decision. A Bible proverb states: "If you falter in a time of trouble, how small is your strength!" (Proverbs 24:10 [NIV]). In other words, spirt (attitude) is important! When faced with life's struggles and tragedies, when faced with times of trouble—people of strong spirit decide to respond in the most positive and proactive manner possible, refusing to be victims of circumstance. People of great spirit will always encounter problems, temptations, and tribulations, but it is their response that sets them apart. They embrace differences and will not abandon a conviction or friendship just because opinions and beliefs differ. They have created effective boundaries to let the good in and keep the bad out. They happily invest in others and often are intimately connected with a greater force, a universal force that provides energy in good times and bad. With this external connection, they forge ahead, "pleasantly, smilingly, non-apologetically," saying no to temptations and yes to their highest priorities—to their fire within. Will your burning yes be the drive to leave a legacy by unleashing your good spirit to ignite the spirit of others?

You will always harvest what you plant. Those who live only to satisfy their own sinful nature will harvest decay and death from that sinful nature. But those who live to please the Spirit will harvest everlasting life from the Spirit.

Gal. 6:7–8

Choices Are Linked to the Well-Being of Our Spirit

Today I choose life. Every morning when I wake up I can choose joy, happiness, negativity, pain...To feel the freedom that comes from being able to continue to make mistakes and choices—today I choose to feel life, not to deny my humanity but embrace it.

Kevyn Aucoin

When you wake up every day, you have two choices. You can either be positive or negative; an optimist or a pessimist. I choose to be an [pragmatic] optimist. It's all a matter of perspective.

Harvey Mackay

Remembering that I'll be dead soon is the most important tool I've ever encountered to help me make the big choices in life. Because almost everything—all external expectations, all pride, all fear of embarrassment or failure—these things just fall away in the face of death, leaving only what is truly important.

Steve Jobs

One's philosophy is not best expressed in words; it is expressed in the choices one makes...and the choices we make are ultimately our responsibility.

Eleanor Roosevelt

Billy Moore, a twenty-two-year-old army private, was training to become an electrical engineer based at Fort Gordon, Georgia. It was 1974, and he had just returned to Georgia from his deployment in Germany to find his wife involved with a drug dealer and addicted to heroin. Billy wasted no time: he moved his preschool-aged son into a trailer, away from the dangerous environment his wife had created for their son.

Billy's paychecks, however, were in his wife's name, and the army required ninety days to make any change. Billy unsuccessfully sought help from various charities and pleaded with the military to expedite the process. He explained that his paychecks were required to care for his son, but they could move no faster (Richardson). Billy had become desperate when one night, a drinking buddy told him about seventy-seven-year-old Fred Stapleton. "He told me that Mr. Stapleton kept between twenty and thirty thousand dollars in his house," Billy later reported. "I borrowed a gun, and after drinking beer and a bottle of Jack Daniels, I followed my friend to the house." The two would-be robbers were thwarted by a locked door, but Billy later returned alone. Recalling the incident, he said, "I had intended to go home, but then, somehow, I found myself outside Mr. Stapleton's house. I went inside and it was pitch black. I moved around trying doors, and then I heard a door open and felt something against my leg. It was a shotgun. Suddenly, it exploded. I grabbed hold of the shotgun, pulled my gun out of my pants and shot back. I heard a thump to the floor and when I turned on the light, there he lay. There was no blood that I could see. He was just lying still" (James 2008). Billy grabbed a couple of wallets and the shotgun before fleeing the scene.

Billy believed he would walk into Stapleton's house, take the money, and run. He did not intend to kill anyone. He returned home, sobered up, and realized that he was a murderer. Billy was horrified. With one heinous act, he had in effect abandoned his son, and as this realization took hold, it crushed his spirit. Billy was so devastated that he was actually relieved when he was arrested the next day. The sheriff, righteously angered by the murder of the elderly Stapleton, informed Billy that he would not stop until Billy received a death sentence. Billy was devastated by the weight of his crime and was not fazed by the sheriff's promise; he wanted to die. Billy confessed to the murder, was quickly found guilty, and was sentenced to death.

Before moving from California's Silicon Valley to Washington State, my family and I attended the First Community Church, led by Pastor Bill Bucholtz, who professed routinely that we are all born with a God-shaped hole in our hearts and that only one thing can fill a God-shaped hole. The problem is that many, if not most, try to fill this emptiness by other means: fancy clothes, nice cars, food, sex, drugs, alcohol, our children, marriage, church, politics, or even our job. Notice that not all of these are "bad" things, but what happens when we raise good things to the level of idolatry? What happens in a marriage where one spouse places the needs of the children above all else? What happens to relationships when one person in the relationship places his or her job at the center of life, as his or her most valued possession? What happens to friendships when one becomes obsessed with drugs, alcohol, money, or success? What happens when a wife becomes obsessed with drugs and then becomes disloyal to her husband to support her habit? What happens to her child, her marriage, and her home? What happens when the father turns to alcohol as a means of escape when he cannot seem to resolve his problems? Bad things happen, even to "good" people. In the case of Billy Moore, theft and murder happened. He became a confessed murderer sentenced to death. He had forfeited his life and abandoned his son. What might have happened had he tried to fill the God-shaped hole in his life with God instead of alcohol, self-pity, and bad advice from a poorly informed friend?

Many, if not all, grapple with the issue of a God-shaped hole, and I believe that in some way, each of us longs for a reason to exist and likely for a relationship with and better understanding of our creator (though some may profess we were not created, there is still a longing that cannot be appeased by the material comforts of this world). We witness the grand design of our world each day from the seas to the mountains, from the expanse of the heavens to the microscopic mysteries of the individual atom. We wonder how this could all be an accident spawned from random interactions of inert matter. We long for something that we do not understand. How do we fill this void? How do we resist temptations and successfully cull the invitations to do what is right from those to do what is wrong? We are influenced by many things—by both our earthly idols and our spiritual creator. How do we avoid placing an idol at the center of our lives and realize when we have done exactly that?

Arthur Gordon is the author of fourteen books and a former editor of *Good Housekeeping, Cosmopolitan,* and *Guideposts* magazines, as well as a contributing author to such publications as *Reader's Digest, Esquire, Collier's,* the *Saturday Evening Post, McCall's,* and *Redbook.* Gordon was born in Georgia into a well-known family: his great-grandfather, William Gordon, founded the Georgia Railroad, and his aunt, Juliette Gordon Low, started the Girl Scouts. Arthur Gordon graduated from Yale University and spent two years at Oxford as a Rhodes scholar, after which he found work at *Good Housekeeping.* Within five years, he became the magazine's managing editor. During World War II, Gordon spent three years overseas as an intelligence officer with the Eighth Air Force and met his wife, Pamela Bartlett. Gordon left the service in 1945 as a lieutenant colonel and returned to the publishing business working for the Hearst Corporation as the editor of *Cosmopolitan.* In 1985, he told the *Savannah Morning News,* "It's been a very lucky life, I think. I've been lucky in the things I've been able to do. And I was lucky in my childhood. It was a happy one. A writer is supposed to have all sorts of terrible trauma, but I don't think I had any" (SavannahNow). Gordon was perhaps best known for his book *A Touch of Wonder,* which is a collection of essays describing life along the Georgia coast. In a chapter entitled "The Turn of the Tide," Gordon may not have had all "sorts of terrible trauma," but he describes a period in his life that was trying and bleak, as most of us encounter at one point or another.

Gordon came from a successful family. He was also extremely successful and happy in his own right, with blessings far beyond most. Yet his life became unbalanced; something was wrong, and he felt lost! Gordon felt run-down and struggled during a "sudden drastic dip in the graph of living, when everything [was] stale and flat." When other courses of action were exhausted, Gordon consulted his family doctor, informing him that he had lost enthusiasm and felt that his writing efforts were useless; the situation was worsening each day. After ruling out any serious physical ailments, his doctor suggested that Gordon spend a day away from home, phones, people, and tasks in a place that had made him happy during his youth. Gordon agreed he would; the doctor scribbled out four prescriptions, each to be read at three-hour intervals, starting at nine o'clock the next morning.

Gordon faithfully went to one of his favorite beaches along the Georgia coast the following morning. At nine o'clock, he dutifully opened the first prescription and read, "Listen carefully." Gordon sat and did as instructed. He wondered how he could sit and just listen for three entire hours. Soon the sounds of the seabirds singing, the waves rolling in and out, and the breeze gusting gently filled his ears and his heart. As he listened intently, he felt peace and warmth growing within. He contemplated and relished this feeling. To his surprise and chagrin, noon came all too quickly.

He opened the second prescription: "Try reaching back." As Gordon considered the meaning of the prescription, he worried that three hours of "reaching back" was far too long. The gentle sounds of the beach once again filled his being. He pondered the prescription further, and soon memories of happy occasions and life's lessons began to resurface. His recollections began slowly, but soon they were flooding back. He relived times of happiness, sorrow, achievement, fulfillment, and struggle. These memories were accompanied by a sense of warmth, satisfaction, fulfillment, and confidence.

15

Three o'clock came quickly. Gordon was excited for the third prescription: "Examine your motives." The first two prescriptions had not been difficult, but this third was quite trying. What did the doctor mean? Gordon deliberated. He was initially defensive. He justified his desires for success, recognition, and security. But as he thought more deeply, it gradually dawned on him that his present endeavors, primarily aimed at satisfying his own needs, were somehow not enough. This gap, this void in contribution, was the cause of his "bleak" situation. He contemplated his motives more deeply. His deepest thoughts, memories, and core motivations became more tangible, and in a sudden moment of clarity, he found his answer: "In a flash of certainty I saw that if one's motives are wrong, nothing can be right. It makes no difference whether you are a mailman, a hairdresser, an insurance salesman, a housewife—whatever. As long as you feel you are serving others, you do the job well. When you are concerned only with helping yourself, you do it less well—a law inexorable as gravity."

Finally, at six o'clock, Gordon opened the final prescription. Gordon later recalled the moment: "The western sky was ablaze as I took out the last slip of paper. Six words this time. I walked slowly out on the beach. A few yards below the high-water mark, I stopped and read the words again, 'Write your worries in the sand.' I let the paper blow away, reached down and picked up a fragment of shell. Kneeling there under the vault of the sky, I wrote several words, one above the other. Then I walked away, and I did not look back. I had written my troubles on the sand. The tide was coming in" (Gordon 1974).

Gordon's story is inspiring. It is a feel-good story, but there is a great risk that it remains just that—a feel-good story tucked away in the recesses of our minds. To the contrary, however, his story may be a call to action if we use this inspiration as a springboard to vault us over our personal hurdles and burdens. There are several key lessons from Gordon, that—if internalized—will change our lives. The foremost lesson is that spiritual renewal is difficult; it requires time filled with deep, honest thought. Deep, honest thought requires that we isolate ourselves from the hustle and bustle of everyday life, escaping even the grasp of mobile phones. We must continuously examine our motives, and we must learn to think pragmatically rather than worry incessantly.

Wherever you are on your journey, it is essential (from time to time) to take a day away from home, phone, people, and tasks to follow the prescriptions of Arthur Gordon's doctor. My daughter, Teagan, has learned to take some quiet time every day to reflect on life and on her savior. With sports, Advanced Placement classes, volunteering at church, an Associated Student Body government position, investigating colleges, and preparing for the SAT and ACT, she does not "have time for this," but she understands that without her quiet time, all the "other stuff" can become overwhelming. It is crucial to examine your motives, determine your center, and surrender your worries to a higher authority. Once motives are understood and, if necessary, realigned, your spirit will be renewed. But be wary: you will be tempted to revert to your old ways, and then you will need to start over at step one—deep, honest thought.

Temptations are invitations to do evil. Everyone receives them. Each temptation invites you to destroy your life. Every invitation to do evil, no matter how small, is designed to destroy some valuable part of you. Temptations look good, but they always contain a lie. They don't tell all the truth.

Bob Schultz

Let's reconsider Billy Moore's murder of Fred Stapleton. Put on your creative thinking hat—imagine receiving an optimistic invitation written to evoke positive feelings by identifying all possible benefits to this situation:

Dear Billy,

You are cordially invited to Fred Stapleton's home in order to end your money worries. He will not be home and often leaves the doors and windows unlocked. He keeps $20,000 to $30,000 in his bedroom, not even locked in a safe, so he must not really need it. Given your difficult situation, you should follow me to his house. I will let you in, and you can walk away with the money. Meet me for a few drinks tomorrow night at our usual spot and then follow me to Fred's for an easy night's work.

Your friend,

X

Now let's flip the card over and reread it using our critical-thinking-hat interpretation:

Dear Billy,

I know a way you can steal an elderly man's life savings in order to ease *your own* financial problems. All you have to do is break into seventy-seven-year-old Fred Stapleton's house. Your drinking buddy will show you the way. When you find that the door is locked, your buddy will leave. You will also have second thoughts and leave, only to return. In your drunken stupor, you will not be able to resist the temptation of Stapleton's hard-earned money. When you break in to his home, Fred will try to shoot you, but don't worry; he will fumble around in the dark and miss. Even inebriated, you will be able to easily shoot him down. In your panic, you will grab two wallets with his identification, and his shotgun— so there will be plenty of evidence for a conviction. You will be a sitting duck...and will confess to murder. Incidentally, you will likely receive the death sentence for your crime. Strangely, I know you are still interested. Meet your buddy for drinks—the more drinks, the merrier. I will help you along the way but will leave you once the deed has been completed.

Yours truly,

X

PS.   Please allow me to introduce myself

I'm a man of wealth and taste

I've been around for a long, long year

Stole many a man's soul and faith

And I was round when Jesus Christ

Had his moment of doubt and pain

Made damn sure that Pilate

Washed his hands and sealed his fate

Pleased to meet you

Hope you guess my name

But what's puzzling you

Is the nature of my game

(Mick Jagger, "Sympathy for the Devil")

We all face temptations and challenges. We all require a plan and a support system to respond consistently according to our values and convictions. All invitations to do evil (slight or severe) are indeed opportunities to do the opposite. In order to transform the opportunity, we must be able to decipher the invitation, unravel that which is puzzling us, recognize the pattern, and have a plan (and support system) to convert the situation into an opportunity. Many of faith engage God as part of their support system, but even people of faith often forget to seek help through prayer until they have already given in to temptation and fallen victim to its circumstances.

Recognizing the Invitation to Do Evil

Many are familiar with the story of Adam and Eve. I've included it here for those who have not heard the story and as a refresher for those who are already familiar.

> ...The Lord God took the man and put him in the Garden of Eden to work it and take care of it. And the Lord God commanded the man, "You are free to eat from any tree in the garden; but you must not eat from the tree of the knowledge of good and evil..."

Then the Lord God made a woman...and he brought her to the man...Adam and his wife [Eve] were both naked, and they felt no shame.

Now the serpent was more crafty than any of the wild animals the Lord God had made. He said to the woman, "Did God really say, 'You must not eat from any tree in the garden'?"

The woman said to the serpent, "We may eat fruit from the trees in the garden, but God did say, 'You must not eat fruit from the tree that is in the middle of the garden, and you must not touch it, or you will die.'"

"You will not certainly die," the serpent said to the woman. "For God knows that when you eat from it your eyes will be opened, and you will be like God, knowing good and evil."

When the woman saw that the fruit of the tree was good for food and pleasing to the eye, and also desirable for gaining wisdom, she took some and ate it. She also gave some to her husband, who was with her, and he ate it. Then the eyes of both of them were opened, and they realized they were naked; so they sewed fig leaves together and made coverings for themselves.

Then the man and his wife heard the sound of the Lord God as he was walking in the garden in the cool of the day, and they hid from the Lord God among the trees of the garden...

Gen. 2–3 (NIV)

The serpent who represents evil (a.k.a. Satan, the devil, Lucifer, etc.) uses a multistep entrapment process that is consistent throughout the Bible and in our lives.

Step 1: The serpent identifies a desire from within our hearts. In the case of Eve, she had plenty to eat already; her desire was not for food but for godlike wisdom—to know good and evil. Eve had a desire for knowledge, which is a noble desire. She did not know why, but the desire became overpowering—she needed it now! As

Benjamin so wisely pointed out, "Take time for all things: great haste makes great waste." In Billy Moore's case, Billy desired to care for his son and thus was in need of money. Our inner desires in and of themselves are not necessarily bad; they may be for knowledge or security, or they may be for respect or love. But when exploited, our desires can lead us down the wrong paths. Evil identifies a desire within our hearts—even a noble desire—and warps it into lust, greed, sloth, envy, gluttony, covetousness, anger, or pride, insidiously camouflaging that path as the one more easily navigated. We must be wary of shortcuts and not shy from the road less traveled.

Step 2: The serpent plants a seed of doubt: "Did God really say, 'You must not eat from any tree in the garden'?" The serpent knew this was not what God had said to Eve, yet he twisted God's words to put forth his agenda. Eve corrected him, stating she may eat of any tree but one, or she will surely die. The serpent laughed and said, "You will not certainly die," and the seed of doubt was planted. For Billy, the seed was planted in a similar fashion. The words were in his head: "Billy, you have a right to the money. It is for your son. The old guy doesn't need it. If he did, it would be in the bank or at least locked in a safe." The seed was planted, the supposed easy way out defined.

Step 3: The serpent seeks to deceive using lies of commission, omission, and half-truths: "'You will not certainly die,' the serpent said to the woman. 'For God knows that when you eat from it your eyes will be opened, and you will be like God, knowing good and evil.'" The serpent knew (but did not tell) that to eat of the fruit was to defy God and open the world to sinful ways. Once the door to sin was open, death was defined as the separation of man from God. It was not literal death from poisoning; the serpent knew that the fruit would not poison the body. But it would poison the spirit. Pain and suffering entered the world. Eve was deceived, and Adam stood by passively, forsaking his responsibility as her partner and as a servant to God. Recall that a "real" man rejects passivity; Adam did not. As for Billy, he also allowed himself to be deceived: "This will be a piece of cake. Walk in, take the money, nobody will know, nobody will get hurt." As did Eve, Billy bought in to the lie— hook, line, and sinker.

Step 4: The serpent leads us to disobedience: "When the woman saw that the fruit of the tree was good for food and pleasing to the eye, and also desirable for gaining wisdom, she took some and ate it. She also gave some to her husband, who was with her, and he ate it." Billy robbed and killed Fred Stapleton. Internal desires (even desires for good) interwoven with lies, half-truths, and deception, lead us to fall. Temptation alone is not wrong or evil, but how we respond to temptation is often another story. We choose to do wrong rather than to do right—to take the easy way out rather than the road less traveled.

Step 5: The serpent abandons us to face the consequences of our actions. Adam and Eve became ashamed and not only stopped seeking God but hid from Him. Billy was sentenced to death. The serpent was pleased; his deception was complete. When sin is allowed to grow, it "gives birth to death." Thus begins a vicious cycle. Your spirit becomes damaged or ill, plagued by self-indulgent motivations, which in turn leads to false justification of temptations and poor decisions. Poor decisions lead to a damaged spirit. The cycle continues, and with sound thought temporarily abandoned, evil is certain to return and exploit yet another desire even if we should somehow regain our way (Figure 2).

> When tempted, no one should say, "God is tempting me." For God cannot be tempted by evil, nor does he tempt anyone; but each person is tempted when they are dragged away by their own evil desire and enticed. Then after desire has conceived, it gives birth to sin; and sin, when it is full-grown, gives birth to death. Don't be deceived, my dear brother and sisters. (James 1:13–16 [NIV])

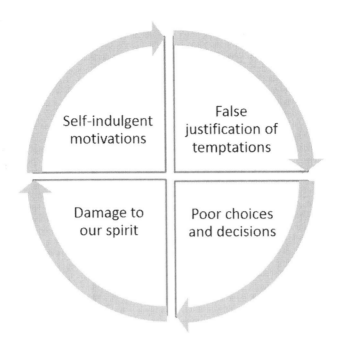

Figure 2: The self-indulgent crazy cycle: Motivation to help only yourself leads to self-indulgent behavior and ultimately to poor decisions; poor decisions harm one's spirit, which feeds self-indulgent motivations. It is a vicious cycle that must be broken.

Recall, from both *VerAegis—Relationships* and *VerAegis—Contribution,* our definition of what it means to be "real": a real man or woman is someone who values relationships; accepts responsibility; rejects passivity; contributes; leads courageously with consideration, passion, and integrity; and believes in grace and mercy.

Accepts Responsibility

Eve did not accept the responsibility of following God's instructions; she accepted the serpent's rationale. Adam did not accept the responsibility of leading Eve away from the devil's invitation. Billy did not accept the responsibility of fending for himself and his child within the realms of decency. He had a strong desire to provide for his son, but Billy allowed the devil to turn this noble desire into something evil. To reject responsibility is to cave in to the dark side.

Rejects Passivity

Adam did not reject passivity. He stood by passively, denying his responsibility to assist Eve in her battle against the devil's ploy. He likely worried that he would appear weak or if he stood against Eve's desires—perhaps like a Goody-Two-shoes. He may have worried that if he took a stance against evil, Eve would disagree, thinking him too cowardly to sample the untried fruit. Whatever emotions he felt, it is clear that he did not muster the courage to discourage Eve. He did not stand for what he knew was right; he caved under peer pressure.

Clearly, neither Adam, Eve, nor Billy refused the invitation to do evil. Could they have done better? Hindsight is twenty-twenty, but by definition, it comes way too late. When we are "under the gun" and embroiled in the heat of the moment, it is difficult to recognize and then refuse invitations to do evil. We need a plan. We need to fight the temptation to remain silent, to remain still...we need to act on our convictions and beliefs.

Refusing the Invitation to Do Evil

We all struggle to resist one temptation after another. Failing to resist temptations leads to poor decisions, and if left unchecked, to a broken spirit. This vicious cycle must be interrupted. Some temptations are small, such as "should I eat that second piece of cake?" Some are not so small, such as "Should I cheat on my spouse? Should I get a divorce?" In book 1 and book 2 of the Legacy Series, *VerAegis—Relationships* and *VerAegis—Contribution,* we addressed the technique of scripting, or creating a plan of action to counter our moments of weakness. Caving to temptation is another weakness we all share, and we need a plan to decline these invitations to do wrong, fight temptation, break the cycle, and heal our spirit.

> **Step 1: Recognize the pattern of temptation.** Don't be puzzled by the "nature of his game." All temptations start with our inner desires.

Step 2: Examine the motives behind your desires. If they are wrong, nothing can be right. Recall the words of Arthur Gordon: "As long as you feel you are serving others, you do the job well. When you are concerned only with helping yourself, you do it less well—a law inexorable as gravity." Once you align your motives and methods with values based on timeless principles, you will be on track to resist temptation. Recall that Billy's motive to help his son was pure, but his methods failed any reasonable test.

Step 3: Do not be intimidated. Do not feel weak or isolated just because you are tempted. We all are tempted. You are no different. Seek solace in a greater force and strength in friendship. "Do not be afraid or terrified because of them, for the LORD your God goes with you; he will never leave you nor forsake you." (Deut. 31:6 [NIV]) Share your desires and motivations with a trusted friend who will help you stand strong "as iron sharpens iron."

Step 4: Be prepared to perform good deeds. Understand which circumstances and desires are your weakest points and thus most likely to lead you astray. "So let us put aside the deeds of darkness and put on the armor of light." (Romans 13:12 [NIV]) Create an action plan of accountability, and most importantly, a plan to do good for others. If you fill your time with good deeds, you will have less time to do wrong. Approach your job with a spirit of service. Volunteer to coach youth sports, teach music, write, tutor, make dinner for your family, work at a local food center, serve at church, or assist at your local school. There are endless good deeds that will benefit others and improve your self-worth in the process. Be prepared to seek forgiveness and reconciliation when you fall. If you do not repair the damage, evil's noose tightens, and the door to temptation widens.

Step 5: Take time to ask God for help. He will often provide an escape route that leads to doing something good. Believers and nonbelievers alike can (and should) ask for help. Often, even believers don't include seeking God as part of their plan to identify and refuse temptation; believers have often learned much more than they have assimilated and are committed to execute. Nonbelievers sometimes think that it is foolish—even childish—to seek God's help. (Guess who planted those seeds of doubt?) Yet can it possibly be more foolish to seek help than it is to yield to destructive temptations? The time of temptation is the time the seek help...the time to "...be strong in the Lord and in his mighty power. Put on the full armor of God, so that you can take your stand against the devil's schemes. For our struggle is not against flesh and blood, but against the rulers, against the authorities, against the powers of this dark world and against the spiritual forces of evil in the heavenly realms. Therefore, put on every piece of God's armor so you will be able to resist the enemy in the time of evil. Then after the battle you will still be standing firm." (Ephesians 6:10--13 [NLT]) At a minimum, seek the help of a good and trusted friend, perhaps someone who can intervene for you. We must not deny the goodness that lives within. We need to perform good deeds; we need to do what is right in order to feel whole.

I know in my heart that man is good. That what is right will always eventually triumph. And there's purpose and worth to each and every life.

Ronald Reagan

Successful implementation of your plan will initiate spiritual healing. Your self-worth will improve. Your motivations will not be self-centered, and when you become more concerned for others, your relationships will improve. So will your decisions, and with clarity of thought, you will be more able to identify and resist temptations. Good decisions, in turn, further strengthen your spirit, confidence, and your motivation to serve others rather than the self (Figure 3). The cycle repeats.

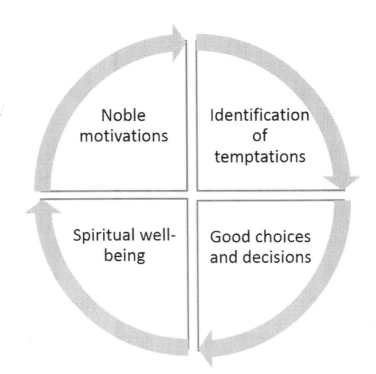

Figure 3: Selfless Renewal: When motivated to help others, we find strength in relationships, which helps us to identify and turn away from temptations. Good decisions further strengthen our spirit, which improves our motivation to serve. The cycle continues.

Is your spirit healthy? Would people describe you as good spirited or ill spirited? Your spirit or temperament shapes your motivations and your desires, which in turn fuel temptations. Decisions then either lift or deflate your spirit, which can negatively influence the spirits of others. The ability (or inability) to lift the spirits of others increases (or decreases) the effectiveness of our relationships and in turn the value of our contributions. When your relationships or contributions suffer, check your motivations—check your spirit. Finally, always remember that no matter how introspective we are, we are dependent upon the support of family, friends, and the strength of our creator in order to repeatedly refuse temptations to do wrong and to consistently choose the path of good over evil.

And It Was Good

I am in politics because of the conflict between good and evil, and I believe that in the end good will triumph.

Margaret Thatcher

The relationship to one's fellow man is the relationship of prayer, the relationship to oneself is the relationship of striving; it is from prayer that one draws the strength for one's striving.

Franz Kafka

"I think our strength is this strong relationship we have all together."

Guy Forget

Then God said, "Let us make human beings in our image, to be like us. They will reign over the fish in the sea, the birds in the sky, the livestock, all the wild animals on the earth, and the small animals that scurry along the ground." So God created human beings in his own image. In the image of God he created him; male and female he created them.

Genesis 1:26–27 (NLT)

From where do we find the strength to combat evil and the preparedness to be ready to perform good deeds? "In his own image...male and female he created them." The fact that God created male and female in His own image implies that God the creator has both male and female characteristics. Thus (depending on our calling), we as humans are potentially not firing on all cylinders until we find a partner who complements our strengths and weaknesses, with whom we can join in a union that more closely reflects a higher spirit than we can achieve alone...an intimate relationship between a man and woman is God's gift and our path to better reflect His image and perform acts of strength and kindness. Through this union, we are better positioned to raise our children and contribute to society. It seems, though, that as we endeavor to fill the voids in our lives with the material world, we devote less thought to both our spiritual lives and to our marital responsibilities.

A woman is the only thing I am afraid of that I know will not hurt me.

Abraham Lincoln

The "boy-girl" partnership grows from a base of trust and desire for mutual benefit (Figure 4). To blossom, the relationship requires openness, courage, and kindness. Mutual consideration leads us to discover the exciting differences between us, and these are the differences that initially (innately) attract us to each other. We instinctively desire someone different to complement our strengths and supplement our weaknesses. Once we have valued and gained mutual benefit from our differences, the relationship reaches a high level of cooperation; we each achieve our highest levels of self-actualization, and we move closer in spirit to God, in love and selflessness. "...then make my joy complete by being like-minded, having the same love, being one in spirit and of one mind. Do nothing out of selfish ambition or vain conceit. Rather, in humility value others above yourselves, not looking to your own interests but each of you to the interests of the others." (Phil. 2:2-4 [NIV]).

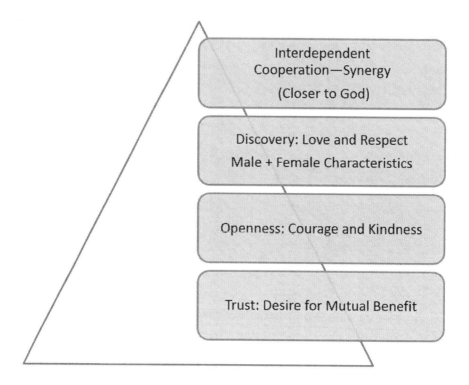

Figure 4: Relationship hierarchy illustrating how trust in relationships leads to openness, openness to discovery of differences that are essential in order to better reflect the true image of God

This concept is not confined to Judeo-Christian cultures. For instance, the Chinese culture has a wonderfully similar concept:

- The symbol 女, pronounced nǚ (or *new* in a tone that falls then rises), means "girl" or "female."
- The symbol 子, pronounced zǐ (or *zee* in a tone that falls then rises), means "boy" or "male."

- The two symbols combined into one as 好, pronounced hǎo (or *how* in a tone that falls then rises), means "good" in the sense that the synergy between male and female is good.

The relationship we share with our "significant other," when bound by the spirit of God, the spirit of goodness, is more durable and able to withstand the negative stresses of our material world. In order to adequately counter these negative influences, we must actively seek to identify the forces that try to divide us, weaken our resolve, and diminish our capacity to act with courage, kindness, and consideration (refer to "Emotional Maturity" in *VerAegis—Relationships*). Let's reexamine the case of Billy Moore.

Billy Moore had broken relationships, especially with his wife. He also had a broken spirit, but he was loved! Billy's death sentence shook his family. Especially distraught were his sister, who had originally paid $9,000 for an attorney to represent Billy, and his aunt. His aunt, a Christian woman, prayed passionately for Billy to accept Jesus as his savior. She requested that her pastor and his wife visit her nephew in prison. Imagine how Billy's life might have been if he had sought the strength of these two women, if he had shared his motivations and ill-conceived plans rather than taking the path of least resistance. Seven days before Billy's scheduled execution, the pastor and his wife met with Billy. Billy clearly remembers the pastor professing to Billy that Billy was loved and God is just. Jesus loved him, his aunt loved him, and the pastor and his wife loved him.

> I was like, "What?" I had never heard about Jesus from the perspective that they talked about it...And I could feel the Holy Spirit. I didn't know what it was, but I could feel that peace as they were telling me that God loved me. He knew what I did and He still loved me and He died for me. That just blew me away. (Richardson)

Billy prayed with them and accepted Jesus as his savior. He was baptized that day in prison, and he knew in his heart that a real change had taken place. As in steps three and five in "Choices Are Linked to the Well-Being of Our Spirt" Billy sought and accepted help.

> The guilt about the crime was gone; not the memory—I still remember it. But the guilt that Satan was using to kill me with was gone...Finally, I had peace. When I went back upstairs, I'm dripping wet, and the inmates said, "Man, what happened to you?"

"I got baptized…You can say what you want. I have finally done something that I know…is right. I know this is what I'm supposed to do." (Richardson)

The day of his execution, September 13, arrived. Billy prepared to die, but the day came and went without incident. In his confusion, Billy prayed and thanked the Lord.

So on Friday, September the 13th, I'm sitting in my cell on my bed waiting to be executed. I'm waiting for the guards to come and get me. Nobody says anything to me about it. Well, nothing happens. None of the guards come by. Nobody stopped by my cell, and, of course, I don't flag anybody down. I don't say, "Hey, did you all forget me?" I don't do it. (Moore)

It turns out his lawyer had forgotten to inform Billy that his case had gone to an automatic appeal with the Georgia supreme court. On Monday, Billy received a letter from his lawyer informing him that his execution would be stayed and that he needed Billy to request that his sister send $3,000 to appeal the case to the Georgia supreme court. But Billy found that there was an automatic appeal for all death sentences and convinced his sister not to send the money; he began to represent himself. With access to his records, Billy decided to write to Fred Stapleton's family members seeking forgiveness (recall step four in the process to refuse the invitation to do evil regarding forgiveness and reconciliation). Billy did not have his plan in place before temptation hit, but he was now working backward, knowing he could not fix the wrong he had committed but that he could prevent it from becoming worse. Billy's relationship with Jesus grew stronger, and he prepared himself to do good deeds. He studied the Bible, conducted Bible studies with fellow inmates, and even earned his bachelor's degree from a Bible college.

I knew that I needed to write these people and apologize. I wrote them, I apologized, and I told them, "I'm sorry, I didn't mean to cause the death of your uncle, your brother, but I did do it. If you can find it in your heart to forgive me I would truly appreciate it. But if I were you, I wouldn't forgive me. If I were you, I would throw this letter away." Well, the very next week I begin to get letters back. They wrote me to say they were Christian people and we forgive you. And it wasn't just lip service. You know, a lot of people say, "I forgive you, but I don't want to be around you—I forgive you but don't talk to me." We continued to write and for that whole time on death row...we wrote letters back and forth. (Moore)

Billy led other inmates to Jesus, helping to create a more tolerable environment for them. But regardless of how he filled his days, his inevitable execution weighed heavy on his conscience. He was always aware that one day, just like the thirteen inmates who disappeared from his cellblock (some members of his Bible study), he too would be strapped to the electric chair and executed.

In 1984, after over ten years on death row, the time had come. Billy was certain there would be no more appeals, no more stays of execution. He had pled guilty, and there were no remaining legal maneuvers. The Eleventh Circuit refused to hear the case for a fourth time, but seven short hours prior to the scheduled time, his execution was stayed once again. Fast-forward to 1990, sixteen and a half years after first being sentenced to death and six years after his down-to-the-wire wait: Billy was faced with yet another execution date.

I finally lose [my appeals] after six [more] years, and I get a new execution date. My lawyers tell me that, "Your case is going to go to the parole board." I said, "That's fine." What we found out is—when the victim's family found out that my case was going to the parole board, they all got together, they got a bus, and everybody in their community who knew the man that I had killed, they all went to the parole board. They told members of the parole board, "Listen, Billy is our brother, and you cannot execute him." Even a friend of mine who is a Jesuit priest that knew Mother Teresa...called her and told her about my case, and the word got to the parole board that she wanted to talk to them. The parole board called her in India and asked her what [she wanted]. She told them that they needed to do what Jesus would do.

They commuted my sentence from a death sentence to a life sentence and said that I would have to do twenty-five years before being eligible for parole. This was in '90. I was sent to the state prison in '91. Just 13 months later, the 11th Circuit made another ruling, in a case not related to my case, that allowed me to come up for parole. As soon as my name came up for parole I was paroled out of prison. (Moore)

Upon his parole, Billy became the only confessed murderer ever in US history to be released from death row (Staff 2012). Initially, Billy had not taken the steps to refuse the invitation to do evil, but he later accepted responsibility to refuse follow-up invitations. After his initial failure, Billy took the necessary steps (in reverse order) to improve a bad situation:

Step 5: He took time to ask God for help. Billy responded to the God-shaped hole in his heart; he felt Jesus's presence and accepted Him as his creator and savior. God provided an escape route and motivated Billy to do good for others.

Step 4: Billy prepared to perform good deeds. Billy studied the Bible and became educated in prison. He volunteered to conduct Bible studies and teach other inmates. Billy recognized that he had fallen far and was prepared to seek forgiveness. When the opportunity presented itself, Billy humbly requested forgiveness even as he professed that forgiveness was not deserved. By confessing his sins and seeking forgiveness, he was afforded the strength to prevent evil from tightening its grip on his spirit. He clung to good; he fought to heal his broken spirit.

Step 3: Billy was scared but would not be intimidated or feel weak just because he had given in to evil temptations. He contemplated suicide, but as his strength and resolve faltered, he relied on the strength of Jesus to lift him up.

Step 2: Billy reexamined the motives behind his desires. As a result, he devoted much of his time to serving others. The new Billy was more concerned with helping others than he was in serving his own needs. He served happily and he served well. Billy realigned his motives to his new Christian values, which were based on timeless principles. His realigned motives, which enabled him to stay on track, fortified him against the temptations to give up, to be a victim, and to resent his captors. He was able to fill his heart with love rather than hate, with courage rather than fear, and with respect rather than contempt.

Step 1: Billy remained vigilant and sought to recognize the pattern of temptation with the intent to avoid its icy-cold talons and prevent relapse into his destructive ways.

As it was for Billy, the choice is ours to initially refuse the temptation to do evil, to remain steadfast and vigilant. And like Billy, we too have the choice to recover when we fail. We may not always have the strength, but we can find that strength in others and in our creator. We cannot simultaneously be good and evil, but we have been given the freedom to be alternately either, as we so choose.

Values and Principles

We hold these truths to be self-evident, that all men are created equal, that they are endowed by their Creator with certain unalienable Rights that among these are Life, Liberty and the pursuit of Happiness.

Thomas Jefferson, in the Declaration of Independence

Darkness cannot drive out darkness; only light can do that. Hate cannot drive out hate; only love can do that.

Martin Luther King Jr.

Arthur Gordon asserted that if as we strive to help others our strength is increased and we do the job well, but if we are consumed only with helping ourselves, we fare less well, and he declared this to be a law inexorable as the principle of gravity. Principles (fundamental truths) are universal and unchanging. The United States of America was founded on the principle that all men are created equal, with the rights to life, liberty, and the pursuit of happiness. Yet slavery, clearly a denial that all men are created equal with these unalienable rights, existed in the United States until the Civil War (1861–1865). President Abraham Lincoln issued the Emancipation Proclamation on January 1, 1863. Fearing that the proclamation would be overturned once the war ended, Congress formally proposed the Thirteenth Amendment, outlawing slavery, on January 31, 1865; it was ratified on December 6, 1865.

If these principles of equality and life were indeed self-evident, why did abolishing slavery in the United States require nearly nine decades (1776–1865)? Why were these principles not self-evident to all, and if they were self-evident, why were they denied? Principles that are "natural" laws, such as gravity, are more difficult to refute. Social principles, on the other hand, seem subjective and are not easily agreed upon. Social principles are moral laws, fundamental truths that unfortunately are (at times) found to be at odds with social values (society's judgment of what is important in life). The social values prevalent in many states during the eighteenth century were definitely not aligned with the principles outlined in the Declaration of Independence—perhaps confirming that these were subjective social values rather than self-evident truths. How do we know when a principle is a principle and not just a different set of values? One litmus test is posterity: principles are universal and unchanging, and thus stand the test of time. Does the principle you are testing seem to have withstood the test of time? Yet another test can be performed by arguing the opposite point of view (e.g., gravity pushes objects away from the earth—which we know to be absurd).

My father loved to argue and debate. He would choose a controversial topic and jump headlong into a heated discussion. Occasionally, he would stop midstream and announce that it was time to argue the other point of view—never fun if you were bent on winning, but thought provoking if you donned your creative-thinking hat. This process facilitated the ability to understand others' points of view, but it was not easy. It could also be used to see if an opposing argument (for instance, one for or against a principle or truth) holds any legitimacy. The more legitimate the opposing argument, the less likely that the primary statement is an objective principle.

Let's rewrite Thomas Jefferson's "truths" to align with the values that existed during the formative years of the United States (and those of many other countries throughout the history of man), which in turn allowed slavery to exist in the United States for nearly ninety years (please note that this is for argument only and does not reflect my own belief): "We hold these truths to be self-evident, that all men are *not* created equal, that they are *not* endowed by their Creator with certain unalienable Rights, and that among the Rights, they are *not endowed to possess* are Life, Liberty, and the pursuit of Happiness."

How can one logically argue that someone is born but does not possess the right to life? Since the act of being born alive proves that we are born with the right to life, is the next logical step to assume that some should be born to a life without freedom or without the right to pursue happiness? Is it logical to assume that we are each valued differently by our creator? No, in fact, it is declared the He loves us all, that we each are His children despite (not because of) our actions. Since arguing that the opposite seems to be quite illogical, we can be confident that all men are created equal, that they are endowed with the rights of life, liberty, and the pursuit of happiness. Being created equal, does not mean we are created to be the same. No...we are different, but born with equal rights. This does not mean we are entitled...and that someone owes us something, only that we have rights and it is our responsibility to act accordingly.

Just as Adam and Eve were given the right to choose to eat the fruit of knowledge of good and evil, humans have the ability to choose based on their values. Unfortunately, the temptations of material goods, the proverbial "sex, drugs, and rock 'n' roll," drive humans to make decisions based on ill-conceived values rather than time-tested principles. Feelings of greed, entitlement, gluttony, lust, contempt, and pride have too often replaced the spirit of courage, responsibility, stewardship, kindness, love, and respect. In these instances, we have failed to execute a plan to refuse the invitation to do evil, and we have failed to fill our time with good deeds.

I cannot read the timeless words of Lincoln's Gettysburg Address without sensing his spirit, without grasping the spirit of a nation, and without feeling the Spirit of God, the spirit of good—without feeling courage, responsibility, kindness, love, and respect.

Four score and seven years ago our fathers brought forth on this continent, a new nation, conceived in Liberty, and dedicated to the proposition that all men are created equal.

Now we are engaged in a great civil war, testing whether that nation, or any nation so conceived and so dedicated, can long endure. We are met on a great battle-field of that war. We have come to dedicate a portion of that field, as a final resting place for those who here gave their lives that that nation might live. It is altogether fitting and proper that we should do this.

But, in a larger sense, we cannot dedicate, we cannot consecrate, we cannot hallow this ground. The brave men, living and dead, who struggled here, have consecrated it, far above our poor power to add or detract. The world will little note, nor long remember what we say here, but it can never forget what they did here. It is for us the living, rather, to be dedicated

here to the unfinished work which they who fought here have thus far so nobly advanced. It is rather for us to be here dedicated to the great task remaining before us—that from these honored dead we take increased devotion to that cause for which they gave the last full measure of devotion—that we here highly resolve that these dead shall not have died in vain— that this nation, under God, shall have a new birth of freedom—and that government of the people, by the people, for the people, shall not perish from the earth.

Abraham Lincoln

Just as Abraham Lincoln's spirit is revealed by the character of his timeless words, your character is a reflection of your true spirit, and it is this spirit that ultimately shines through, revealing the "real" you. No matter how charming one is during the moment of "first impression," all lasting relationships and legacies are based on a true inner spirit, and it is by this true inner spirit that we choose to fight or flee from our greatest battles.

Men like Jefferson, Washington, Lincoln, and many before and since, have made it clear to all: once one is born, the right to life is a principle that must be protected, and this principle has endured the test of time. It has endured but not without challenges of genocide and mass murder by men such as Hitler, Stalin, Mao, and many, many more. It pains me to stain these pages with the words of such men, but it would pain me more to turn a blind eye. By including these words, I pray that it will become evident that values not founded on principles stand like a house built on sand. Further, I hope that together we can prevent more of these shallow leaders from blemishing our great earth with their atrocities. Following are a few quotes and brief historical summaries of Adolf Hitler, Mao Tse-tung, and Joseph Stalin that shed light on their values and true spirits:

Adolf Hitler: His Words Reflect His Inner Spirit

Humanitarianism is the expression of stupidity and cowardice.

Success is the sole earthly judge of right and wrong.

I do not see why man should not be just as cruel as nature.

How fortunate for governments that the people they administer don't think.

If you tell a big enough lie and tell it frequently enough, it will be believed.

It is not truth that matters, but victory.

Adolf Hitler

Hitler's Legacy (1889–1945)

Adolf Hitler, elected German chancellor in 1933, was dictator of Nazi Germany from 1934 to 1945. Under Hitler's rule, the Nazis murdered nearly six million Jews and approximately five million others deemed inferior (gypsies, Jehovah's Witnesses, Poles, Soviet prisoners, homosexuals, communists, and other political opponents). In 1939 Hitler declared that Britain was the main enemy to be defeated and that the obliteration of Poland was necessary as a means to his ultimate goal. Accordingly, Nazi forces mobilized against Poland in August 1939, marking the beginning of World War II, which resulted in as many as fifty-five million deaths. In 1945, with Soviet forces only blocks from his bunker, Hitler committed suicide on April 30 with his wife of two days and longtime partner, Eva Braun. Their bodies were taken outside to the bombed-out garden behind the Reich Chancellery, placed in a bomb crater, doused with fuel, and burned.

Joseph Stalin: His Words Reflect His Inner Spirit

The death of one man is a tragedy. The death of millions is a statistic.

Death is the solution to all problems. No man—no problem.

Ideas are more powerful than guns. We would not let our enemies have guns, why should we let them have ideas.

When we hang the capitalists they will sell us the rope we use.

The people who cast the votes don't decide an election, the people who count the votes do.

Joseph Stalin

Stalin's Legacy (1879–1953)

Upon Vladimir Lenin's death in 1924, Joseph Stalin became the Soviet leader and within six years became the unrivaled dictator from 1930 to 1953. Stalin forced rapid industrialization and usurped agricultural land to convert it from private to government-run farms (a policy known as collectivism), resulting in the deaths of as many as five million Soviet citizens due to famine from 1932 to 1933. Political purges and forced labor camps were responsible for the deaths of as many as an additional seven million Soviet citizens. Stalin's diplomatic and military blunders (especially with Hitler) contributed significantly to the twenty million WWII military and civilian Soviet casualties.

Stalin first gained infamy by his association with the 1907 Tiflis bank robbery, which resulted in several deaths and the theft of 250,000 rubles ($3.4 million). Between 1902 and 1913, he was arrested and jailed seven times.

Mao Tse-tung: His Words Reflect His Inner Spirit

Classes struggle, some classes triumph, others are eliminated. Such is history; such is the history of civilization for thousands of years.

People like me sound like a lot of big cannons.

The atom bomb is a paper tiger which the United States reactionaries use to scare people. It looks terrible, but in fact it isn't.

Every Communist must grasp the truth; political power grows out of the barrel of a gun.

In class society, everyone lives as a member of a particular class, and every kind of thinking, without exception, is stamped with the brand of a class.

Mao Tse-tung

Mao's Legacy (1893–1976)

Mao Tse-tung became the leader of the Chinese Communist Party in 1935 and founded the People's Republic of China in 1949, formerly known as the Republic of China, which he ruled until his death in 1976. Mao was aligned with Joseph Stalin's industrialization and land-reform strategies and initiated programs such the Great Leap Forward and the Cultural Revolution, during which thirty to seventy million people starved to death or were murdered by Mao's government and its policies. Chang and Halliday, *coauthors of Mao: The Unknown Story*, claim that Mao was responsible for well over seventy million deaths. In 1980 Hu Yaobang, a high ranking official of the People's Republic of China, estimated that the famine created by the Great Leap Forward alone accounted for twenty million deaths; in 2000, journalist Philip Short estimated the number to be between twenty and thirty million, while Chang and Halliday estimated approximately thirty-seven million, and Yang Jisheng, a Communist Party member and former reporter for *Xinhua*, put the number at approximately thirty-six million. Millions of others were jailed and executed during political purges and "reeducation" programs that targeted those who were considered to hold views contrary to Maoist ideals. Mao's supporters claim that he was the unifying force in China and that his methods were essential to jump-start China's economic growth.

What Lies within You?

Who you are speaks so loudly I can't hear what you're saying.

Ralph Waldo Emerson

What lies behind you and what lies in front of you, pales in comparison to what lies inside of you.

Ralph Waldo Emerson

Hitler, Stalin, and Mao each had values, but many of their values were not and are not founded on enduring principles. Their inner spirits were poisoned with lust for power, greed and contempt. Their values did withstand the test of time. Their tragic legacies each stand as living testimonies to the necessity of recognizing and reacting when one's values are not aligned with lasting principles. Their stories also exemplify why those of sound character and spirit need to reject passivity, accept responsibility, and contribute to the greater good! Fortunately, such ill-founded values will not withstand the test of time and are ultimately doomed to fail, but too many have suffered (and will suffer) when faith is placed in undeserving leaders.

Whether one leads a nation, a business, a team, or a household, only leadership based on lasting principles will withstand the test of time and leave the legacy you wish to leave. The same philosophy holds true when choosing a leader to follow. As you seek to understand your own motives, so too should you seek to understand the motives of those you choose to follow. Test their values. Do those leaders have respect for you? Do they have respect even for competitors or enemies? Are they loud and bombastic like cannons? Do they believe that often-told lies will become your new truth—your new hope? Are they confident, courageous, and open with the truth? Do they respect the truth? Do they think that might makes right, that the ends justify the means, and that power grows from the barrel of a gun? If there is not a deep-rooted integrity and fundamental goodness at the core of what you and they do, ill-conceived motives will surface, and short-term successes will give way to long-term failure. Aesop's fable depicting the battle between the wind and sun illustrates, in an analogy collapsed in time but potent in its message, how strength is not always what it seems:

> The North Wind and the Sun disputed as to which was the most powerful, and agreed that he should be declared the victor who could first strip a wayfaring man of his clothes. The North Wind first tried his power and blew with all his might, but the keener his blasts, the closer the Traveler wrapped his cloak around him, until at last, resigning all hope of victory, the Wind called upon the Sun to see what he could do. The Sun suddenly shone out with all his warmth. The Traveler no sooner felt his genial rays than he took off one garment after another, and at last, fairly overcome with heat, undressed and bathed in a stream that lay in his path.
>
> Influence is better than force. (Townsend)

"Influence is better than force." Lasting effectiveness requires mutual benefit. When you are motivated to do something and a leader purposefully avoids behaviors and endeavors that demotivate, you both benefit. If you are undermined and become demotivated by your leader's actions, you will find another way and another leader—if not today, then eventually—and neither benefit, just as in this tale told by Aesop:

> A Cottager and his wife had a Hen that laid a golden egg every day. They supposed that the Hen must contain a great lump of gold in its inside, and in order to get the gold they killed it. Having done so, they found to their surprise that the Hen differed in no respect from their other hens. The foolish pair, thus hoping to become rich

all at once, deprived themselves of the gain of which they were assured day by day. (Townsend)

The foolish cottager and his wife did not seek a mutually beneficial situation with their extraordinary hen. They did not act with courage and consideration and did not test their motives nor seek to understand their methodologies. They did not nourish and care for the hen (relationship and spirit) that could have been such a blessing if treated well. They ended any possibility of a lasting relationship because they gave in to greed, fear, and ignorance. They did not recognize the symptoms of temptation and were not prepared to decline its ugly invitation. They did not follow the golden rule. Their lives were worse because of it.

Liberty, the pursuit of happiness, and the unalienable right to life are principles, as are the equal rights of men and women of all races alike. Different cultures and religions may express these principles in various ways, but it is evident that all of them are embodied in the golden rule, which is a universally documented (if not accepted) principle found in all major (and many of the minor) religions of the world:

Baha'i: "And if thine eyes be turned toward justice, choose thou for thy neighbor that which thou choosest for thyself" (Epistle to the Son of the Wolf).

Buddhism: "Hurt not others in ways you yourself would find hurtful" (Udanavarga 5:18).

Christianity: "In everything do to others as you would have them do to you; for this is the law and the prophets" (Matthew 7:12).

Confucianism: "Do not unto others what you do not want them to do to you" (Analects 15:13).

Hinduism: "This is the sum of duty: do naught unto others which would cause you pain if done to you" (Mahabharata 5:15).

Islam: "Not one of you is a believer until he loves for his brother what he loves for himself" (Fortieth Hadith of an-Nawawi 13).

Jainism: "A man should wander about treating all creatures as he himself would be treated" (Surtrakritanga 1:11:33).

Judaism: "What is hateful to you, do not do to your neighbor: that is the whole of the Torah; all the rest of it is commentary" (Shabbat 31a).

Native American: "Respect for all life is the foundation" (The Great Law of Peace).

Sikhism: "Treat others as thou wouldst be treated thyself" (Adi Granth).

Taoism: "Regard your neighbor's gain as your own gain and your neighbor's loss as your own loss" (T'ai Shang Kan Ying P'ien).

Zoroastrianism: "That nature alone is good which refrains from doing unto another whatsoever is not good for itself" (Dadistan-I-Dinik 94:5).

The golden rule for Christians does not state that you do to other Christians as you would have them do to you, just as the golden rule of Islam does not state that not one of you is a believer until he loves for his Muslim brother what he loves for himself. These golden rules do not distinguish between religions or race. They are universal and timeless. This basic principle does not have a beginning or end; it was applicable when first conceived, it is applicable now, and it will be applicable in the future. Christian doctrine calls men to love their women as Jesus loved his church, and women to honor their men. These concepts are founded in the principle of mutual love and respect.

A FATHER had one son and one daughter, the former remarkable for his good looks, the latter for her extraordinary ugliness. While they were playing one day as children, they happened by chance to look together into a mirror that was placed on their mother's chair. The boy congratulated himself on his good looks; the girl grew angry, and could not bear the self-praises of her Brother, interpreting all he said (and how could she do otherwise?) into reflection on herself. She ran off to her father, to be avenged on her Brother, and spitefully accused him of having, as a boy, made use of that which belonged only to girls.

The father embraced them both, and bestowing his kisses and affection impartially on each, said, "I wish you both would look into the mirror every day: you, my son, that you may not spoil your beauty by evil conduct; and you, my daughter, that you may make up for your lack of beauty by your virtues." (Townsend)

Notice the father's response: he embraced both children. He loved and valued both. He valued their differences and suggested not only how strengths could become weaknesses if not countered by humility, but how weaknesses could be overcome by strengths when appropriately countered by perseverance, integrity and fortitude. He valued both children based on the principle that they each should be treated with equal respect and consideration. The father's inner strength and spirit shines through in his powerful yet loving response. He emphasizes to his children that their inner spirits and God-given gifts are core to who they are and should be their focus.

We were created as equals in God's eyes, with the right to be treated well. Man and woman in his image were created equal. Jews and gentiles were created equal. We were created equal—not the same, not with identical gifts—but with an infinite variety of gifts—gifts specifically designed for each of us. These differences are not wrong nor are they mistakes. We are different, but we are equally valued by our creator. We need to learn to use our gifts, value our differences, and embrace our equality. Embracing equality of all in the face of such variation, accepting all as through the eyes of our creator, is challenging, and even more so when one places no faith in a creator. Where do you stand?

Complacency Is Not an Option

Things may come to those who wait, but only the things left by those who hustle.

Abraham Lincoln

When the solution is simple, God is answering.

Albert Einstein

When you focus on being a blessing, God makes sure that you are always blessed in abundance.

Joel Osteen

That deep emotional conviction of the presence of a superior reasoning power, which is revealed in the incomprehensible universe, forms my idea of God.

Albert Einstein

Before the throne of the Almighty, man will be judged not by his acts but by his intentions. For God alone reads our hearts.

Mahatma Gandhi

...Our great desire is that you will keep on loving others as long as life lasts, in order to make certain that what you hope for will come true. Then you will not become spiritually dull and indifferent. Instead, you will follow the example of those who are going to inherit God's promises because of their faith and endurance.

Hebrews 6:11-12 (NLT)

Albert Einstein thought deeply about the universe, ultimately arriving at the conclusion that the universe has a creator and that only a higher reasoning power could have created such *natural* wonders. What do you believe? Are you actively seeking to understand? Have you taken a leap of faith in your belief system, whatever it may be? Recall our visionary statement for a "real" man or woman: a real man or woman is someone who values relationships; accepts responsibility; rejects passivity..."

Complacency is not an option. Seek to understand first, and then take a leap of faith in one direction or the other—but do not remain dormant. Your belief system is vitally important to the well-being of your spirit and should not be neglected or taken for granted. It would take volumes to cover such a broad and rich philosophical topic as the creation of the universe and the existence (or not) of a creator, so instead I will try to share some of the information I have gathered and insights I have gleaned over the past several decades.

Is There a Creator?

Any examination of the existence of the creator is facilitated by examining creation itself. Let's begin with a philosophical review of our universe. Either the universe is eternal, with no beginning or end, or it had a beginning and someday will end. It follows that if the universe is not eternal, then it had a beginning and either emerged from nothing or was created by an entity that preexisted its creation.

For the universe to be eternal, it would have to exist in a state of relative equilibrium; otherwise, if in a state of decay—however minute—for an infinite amount of time, it would cease to exist. In other words, in order to be eternal, the universe needs to be unchanging—constant. There are at least three sound scientific principles or facts that need to be proven false in order to prove that the universe is unchanging.

1. The second law of thermal dynamics states that the entropy of an isolated system is always increasing—or in other words,

the system naturally tends toward a less ordered state. The law of entropy suggests that the universe is wearing out; it does not support an infinitely old, unchanging universe.

2. Stars (including our sun) convert hydrogen to helium via the process of nuclear fusion. If the universe is infinitely old (a.k.a. eternal), the hydrogen (in absence of a source external to our universe) would be scarce. But there is an abundance of hydrogen in the universe, indicating that the universe is not infinitely old.

3. Hubble's law, which suggests that the universe is uniformly expanding in all directions, led to George Gamow's big bang theory, which when combined with the additional discovery in 1965 of omnidirectional background radiation in the universe, all support the conclusion that the universe was once dense and hot, having a definite beginning, and thus is not eternal (Boa 1982).

It is now generally accepted that the universe has not always existed. The big bang theory suggests that the universe originated from an extremely dense and hot clump of matter. Nearly fourteen billion years ago, it suddenly exploded with a "big bang," expanding nearly instantly from smaller than a single atom to bigger than a galaxy, after which it has continued expanding at a slower rate. This theory leads to the conclusion that the universe has a beginning and either emerged from nothing by nothing or was created by something that preexisted its creation. The first law of thermal dynamics states that energy or matter can be neither created nor destroyed, which strongly suggests that creating something from nothing by nothing is not possible. Additionally, all human experience suggests that something cannot be created from nothing. Even the creation of an idea requires energy and a living mind. There are many who argue, in fact, that the big bang theory is a violation of the first law of thermodynamics, if indeed there was neither matter nor energy prior to the bang—though supporters contend that the theory supports the evolution of the universe from existing matter rather than the creation of matter from nothing

(Strickland). Strickland lists many other theories regarding the development of the universe, but none has gained wide acceptance. For the sake of this discussion, we need not argue the exact mechanism, as I believe it is fairly safe to assume that nothing from nothing leaves nothing—meaning the universe needs to have come from *something*, and that *something* needs to have predated the universe.

If the universe did begin at a specific point in time, whether with a big bang, a little whistle, or a silent gasp, what initiated the process? Newton's first law of motion states that objects at rest tend to stay at rest unless acted on by an external force, and thus, an extraordinarily dense mass (the mass of the entire universe) at rest would take quite a bit of force to create motion. Newton's third law suggests that for every action, there is an equal and opposite reaction. If the expansion of the universe was the reaction, what was the action? What could have caused the explosion? Remarked Nosowitz, "We have no idea what would trigger an ultra-dense pinpoint of matter to explode outwards" (2013). We may not be able to answer this question definitively, but we can conclude that whatever created the big bang or initiated the creation of the universe necessarily predated the universe and thus is likely to be eternal and possess the ability to impart an enormous amount of energy in order to accelerate all the mass of the universe into its ever-expanding present-day form. Thus, we have arrived at two characteristics of an entity that may be responsible for the creation of the universe:

1. Existed before the universe (**eternal—unchanging**)

2. Extraordinarily powerful, unlike anything known to mankind (**omnipotent**)

If matter cannot be created or destroyed, then matter and energy must be eternal and thus would predate the beginning of the universe. The initiation of our universe required a triggering event. What was the nature of that triggering event? Either the initiation was random, or it was intelligent and purposeful. In order to answer this question, it is useful to narrow the focus of inquiry from the entire universe to the realm of life on Earth, and even more specifically to the creation of the first single-celled being, and then to the transition from that single cell to the plants, animals, insects, and human beings that today coexist on Earth.

To facilitate this part of our journey, I would like to introduce Lee Strobel. Lee is a journalist, author, former legal editor, and investigative reporter of the *Chicago Tribune*. Lee has dedicated his career to investigating and solving mysteries. He was a hard-hitting reporter who was once antagonistic toward God and people of religion. His wife, Leslie, was more of an agnostic and was confused about issues concerning God and creation. Lee and Leslie lived a carefree, upwardly mobile life and admittedly had no time for God. Lee spent much of his time endeavoring to break cases and write story after story. This was the life he loved, but all of a sudden, it was flipped on its head:

> Leslie stunned me in the summer of 1979 by announcing that she had become a Christian. I rolled my eyes and braced for the worst, feeling like the victim of a bait-and-switch scam. I had married one Leslie—the fun Leslie, the carefree Leslie, the risk-taking Leslie— and now I feared she was going to turn into some sort of sexually repressed prude who would trade our upwardly mobile lifestyle for all-night prayer vigils and volunteer work in grimy soup kitchens. (Strobel 2007)

When Leslie invited Lee to go to church with her in 1980, he agreed, and armed with his reporter's notebook, he committed to "get her out of this cult…she had gotten involved in" (Strobel 2007). Lee had not signed up for a religious Leslie and was convinced that by using his investigative techniques, it would be easy to dissuade her and others from following a fallacious God. He remarked, "I plunged into the case with more vigor than with any story I had ever pursued. I applied the training I had received at Yale Law School as well as my experience as legal affairs editor of the Chicago Tribune."

From his high school days, Lee knew that the creation of life did not begin as described in the Bible, and so he endeavored to demonstrate that life was random and thus did not have a creator. Recalling his high school lessons, he began probing the famous Stanley Miller experiment. Stanley Miller is considered to be the father of prebiotic chemistry—the synthetic organic chemistry that takes place under natural conditions in geocosmological-chemical environments. In 1953, while a graduate student, Miller had published a paper on the synthesis of amino acids under early Earth conditions; it had a "tremendous impact and immediately transformed the study of the origin of life" (Bada 2012). The natural synthesis of amino acids is the first step of several required to form the first single-celled organism and thus proof that such synthesis did not require an intelligent source is crucial to support any theory that life on Earth began as a random unplanned event. Lee knew in his gut, from the moment he first learned of Miller's success, that if the origin of life could be explained with natural (random) processes, then "God was out of a job":

> After all, there was no need for a deity if living organisms could emerge by themselves out of the primordial soup and then develop naturally over the eons into more and more complex creatures....In my quest to determine if contemporary science points toward or away from God, I knew I had to first examine the claims of evolution in order to conclude once and for all whether Darwinism creates a reasonable foundation for atheism. That's because if the materialism of Darwinian evolution is a fact, then the atheistic conclusions I reached as a student might still be valid. (Strobel 2004)

This crucial point was not lost on Charles Darwin who recognized that the ability to produce life from inanimate material was a gap in his theory of evolution. Darwin wrote to Joseph Hooker in 1871:

If (and oh! What a big if!) we could conceive some warm little pond, with all sorts of ammonia and phosphoric salts, light, heat, electricity, etc. present, that a protein compound was chemically formed ready to undergo still more complex changes, at the present day such matter would be instantly absorbed, which would not have been the case before living creatures were found. (Peet)

Evolutionists theorize that life sprang into existence when a bolt of lightning struck the prebiotic soup (the ocean) that was teeming with the chemical compounds that would eventually become the building blocks of life. Miller sought to reproduce Darwin's "warm little pond" on his laboratory benchtop. Lee's investigation in the early 1980s, like that of many other inquiring minds, uncovered some surprisingly interesting data regarding Miller's experiment, as well as those of other icons of evolution, and two decades later, Lee decided to dig even deeper. His investigation led him to Jonathan Wells. Wells had completed his undergraduate studies at UC Berkeley with a degree in geology and physics and a minor in biology. At Yale, he had earned a doctorate in religious studies, specializing in the nineteenth-century controversies surrounding Darwin, and in 1994, he had received a second doctorate in molecular and cell biology from Berkeley, where he focused on vertebrate embryology and evolution.

Miller's Experiment

Miller assembled a closed, sterile array of glass flasks connected in a loop, consisting of a heated flask half-filled with water, which represented the primordial pond, configured with gas input tubes, and a second flask containing Miller's "atmosphere," configured with electrodes as an energy source to simulate lightning. One tube directly connected the two flasks. A second U-shaped tube led from the atmosphere flask through a "cold trap," used to collect liquid products and condense water, before returning to the water flask. Miller's atmosphere consisted of methane, ammonia, and hydrogen, which were heated and cooled as the atmosphere was continuously pumped through the system and repeatedly exposed to electrical discharges.

After two days of sparking the gaseous mixture, Miller was able to synthesize glycine, and after repeating the process for an entire week, he reported that the flask was coated with a dark, oily substance, and the water had become yellow-brown in color. Upon further analysis, Miller reported that he had synthesized glycine and several other amino acids (Bada 2012).

Miller's findings have been taught in high schools and colleges, and as stated above, have profoundly influenced the field of study of the origin of life. Lee Strobel knew instinctively that atmospheric conditions were a linchpin in Miller's thesis. He posed the question to Jonathan Wells: had Miller adequately duplicated the primordial atmospheric conditions in his test lab?

Wells admitted that no one is certain what the atmosphere was like on prelife Earth but stated that the consensus is that the atmosphere was not at all like the atmosphere Miller used. Wells explained that Miller chose a hydrogen-rich mixture of methane, ammonia, and water vapor, which was consistent with contemporary scientific thought at the time of his experiment. Wells continued as follows:

> But scientists don't believe that anymore. As a geophysicist with the Carnegie Institution said in the 1960s, "What is the evidence for a primitive methane-ammonia atmosphere on earth? The answer is that there is no evidence for it, but much against it."

> By the mid-1970s, Belgian biochemist Marcel Florkin was declaring that the concept behind Miller's theory of the early atmosphere "has been abandoned." Two of the leading origin-of-life researchers, Klaus Dose and Sidney Fox, confirmed that Miller had used the wrong gas mixture. And *Science* magazine said in 1995 that experts now dismiss Miller's experiment because "the early atmosphere looked nothing like the Miller-Urey simulation."

> The best hypothesis now is that there was very little hydrogen in the atmosphere because it would have escaped into space.

Instead, the atmosphere probably consisted of carbon dioxide, nitrogen and water vapor. (Strobel 2004)

Wells explained further that when Miller's experiment is repeated with an atmosphere of carbon dioxide, nitrogen, and water vapor, organic molecules are synthesized, but those molecules are cyanide and formaldehyde, both deadly to embryos and hardly conducive to the creation of life. Wells added for emphasis that "to suggest formaldehyde and cyanide give you the right substrate for the origin of life...well, it's just a joke. Do you know what you get? Embalming fluid!" (Strobel 2004).

No, formaldehyde and cyanide are not the building blocks of life. We know today that in addition to amino acids, the building block of life, DNA, consists of two chains of nucleotides, which are bonded together in the structure of a double helix. Adenine, thymidine, cytosine, and guanine are the "letters" that make up the genetic code. Still, scientists around the world have continued to experiment under varied atmospheric conditions to create amino acids. Even under ideal laboratory conditions, these efforts have been in vain. "After nearly four decades of trying, with the best equipment and the best minds in chemistry, not even the 'letters' of the genetic code have been produced by *random* chemical processes. If the letters cannot be produced [under ideal lab conditions] by doctorate-level chemists, how can we logically assume that they arose by chance in a chemical quagmire?" (Eastman).

What's the Probability of That?

There are additional problems that must be explained when proposing the spontaneous occurrence of life, one being probabilities. What are the odds of the spontaneous occurrence of life forms? Many espouse hand-waving arguments that, given enough time, even the most improbable events become likely. Consider George Bernard Shaw's hypothesis that if a million monkeys pounded on keyboards for a long enough time, one would eventually arrive at a Shakespearean play. To many, his assertion seemed preposterous, but to others, though humorous, it was considered quite feasible. So is this assertion plausible, or does it fall into the category of a lie told often enough that it is accepted as truth?

What happens when the numbers are crunched and the probabilities considered? Today the average person types from twenty to forty words per minute, with professional typists weighing in at fifty to eighty words per minute. Let us assume our million monkeys are unfettered by thought and can type an average of one hundred words per minute, and that each word in the play contains only four letters (both generous assumptions!). Using probability and statistics, one can arrive at the time required for these million monkeys to produce words of meaning. One million monkeys each typing one hundred words per minute would bang out the equivalent of one hundred million words per minute and in a mere twelve seconds, one of the monkeys would pound out the first four-letter word of the play. However, it is much more difficult to link two cohesive words together and for this five days would be required; the first four words of the play would require a staggering one hundred billion years—and a lot of monkey food. The time required for the first scene alone is beyond staggering, and no one could imagine the time required to compose an entire play (Boa 1982). For reference, though there is not a consensus on Earth's age, the oldest estimates are four to five billion years—far less than the hundred billion years required for the million monkeys to produce a statement consisting of merely the first four cohesive words of our Shakespearian play. We can conclude that creating stories without intelligence is implausible and not enough time will ever elapse for the most improbable events to become likely.

In the 1970s, British astronomer Sir Frederick Hoyle, using laws of chemistry, thermodynamics, and mathematical probabilities, endeavored to calculate the likelihood of the spontaneous generation of life from the primordial soup:

Hoyle and his associates knew that the smallest conceivable free-living life form needed at least 2,000 independent functional proteins in order to accomplish cellular metabolism and reproduction. Starting with the hypothetical primordial soup, he calculated the probability of the spontaneous generation of just the proteins of a single amoeba. He determined that the probability of such an event is one chance in ten to the 40 thousandth power (1 in $10^{40,000}$). Mathematicians tell us that if an event has a probability which is less likely than one chance in 10^{50}, then that event is mathematically impossible; such an event, if it were to occur, would be considered a miracle. Prior to this project, Hoyle was a believer in the spontaneous generation of life. This project, however, apparently changed his opinion 180 degrees. (Eastman)

Sir Frederick Hoyle found that it would take more than a miracle for the spontaneous generation of just a protein, which is a small building block. Consider a simplified sequence of events that need to be executed in order to produce a living cell:

1. Random atoms need to combine to form an amino acid.

2. Amino acids need to form chains, creating polypeptides.

3. Twenty different amino acids must join in specific order in notably long chains (hundreds of amino acids altogether) to create a simple protein molecule.

4. More complex proteins must be created.

5. DNA must be formed and maintained.

6. A staggeringly complex chemical factory must then be assembled, complete with enzymes, proteins, DNA, RNA, ribosomes, and a cell wall.

7. Finally, this single cell needs to be equipped with a mechanism that allows it to reproduce itself.

Jonathan Wells discussed the improbability the spontaneous occurrence of this sequence of events with Lee Strobel. Wells showed a video of a cell moving through a liquid. The cell wall is pierced, and all its contents spill into the liquid. Wells explained that even with all the components necessary to re-create this single-cell organism in an ideal vile of sterile liquid, with the accumulated intelligence humankind, we are not able to reconstruct this cell.

> Even if Miller's experiment were valid, you are still light-years away from making life. It comes down to this: No matter how many molecules you can produce, with early earth conditions, plausible conditions, you're still nowhere near producing a living cell. And here's how I know, if I take a sterile test tube, and I put in a little bit of fluid with just the right salts, with just the right balance of acidity and alkalinity, at just the right temperature...the perfect solution for a living cell...and I put in it one living cell. This cell is alive. It has everything it needs for life. Now I take a sterile needle and I poke that cell [the video shows a cell as its wall is broken and its insides leak out] and all its stuff leaks out into this test tube. You have all in this nice little test tube all the molecules you need for a living cell, not just the pieces of the molecules, but the molecules themselves, and you cannot make a living cell out of them. You can't put Humpty Dumpty back together again. (Strobel 2008)

Robert Shapiro, in his book *Origins: A Skeptic's Guide to the Creation of Life on Earth*, provides a realistic illustration of how one might attempt to understand the enormity of spontaneous generation of life on Earth. Shapiro notes that twenty minutes is required for a single bacterium to duplicate. He assumes the first cell would be much simpler and thus require only one minute for a trial assembly, which would allow for approximately 5×10^{14} trials in one billion years. Next, he assumes Earth's entire oceans would be the "reactor chambers," which if divided into flasks with volumes the size of a single bacterium, would yield 10^{36} separate chambers. His next assumption is that each reactor chamber is stocked with all the necessary components to create life and can be restocked as necessary. Then each is allowed to run the one-minute trial assemblies for a period of one billion years. With all of these generous assumptions, Shapiro found that there would be time available for 10^{51} trials during one billion years. Hoyle's calculations of the improbabilities (1 in $10^{40,000}$) did not include any steps beyond the proteins. Harold Morowitz, a Yale physicist, calculated that the odds of a single bacterium spontaneously assembling itself by chance, even in an environment that consisted of all the necessary components, are only 1 in $10^{100,000,000,000}$. With only 10^{51} trials feasible in one billion years and with these probabilities, the time required for spontaneous generation of life would be $10^{99,999,999,949}$ billion years—which is unfathomable. In the words of Francis Crick, winner of the Nobel Prize in Biology, "An honest man, armed with all the knowledge available to us now, could only state that in some sense, the origin of life appears at the moment to be almost a miracle, so many are the conditions which would have to be satisfied to get it going" (Crick 1982).

We have previously established that whatever initiated life on Earth existed before the universe, was extraordinarily powerful, and was either random or purposeful. With the evidence and probabilities presented by Strobel, Wells, Peet, Crick, Hoyle, Morowitz, Boa, and more, it is apparent that the likelihood of spontaneous creation has staggeringly lower odds than those of a miracle. Combine the low odds of spontaneous generation of life with the (im)probability of randomly creating the entire universe times the improbability of transitioning from one single-celled organism to all the species that have populated our planet, and the improbability that life and our universe were created from a random, unguided process makes creation by a greater power seem relatively likely and the most probable explanation.

Choose Your Headline

Consider for a moment the search for extraterrestrial intelligence (SETI). Radio experiments are one branch of experiments of the SETI project. Radio frequencies are monitored to detect "nonnatural" radio emissions from a location outside our galaxy. Imagine yourself a radio technician monitoring the airwaves when a series of bleeps and blips commences. The recorders are running as adrenaline courses through your veins. You listen. "Blip-bleep, bleep, bleep. Blip-bleep, bleep, bleep-blip-bleep-blip." Your heart pounds as you realize this may be Morse code. In your excitement, you summon all your colleagues, who come as quickly as they can. "Blip-bleep, bleep, blip-bleep." They crowd around a whiteboard as you translate the Morse code in real time. "Bleep, bleep-bleep-blip, bleep-bleep-blip."

ATT, ATC, ATA, TGG...

The excitement is palpable. This has to be Morse code, but what does the strange pattern of letters mean? It certainly does not seem to be random, yet it also does not seem to form words. A biologist who has been studying how life may have evolved on Mars rushes to the board, circles your first three groups of letters, and under them scribbles "isoleucine." She then circles "TGG" and scribbles "tryptophan." By that time, you've written two more groups of three. Next to them, she writes "phenylalanine." The process continues until she has written twenty words, and she excitedly explains that these are the DNA codons of the twenty amino acids that are found in proteins. The pattern of blips and bleeps begins to repeat. You and your colleagues confirm that the transmission originates from a location outside our galaxy. You pause, take a deep breath, and ponder your next move. Imagine what you would announce to the press. What would the headlines read? What would be the conclusion of the SETI team?

SETI Researchers Declare Extraterrestrial Transmission of DNA Codons for Twenty Amino Acids a Random Event

OR

SETI Researchers Confirm Extraterrestrial Intelligence!
List of DNA Codons Sent from beyond Our Galaxy: No Random Event.

The Evidence Points to Intelligence

We know instinctively that such an extraterrestrial radio message would confirm that intelligence existed beyond our galaxy. Yet this same message and messages infinitely more complex (genetic codes for wheat, corn, and all plant, animal, and human life, for example) are thought by many to be random events rather than messages from an intelligent source. **Considering the probabilities, more faith is required to believe that order and life have been created from randomness than is required to believe that order and life have been created purposefully and with intelligence.** It is strikingly clear that the intelligence required to create life (as evidenced by man's collective inability to systematically do so other than via procreation) remains far beyond human intellect. Some take the leap of faith, considering humans the most evolved animals; if the problem is beyond our grasp, it must be a random event. If, however, faith is observing facts, determining where they lead, and then trusting the illuminated path, then faith needs to be placed in the existence of an intelligence beyond our own. As summarized by Sir Frederick Hoyle, "A super intellect has monkeyed with physics, as well as with chemistry and biology...The likelihood of the formation of life from inanimate matter is one to a number of 10 with 40 thousand noughts [zeros] after it. It is enough to bury Darwin and the whole theory of [Macro] Evolution. There was no primeval soup, neither on this planet nor on any other, and if the beginnings of life were not random they must therefore have been the product of a purposeful intelligence" (Hoyle 1981).

We have now arrived at three characteristics of an entity that may be responsible for the creation of the universe:

1. Existed before the universe (**eternal—unchanging**)

2. Extraordinarily powerful, unlike anything known to mankind (**omnipotent**)

3. Possesses extreme intelligence unfathomable by man and has the ability to conceive and author the genetic code for all life forms (**omniscient**)

The Fossil Record: A Brief Excursion

As mentioned, volumes would be required to do justice to the topic of the creation and evolution of life, but to summarize without mention of our fossil record would be remiss. When Darwin published his theory of evolution, he noted two big gaps, the first being the spontaneous generation of life from inanimate matter, which we have already discussed, and the second being the mechanism by which a simple single cell could give birth to higher and higher orders of life, ultimately evolving from mindless inanimate materials to thoughtful, introspective human beings.

Darwin observed change in birds and animals of the same species. He surmised that the slight differences within the same species were due to the ability to adapt to the different influences of their respective environments. For example, he noted that birds of the same species may have slightly different beaks based on the food available within their respective ecosystems. From these observations, he extrapolated that over extremely long periods of time, these cumulative microevolutionary changes could result in the creation of an entirely new species, though he noted at the time that the fossil record did not support such a theory. There is also no explanation as to why this macroevolutionary change process would cease to function; in other words, there is no explanation as to why amoebas, monkeys, and even men would not continually give birth to intermediate species, making slow progress to new species each day, year, decade, century, millennium, and so on. Jonathan Wells noted the following:

> A key aspect of his [Darwin's] theory was that natural selection would act, in his own words, "slowly by accumulating slight, successive, favorable variations" and that "no great or sudden

modifications" were possible...Darwin knew the fossil record failed to support his tree. He acknowledged that major groups of animals (he calls them divisions; now they are called phyla) appear suddenly in the fossil record. That's not what his theory predicts...Darwin believed that future fossil discoveries would vindicate his theory, but that hasn't happened. Actually, fossil discoveries of the last hundred and fifty years have turned his tree upside down by showing the Cambrian explosion was even more abrupt and extensive than scientists once thought. (Strobel 2004)

If all life indeed descended from a common ancestor, the layers of rock all around Earth should be teeming with evidence that supports this gradual transition. The fossil record should demonstrate a series of small changes—single cells transitioning in the deepest layers to subsequently more and more complex organisms through each stratum. Yet fossils discovered and researched for over the past two hundred years do not support the supposition of slow biological changes. The most pervasive contrarian data comes from fossils found from an era now known as the Cambrian explosion. The Cambrian explosion of life, also known as the biological big bang, occurred about 530 million years ago. The Cambrian fossils show that all of the major animal phyla appeared rather suddenly, rather than via a series of slow transitions from one life form to another. Wells illustrates the stark nature of this explosion:

The branching tree pattern of Darwin's theory is actually not seen anywhere in the fossil record...The Cambrian explosion is the most dramatic refutation of the tree of life. If we imagine the whole history of life on Earth taking place in one twenty-four-hour period, the current standard estimates for the origin of life put it at about 3.8 billion years ago; let's say 4 billion. So, if we start the clock then—our twenty-four-hour clock, [at] six hours [still] nothing but these simple single-celled organisms appear. [These are] the same sort that we saw in the beginning. [At] twelve hours [we find the] same thing. [At] Eighteen hours [we find the] same thing. Three quarters of the day has passed, and all we have are these simple single-celled organisms. Then at about the twenty-first hour, in the space of about two minutes: boom! Most of the major animal forms appear in the form that they currently have in the present, and many of them persist until the present, and we have them with us today. Less than two minutes out of a twenty-four-hour day, that's how sudden the Cambrian explosion was. (Strobel 2008)

In what seems to have been a mere heartbeat, the animal kingdom experienced a quantum leap from simple single-celled organisms to extraordinary creatures with spinal cords, articulated limbs, and compound eyes. The stark nature of this leap looks nothing like Darwin's slowly branching tree, which depicts one organism evolving slowly into several divergent branches, with big differences finally appearing at the top. The data actually shows a bunch of different phyla (like Darwin's tree) originating simultaneously, and then perhaps branching out within a phylum—more like an orchard than a single tree.

From the mystical big bang to the extraordinary creation of life and the dramatic Cambrian explosion, we recognize a common fingerprint or signature. NASA astronomer Robert Jastrow wrote, "Now we see how the astronomical evidence leads to a Biblical view of the Origin of the world: the chain of events leading to man commenced suddenly and sharply in a definite moment of time, in a flash of light and energy" (Jastrow 1992). In our brief summary reviewing specific events in time, from the big bang to the appearance of man, we have derived four characteristics of an entity that may be responsible for the creation of the universe and all it contains:

1. Existed before the universe (**eternal—unchanging**)

2. Extraordinarily powerful, unlike anything known to mankind (**omnipotent**)

3. Possesses extreme intelligence unfathomable by man and has the ability to conceive and author the genetic code for all life forms (**omniscient**)

4. Able to successfully "implement" genetic plans quickly and simultaneously, with high yield, over the entire planet (**omnipresent**)

These characteristics point toward an intelligent, powerful, everlasting, and always-present creator. I don't know what you might name an entity with such characteristics, but many have named this being God.

If There Is a God, Then Who Is He?

There are five major religions in the world today: Buddhism, Christianity, Islam, Hinduism, and Judaism. Some dismiss religions as being "the same," whereas others claim that some religions, such as Christianity, are too exclusive and require too many people to be wrong. These two statements cannot both be true; these religions cannot simultaneously be the same and by their doctrine exclude one another from being "right."

Buddhism

Buddhism, founded in India, is based on the teachings of Siddhartha Gautama, also known as the Buddha. Gautama, born the son of the ruler of a small kingdom in 563 BC, realized at age twenty-four that his life was empty and meaningless. He left home in search of enlightenment. After a few years of yoga, extreme self-denial, and meditation, he became enlightened. Gautama developed the Four Noble Truths, which became the core of Buddhism:

1. All living beings suffer.
2. The origin of suffering is desire.
3. Desire can be overcome.

4. There exists a path, the Eightfold Path, that leads to release from desire. The eight "folds" are divided into three categories: anatta, karma, and nirvana.

Buddha denies that there is an everlasting soul (anatta), rejects the existence of a creator, and teaches that one must earn release from an endless chain of reincarnation by following the Four Noble Truths and the Eightfold Path. Karma is based on a person's acts: good deeds are rewarded and evil deeds, punished. Karma determines one's species, wealth, social status, health, beauty, and all other circumstances upon each rebirth. Being from India, Buddha was a theist (he believed in gods); however his teachings are largely non-theistic. As a consequence, some Buddhists are atheists (believe there are no gods) and others believe in many gods known as devas. The ultimate goal of Buddhism is to attain nirvana by achieving complete detachment from the cares of this world.

Christianity

Christianity is based on the teachings of Jesus Christ as documented in the New Testament Bible. Jesus was a Jew, as were his earliest disciples. The Jews taught that all must adhere to God's laws (the laws of Moses) to ultimately be saved by the Messiah. Jesus claimed to be the Messiah, sent as the Son of God to fulfill the prophecies of the Old Testament (Jewish Torah) and cleanse the world of its sins so that man would no longer be separated from God after death. Many Jews were expecting a mighty warrior who would save them by might from the oppression of the Roman Empire. Jesus taught, however, that no man had ever lived a pure enough life to gain admittance into heaven. As a result, he had come to save us from our own sins rather than from the oppression of others, and only by his death and resurrection could our sins be cleansed. Jesus challenged his followers to live good lives and to help one another through good works, but he taught that ultimately, all would fall short of the glory of God, and it would not be through good works but through faith in him, the Son of God, that they would gain entrance to heaven. Jesus claimed that he was one with the Father who sent him in human form to be challenged by all the ways of this world and to be tempted by Satan. After passing all tests on earth without sin, Jesus passed the final and ultimate test: he was sentenced to death by Jewish Pharisees and Sadducees and crucified under Roman rule.

Upon his death, Jesus's frightened disciples were scattered and in denial. They feared for their lives. Christianity is based on the premise that although Jesus was buried in a tomb guarded closely by his enemies, he rose from the grave and walked again among his followers. He was even seen by as many as five hundred Jews at one time. So convinced of Jesus's resurrection were his followers that they moved from denying their affiliation with Jesus to teaching others of Jesus's resurrection and ultimately paying for their belief with their own lives, as they were persecuted and killed because they would not renounce the fact that Jesus rose from the grave. Even the Romans, who crucified Jesus, later divided their calendar to reflect Jesus as the Son of God, dividing history into two periods: BC (before Christ) and AD (*anno Domini*, "the year of the Lord").

Hinduism

Hinduism, the main religion in India, is thought to be one of the oldest religions in the world, dating back to prehistoric times. With no clear founder, Hinduism finds its origins in the religious practices of Aryan tribes that migrated to India from the ancient lands now known as Iran. The Aryans developed a caste system that ranked society into four hereditary classes based on occupation: Brahman (priests), Kshatriya (military, professional, ruling, and governing occupations), Vaisya (landowners, merchants, and business occupations), and Sudra (artisans, laborers, and peasants). Below the Sudra was a fifth group known as the harijans, or "untouchables," which had no social standing and consisted of the lowest occupations. Despite being outlawed by the Indian government in 1948, the caste system still holds import as the manner by which to classify society in India.

Hinduism is characterized by complete freedom of belief, supporting atheism, monotheism, and polytheism. Those who choose monotheism generally devote themselves to either Shiva or Vishnu. The most ancient texts of Hinduism are called the Vedas, and the oldest, Rig Veda, talks of multiple gods, the universe, and creation. Like Buddhism, Hinduism is based on reincarnation and karma—rebirth being determined by moral behavior during one's previous life. Life on earth is viewed as a short-lived burden with the ultimate goal of obtaining liberation from the potentially endless cycle of death and rebirth to a state of moksha, where one attains his or her Supreme Self (Brahman), or oneness with all existence and understanding.

Islam

Islam was founded in Arabia by the prophet Muhammad, who was born in AD 570 to a wealthy family in Mecca. At twenty-five years old, Muhammad joined a caravan traveling from Mecca to Syria, and it was during this trip that he learned of the suffering of others and thus began his search in the desert for personal enlightenment. His ministry began at age forty, after having visions that he gradually came to believe detailed a mission from God to reform religion. He first began to preach in Mecca, but upon being ill received in his hometown, he moved in 622 to the city of Medina, where he was soon thought of as a lawgiver and prophet. By the time of his death in 632, Muhammad was the leader of a strong and growing Arab state and considered by his followers (Muslims) to be the prophet of Allah, the one and only true god.

Muhammad's teachings are found in the Koran, which presents the Five Pillars of Islam as an obligatory framework of worship and a sign of commitment to the faith:

1. Profession of faith (*shahada*)
2. Prayer performed five times a day (salat)
3. Almsgiving to the poor (zakah)
4. Daylight fasting during the month of Ramadan

5. Pilgrimage to Mecca (hajj) at least once in a Muslim's life

Muslims testify that there exist no other deities besides Allah and that Muhammad is His messenger. Muslims believe that God's purpose is creation, sustenance, guidance, and judgment, whereas the main purpose of humanity is to serve and worship God. Muslims believe that by worshiping God and living a moral life according to the Five Pillars and Islamic jurisprudence, they earn their way to heaven.

Judaism

Judaism is also one of the oldest religions of the world. It originated in the Middle East and is based on the existence of one god, Yahweh, who in the twentieth century BC established a holy covenant raising Abraham as the patriarch of Judaism and Abraham's descendants as God's chosen people. Judaism's teachings are found in the Torah, which is part of a larger text known as the Tanakh or Hebrew Bible. The Torah is a combination of historical records, divine laws, and written explanations of God's plans and prophecies based on the cultural norms of two to four thousand years ago. Abraham's line descended through Isaac to Jacob, who fathered the twelve families who ended up slaves after migrating to Egypt and became known as the twelve tribes of Israel. In about 1300 BC, Moses led the Jews out of Egypt and slavery, but for forty years, they wandered the desert until he led them to the promised land of Canaan, where with the Lord's help, they defeated the Canaanites.

After conquering Canaan, the Jews prayed for a monarchy, and God responded by raising Saul as the first king of the Israelites. Saul was succeeded by David and then by David's son Solomon. Saul's and David's reigns were fraught with war, and though David longed to build a house for their god, that task was left for the peaceful times enjoyed by Solomon, who with God's blessings, became known far and wide as one of the wisest and, subsequently, richest men to have ever lived. Upon Solomon's death, Canaan split into Israel in the north and Judea in the south. The famed house of God was destroyed and the

Jews exiled in subsequent conflicts with the Assyrian and Babylonian empires. The Israelites were then subject to centuries of rule by Persians, Egyptians, Syrians, Greeks, and Romans. During this period, many small groups emerged, such as the Pharisees, Sadducees, Zealots, and the Essenes, each offering a different twist on Judaism, though today, the largest Jewish religious movements are Orthodox, Conservative, and Reform Judaism, with the major differences being their approaches to Jewish law, the significance of the State of Israel, and the authority of rabbinic tradition.

Jews believe that salvation is earned by leading a moral life according to God's laws, also known as the laws of Moses. Judaism has strongly influenced Christianity (Jesus Christ was a Jew), Islam, and the Baha'i faith, as well as Western ethics and civil law. The prominent difference between the Jewish and Christian faiths is the belief in a messiah. Jews believe that the Messiah is yet to come, whereas Christians have faith that Jesus is the Messiah and that peace will be attained when he returns.

Summary of Today's Five Major Religions

Each of these religions claims to be correct in its beliefs. Four of the five believe that salvation is attained only through human effort. Buddhists, Christians, Muslims, and Jews all believe that they have found the only true way to God and salvation, whereas Hindus might argue that their beliefs are not exclusive of others because there exist many paths to achieve nirvana. "A closer look...reveals that the Hindu allows for an openness to other faiths but stresses the superiority of his own. There is really only one path by which an outsider can enter the fold. He must live a pious life and then, after many transmigrations, his soul may be at last reborn into a Hindu family" (Boa 1982). Each of these major religions has a different view of who or what God is, of what our ultimate destiny will be, and how we achieve salvation (Figure 5).

How can each religion be exclusive yet correct? Can these religions disagree on who God is, what happens in the afterlife, and how salvation is achieved, and still all be correct? The answer is probably obvious: simply put, they cannot all be so different and yet be simultaneously correct. One may be correct, or all are incorrect or at best partially correct.

View of:	God	Destiny	Salvation
Buddhism:	Varies from atheistic (no gods) to polytheistic (many gods)	Individual consciousness ultimately yields to nirvana, a state of total nothingness (no consciousness).	Release from the endless chain of reincarnation is earned by following the Four Noble Truths and the Eightfold Path.
Christianity:	One true god who presents himself as the Father, the Son (Jesus), and the Holy Spirit (the voice of God)	Believers are destined to spend eternity with God in heaven, while nonbelievers will be separated from God in hell.	Salvation is attained by accepting that Christ died on the cross so that sins would be forgiven.
Hinduism:	Varies from atheistic (no gods), to monotheistic (one god) to polytheistic (many gods)	Individual consciousness yields to oneness with all existence and understanding in a state of moksha (unified consciousness).	Oneness is achieved through a series of reincarnations.
Islam:	One true god	Muslims spend eternity with Allah in heaven, enjoying sensual pleasures.	Salvation is earned by following the doctrines and performing the duties outlined in the Five Pillars.
Judaism:	One true god	Some sects believe that nothing exists after death, while others look forward to spending eternity with the Messiah.	Salvation is earned by living a moral life.

Figure 5: Summary views of the five major world religions

Many people seem to believe that Christianity is the only religion that claims exclusivity, but we can see clearly from the summary above that is not the case. However, Christianity alone is based on the premise that salvation is a gift and not earned. In his quest to free his wife Leslie from this "apparent" cult, Lee Strobel set out to prove God nonexistent and Jesus a fraud. His journey led him to the conclusion that there is a creator, but is Jesus that creator?

Christianity (A Deeper Dive)

Was Strobel able to prove Jesus a fraud? In his quest for truth, Strobel employed his training from Yale Law School and his experience as a legal affairs journalist to investigate the proof (akin to that reviewed in a court of law): eyewitness testimony, documentary evidence, corroborating and rebuttal evidence, circumstantial evidence, and, "yes, even fingerprint evidence" (Strobel 1998).

> As far as Jesus was concerned, I thought that if he existed, and I wasn't sure whether or not he ever did, he was probably a nice guy, he was probably an excellent teacher, but he certainly wasn't the Messiah, and he certainly wasn't the Son of God. Now my wife was more in spiritual neutral, she was more of an agnostic whereas I was more antagonistic toward Christians. (Strobel 1998)

Strobel began his investigation by delving into the Gospel accounts of the New Testament. He did not believe the New Testament to be the word of God, but he did recognize it as a historical document, and so set out to determine if it stood up to the scrutiny of historians. The New Testament Gospels are biographies of Jesus, primarily focused on his ministry, written by four different authors: Matthew, Mark, Luke, and John. The authors are not specifically noted in the texts but have been attributed to each of these four from the earliest times of the Christian era. Who were these men?

- Matthew: Formerly Levi a tax collector who became a disciple of Jesus and an apostle upon being called into the ministry directly by Jesus. A firsthand witness.

- Mark: A colleague of Peter who was a disciple of Jesus. Mark was converted to Christianity by Peter, became an evangelist, and subsequently traveled with the apostle Paul. A secondhand witness.

- Luke: A historian and physician who became an evangelist and was a confidant of the apostle Paul. A secondhand witness.

- John: A disciple and apostle of Jesus who was an eyewitness to the crucifixion and transfiguration of Jesus. A firsthand witness.

Both Matthew and John were among Jesus's twelve closest followers and personally observed most of the events described in their respective Gospels. Mark and Luke were also contemporaries of Jesus, and they wrote their biographies based on information collected from many eyewitnesses. Strobel questioned historians and biblical scholars to ascertain whether or not the Gospels are indeed rooted in eyewitness testimony. What Strobel found began to change his world. He found that the documents were written not only close to the time that Jesus lived but while eyewitnesses were still alive to challenge and correct any potential errors. All the authors were either eyewitnesses or had interviewed and learned from eyewitnesses. They and their colleagues had vested interests in preserving accuracy, even though as proponents of Jesus's ministry, they knowingly placed their lives in considerably risk. Even Jesus's opponents, who desired the truth to be forgotten in order to contain the spread of Jesus's influence after his death, would not stand for lies to spread wantonly.

It is valuable to understand the timeline for a few significant events just prior to and throughout the first century:

- Jesus's birth occurred between 7 and 3 BC, which seems counterintuitive, given that BC stands for "before Christ," but the division of years is based largely on the timing of King Herod's death as correlated to events documented in the Gospels. It is thought that King Herod died between 4 and 1 BC and that Jesus was born two to three years prior to Herod's death—thus, between 7 and 3 BC.

- Jesus's public ministry began between AD 27 and 30.

- Jesus's death occurred between AD 30 and 33.

- The Gospel of Mark was written between AD 60 and 75.

- The Gospels of Matthew and Luke were written between AD 60 and 85.

- The Gospel of John and Revelations were written between AD 65 and 95.

- In AD 70, the Zealots revolted, and Jerusalem and its temple were destroyed.

According to JP Moreland of Biola University, a distinguished professor of philosophy, "It's become evident to scholars of the first century that the Gospels were actually attempts to write biographies of Jesus, but not in the modern sense, because the Gospels are not particularly interested in his early years, but when it comes to Jesus's adult life and his activities, these are biographies. They're very clearly attempts by eyewitnesses to describe exactly what Jesus said and did and the consensus of New Testament scholarship has moved in that direction" (Strobel 2007).

The people in the first century, similar to people today, valued eyewitness testimony, and Luke personally noted that he had carefully documented the details of Jesus's ministry based on the accounts of eyewitnesses: "Many have undertaken to draw up an account of the things that have been fulfilled among us, just as they were handed down to us by those who from the first were eyewitnesses and servants of the word. With this in mind, since I myself have carefully investigated everything from the beginning, I too decided to write an orderly account for you, most excellent Theophilus, so that you may know the certainty of the things you have been taught" (Luke 1 [NIV]).

It was important to early church leaders to accurately determine authorship of the New Testament and to ensure their writings were based on eyewitness testimony. According to Mark Strauss, a biblical scholar and professor of the New Testament at Bethel Seminary in San Diego, "We have, actually, very early attestation of the authorship of the Gospels. The early church father Patheus, for example, as recorded by the church historian Eusebius, identifies Mark's Gospel as essentially the eyewitness account of Peter. Patheus was a disciple of the apostle John" (Strobel 2007). Craig Bloomberg of the Denver Seminary, one of the foremost experts on the biographies of Jesus, stated, "Within the first two years after his death, significant numbers of Jesus followers seem to have formulated a doctrine of the atonement, were convinced that he [Jesus] had been raised from the dead in bodily form, associated Jesus with God, and believed they found support for all these convictions in the Old Testament" (Strobel 1998). Two years is not nearly enough time for legend to have developed and wiped out the solid core of historical truth; too many witnesses were yet alive!

Some argue that there are too many inconsistencies in the Gospels for them to be accurate biographies, while others suggest that the content is fabricated; however, most of the inconsistencies can be explained by the differences in each author's perspective, style, and emphasis. For instance, Matthew tells the story of two blind men being healed, whereas Mark tells of only one. The reason is that Mark focused only on the most prominent man, as he was the man of most societal import, while Luke, a doctor, naturally included more detail regarding ailments. In fact, most discrepancies in the Gospels are quite similar, and if all the accounts were exactly the same, it would suggest collusion rather than agreement. After reviewing the evidence, Strobel stated, "It's natural when you have multiple eyewitnesses to the same event you're going to get different perspectives, and that's okay; you want that. What you're looking for is a core to the testimony that's the same, that's consistent, even though there might be some variation in the incidental details. If you are in a court of law and you have multiple witnesses that come in and testify to the exact same thing, the first objection that's brought up is to say 'Collusion! They got together. They orchestrated their testimony!' And their credibility is shot" (Strobel 2007).

Dr. Simon Greenleaf was one of the principle founders and Royal Professor of Law at Harvard University, and author of the famous legal document *A Treatise on the Law of Evidence* (considered by many to be the greatest legal volume ever written), believed the resurrection of Jesus Christ to be a hoax, and like Strobel, was determined to expose the "myth" once and for all. Greenleaf set out to subject the four Gospels to tests similar to those used during modern-day trials, and though he set out to prove them invalid, he strived to remain objective; he wrote eloquently of the Gospels and their authors in *Testimony of the Evangelists*. In the course of his investigation, Greenleaf reviewed the integrity of the documents themselves, the four authors' backgrounds, their target audiences, their personal integrity, and their capability before arriving at his final conclusion.

Integrity of the New Testament Documents

Both Strobel and Greenleaf found the New Testament to be extremely sound and of the highest integrity. Strobel interviewed experts who showed that not only do we have more ancient manuscripts for the New Testament than for any other ancient text, but the New Testament is the only such text written by contemporaries and eyewitnesses to the events documented. Recall that all four Gospels were written in the first century and less than seventy years after Jesus's crucifixion by the Romans, and they were thus subjected to the scrutiny of contemporaries both for and against Jesus's doctrine. Strobel requested that Bloomberg provide a comparison to illustrate how much time elapsed between the actual events and the time they were documented in other ancient texts. Bloomberg responded confidently, "The two earliest biographies of Alexander the Great were written by Arrian and Plutarch more than four hundred years after Alexander's death in 323 BC, yet historians consider them to be generally trustworthy. Yes, legendary material about Alexander did develop over time, but it was only in the centuries after these two writers" (Strobel 2007). Further, Greenleaf found that the documents withstood the legal test of genuineness and authenticity:

> Are they worthy of implicit belief, in the matters which they relate?...They are received as the plain narratives and writings of

the men whose names they respectively bear, made public at the time they were written; and though there are some slight discrepancies among the copies subsequently made, there is no pretense that the originals are lost, and that copies alone are now produced...These copies of the Holy Scriptures having thus been in familiar use in the churches, from the time when the text was committed to writing; having been watched with vigilance by so many sects, opposed to each other in doctrine, yet all appealing to these Scriptures for the correctness of their faith; and having in all ages, down to this day...it is quite erroneous to suppose that the Christian is bound to offer any further proof of their genuineness or authenticity. (Greenleaf 1846)

Integrity of the Four Evangelists

In order to evaluate the consistency and integrity of the Gospels, Greenleaf evaluated each author's background, perspective, and primary target audience. Understanding the author's intended audience is key to unraveling differences between the Gospel's in both tone and content.

Matthew

Background: Matthew, also known as Levi, was one of Jesus's twelve disciples and traveled with Jesus throughout his ministry. Prior to joining Jesus, Matthew was a Jew who became a tax collector for the Roman conquerors. He collected taxes within his district as well as customs levied on goods and travelers passing in and out of his district and province. Matthew became a faithful follower of Jesus until Jesus's crucifixion and ascension, after which he preached with the other apostles throughout Judea for about fifteen years before spreading his ministry to gentiles: Macedonians, Persians, and Parthians. Finally, Matthew traveled to Ethiopia, where he became acquainted with the queen of Ethiopia, who had been influenced by her treasurer, who, as is documented in Acts 8:26–40, had been baptized by Philip, a convert of Jesus. Early church historians documented that Matthew was later killed by order of the king of

Ethiopia, whom Matthew had rebuked for lusting over his own niece, a convert and nun devoted to Christ. Matthew protected her despite the risk and died a martyr's death at the hands of the king's men.

Perspective and primary audience: Being a native Jew, Matthew was familiar with the traditions, opinions, and customs of his fellow Jews. He was conversant with the sacred writings and was thought to be a trustworthy man of common sense (thus his appointment as a tax collector). Beyond knowledge of the Old Testament, he was not considered to be a well-educated man, but being a tax collector, he was well versed in the ways of his countrymen. Greenleaf found that Matthew wrote with conviction based on personal experiences as well as experiences shared by other firsthand witnesses, and without any intent of self-profit. According to Greenleaf, "[these] are facts which we may consider established by internal evidence. It is deemed equally well proved, both by internal evidence and the aid of history that he wrote for the use of his countrymen the Jews." Greenleaf explained that Matthew took care to document each circumstance which might win over his fellow Jews and omitted "every unnecessary expression" that may cause confusion. For example, Matthew took special care to document that Jesus was descended from King David and born in Bethlehem to illustrate that Jesus did, in fact, fulfill their expectations of the Messiah based on prophecies of the Old Testament. Because he was a tax collector for the Romans, Matthew was considered by his fellow countrymen to have *cooperated with the enemy*. Despite that knowledge, he did not sway from writing his Gospel in a manner that was clearly addressed to his fellow Jews. His was the only biography of Jesus written in Hebrew and is filled with events and commentary designed to profess to God's chosen people the good news—that their messiah had come.

Capability and opportunity: During the day-to-day execution of his duties, Matthew was responsible for the assessment and collection of taxes that were not voluntarily paid by the conquered Jews to the conquering Romans. Thus, it is believed that Matthew was accustomed to evasions and frauds, while he remained responsible for diligent exaction. Under these circumstances, monitoring and taxing trade among Jews, Greeks, and Romans, Matthew gained the trust of both the Romans and Jesus. Matthew was considered astute, capable of "reading" and negotiating with both honest and potentially fraudulent men.

> At this period, a considerable portion of the commerce of that part of the world was carried on by the Greeks, whose ingenuity and want of faith were proverbial. It was to such an employment and under such circumstances, that Matthew was educated; an employment which must have made him acquainted with the Greek language, and extensively conversant with the public affairs and the men of business of his time; thus entitling him to our confidence, as an experienced and intelligent observer of that day were, as in truth they appear to have been, as much disposed as those of the present time, to evade the payment of public taxes and duties, and to elude, by all possible means, the vigilance of the revenue officers, Matthew must have been familiar with a great variety of forms of fraud, imposture, cunning, and deception, and must have become habitually distrustful, scrutinizing, and cautious; and, of course, much less likely to have been deceived in regard to many of the facts in our Lord's ministry, extraordinary as they were, which fell under his observation. (Greenleaf 1846)

Conclusion: Matthew was not likely deceived by the fraud of his fellow man, for his Roman employers would not have suffered his failure to collect appropriate taxes, and it follows that he was not likely deceived by Jesus. In fact, Jesus's selection of a man with such powers of observation and knowledge of the Jewish community—and in the difficult position of extracting payment for the conquering rulers, moreover—highlights Jesus's wisdom. Greenleaf concludes, "This circumstance shows both the sincerity and the wisdom of Jesus, in selecting him for an eye-witness of his conduct, and adds great weight to the value of the testimony of this evangelist."

Mark

Background: Mark was converted to Christianity by Peter, a disciple of Jesus. Mark became an evangelist and subsequently traveled with the apostle Paul and Barnabas, his uncle. It was at Mark's home that early Christians often assembled. Subsequent to travels with Paul and Barnabas, at Paul's request, Mark traveled with the disciple Timothy to Rome. From Rome, he traveled to Asia, where he joined Peter. Together, they returned to Rome, where Mark wrote and published his Gospel. Finally, Mark established a church in Alexandria, where he died.

Perspective and primary audience: Mark wrote his Gospel in order to convert gentiles (non-Jews) to Christianity both in Rome and Egypt. We ascertain this in part through Mark's allusions to Roman colloquialisms in his Gospel that would have been meaningless to his Jewish contemporaries. Greenleaf explained that "[many of Mark's explanations] would have been useless to a Jew." Greenleaf further asserted that Mark explicitly targeted conversion of Romans: "[Mark's Gospel] was composed for those at Rome, is believed, not only from the numerous Latinisms it contains, but from the unanimous testimony of ancient writer, and from the internal evidence afforded by the Gospel itself."

Capability and opportunity: Mark was converted to Christianity by Peter who was one of Jesus's twelve disciples. Mark was trained by Paul and his uncle, Barnabas, and later, while writing his Gospel, he was a scribe to Peter. Peter was quite close to Jesus and was an eyewitness to most of the events of Jesus's ministry. Greenleaf discussed the similarities and differences between Matthew's and Mark's Gospels:

> The striking coincidences between them, in style, words, and things, in other places, may be accounted for by considering Peter, who is supposed to have dictated this Gospel to Mark, was quite as intimately acquainted as Matthew with the miracles and discourses of our Lord; which, therefore, he would naturally recite

in his preaching; and that the same things might very naturally be related in the same manner...Peter's agency in the narrative of Mark is asserted by all ancient writers. (Greenleaf 1846)

Greenleaf asserts that Peter's humility is evident throughout Mark's Gospel. Any commentary regarding Peter's weaknesses is fully disclosed, whereas examples of his value and valor are either skimmed over or not even included. He notes further that Mark did not write much about Jesus that did not directly involve Peter and that, in fact, Mark captured minute details that strongly indicated that he was learning from an eyewitness.

Conclusion: Strobel and Greenleaf arrived at the same conclusion: Mark's Gospel is an original composition of eyewitness testimony, especially that of Peter, who was a disciple of Jesus: "We may, therefore, regard the Gospel of Mark as an original composition, written at the dictation of Peter, and consequently as another original narrative of the life, miracles, and doctrine of our Lord" (Greenleaf 1846).

Luke

Background: Luke was well educated and a physician by trade. He was born to gentile parents, but in his youth, he embraced Judaism before becoming a Christian convert. Luke became a companion of the apostle Paul and was first mentioned during Paul's travels to Troas, Jerusalem, and Judea. He also stayed with Paul while he was a prisoner for two years in Rome. Unlike many of his contemporaries, Luke was apparently not killed for his belief in Jesus as the resurrected Messiah: "As none of the ancient fathers have mentioned his having suffered martyrdom, it is generally supposed that he died a natural death" (Greenleaf 1846). It is important to note that being a Christian in these times was so hazardous to one's health that dying of natural causes was out of the norm for early church leaders. Men and women risked their lives each day for their belief in the risen Jesus.

Perspective and primary audience: Luke addressed his Gospel to Theophilus and was mindful of addressing topics that would be conducive to teaching "outsiders" rather than Jews, leaving no doubt that his audience was primarily gentile. For example, he describes Jesus's lineage backward from Jesus to Adam rather than forward from Adam to Jesus, as practiced by his fellow Jews. He marks major events by the reigns of Roman emperors and includes many parables of the "lost" (all gentiles were considered lost) being "found" (e.g., the stories of the prodigal son and the lost silver coin).

Capability and opportunity: Trained as a physician, Luke was a keen and astute observer, highly capable of scrutinizing and commenting on Jesus's healing ministry. Luke reported minor nuances of Jesus's healing events that went unnoticed by others, such as handedness, causes of extreme weariness, and even the fact that Jesus "sweated blood" in the garden of Gethsemane. Much later, Leonardo da Vinci described a soldier who sweated blood before a battle, and today, sweating blood (known as hematidrosis) is an unusually rare condition that is believed to be brought on by extreme stress (Jerajani 2009):

> That Luke was a physician...and had given particular and even professional attention to all our Savior's miracles of healing. Thus, the man whom Matthew and Mark describe simply as a leper, Luke describes as full of leprosy; he, whom they mention as had having a withered hand, Luke says had his right hand withered...He alone, with professional accuracy of observation, says that virtue went out of Jesus, and healed the sick; he alone states the fact that the sleep of the disciples in Gethsemane was induced by extreme sorrow; and mentions the blood-like sweat of Jesus, as occasioned by the intensity of his agony; and he alone relates the miraculous healing of Malchus's ear. (Greenleaf 1846)

Conclusion: Luke wrote his Gospel while in Greece, specifically for gentiles, with the intent to replace incomplete and inaccurate narratives that had preceded his visit. Greenleaf concluded that Luke was fully capable of delivering to Theophilus (and others) a full and authentic account of Jesus's life, ministry, death, and resurrection. Luke does not literally name himself as an eyewitness to these events, but the specific details he includes, combined with his statement of perfect understanding, have led Greenleaf and others to conclude Luke to be a firsthand witness. Greenleaf concluded that if Luke's Gospel were merely the work of a historian, it would be deemed reliable, and went on to emphasize that Luke's work is much more, stating, "But it is more than this. It is the result of careful science, intelligence and education, concerning subjects which he was perfectly competent to peculiarly skilled, they being cases of the cure of maladies; [and] it would not be for the interest nor safety of the writer to deceive or mislead. Such a document certainly possesses all the moral attributes of an inquest of office, or of any other official investigation of facts."

John

Background: John, the son of Zebedee, a respectable fisherman with his own boat in the town of Bethsaida on the Sea of Galilee, was among the first followers to answer the call of Jesus. John was intimately close to Jesus, rounding out his inner circle along with Peter and James.

Perspective and primary audience: After Jesus's crucifixion, resurrection, and ascension, John began his ministry in and around Jerusalem, until the death of Jesus's mother, Mary, at which time he took his ministry to Asia Minor, where he founded and presided over seven churches in seven different cities, the gentiles comprising his primary audience in church and subsequently his Gospel. During Domitian's reign, John was banished to the Isle of Patmos, where he wrote Revelations, the final book of the New Testament. Greenleaf inferred that John's Gospel targeted gentiles, "That [John's Gospel] was written either with especial reference to the Gentiles, or at a period when very many of them had become converts to Christianity, is inferred from the various explanations it contains, beyond the other Gospels, which could have been necessary only to persons unacquainted with Jewish names and customs."

Capability and opportunity: John was joined by his mother as a follower of Jesus. The youngest of the disciples, John was welcomed by Jesus into his inner circle, and due to his closeness with Christ, he was often afforded unique opportunities to gain and record intimate knowledge. John was present with only Peter and James when Jesus resurrected Jairus's daughter at the transfiguration on the mount, and when Jesus prayed under great stress in the garden of Gethsemane prior to his crucifixion. John was the sole apostle to follow as Jesus carried his cross to Calgary Hill, and Jesus requested John to look after his mother, Mary, as he hung on the cross. John was the first of the apostles at Jesus's tomb and was present at the several appearances of the risen Jesus after his resurrection.

Conclusion: Based on John's inclusion in the inner circle and his decidedly close relationship with Jesus's mother, Mary, Greenleaf concludes that John was especially qualified as a firsthand witness to the events of Jesus's ministry. Further, since John's was the final of the four Gospels, he was able to "fill in the blanks" and omit topics that were already well covered. John was capable and had ample opportunity to witness and discuss firsthand events. His writing was accurate, timely, and personal.

> These circumstances, together with his intimate friendship with the mother of Jesus, especially qualify him to give a circumstantial and authentic account of the life of his Master...from his care to mention several incidents which were known to him, is too evident to admit of doubt; while his omission to repeat what they had already stated, or, where he does mention the same things, his relating them in a brief and cursory manner, affords incidental but strong testimony that he regarded their accounts as faithful and true. The learned are not agreed as to the time when the Gospel of John was written; some dating it as early as the year 68, others as late as the year 98; but it is generally conceded to have been written after all the others. That it could not have been the work of Some Platonic Christian of a subsequent age, as some have

without evidence asserted, is manifest from references to it by some of the early fathers, and from the concurring testimony of many other writers of the ancient Christian church. (Greenleaf 1846)

The Four Evangelists

Upon evaluation of each author, Greenleaf assessed the entirety of the Gospel authors' honesty and abilities, as well as the consistency, conformity, and circumstances of their testimonies.

Honesty: Greenleaf could find no reason to doubt the honesty and integrity of these men and their Gospels. In fact, he found that Jesus's followers were devastated when they realized the error of their belief that Jesus had come to liberate by force the Jews from Roman rule. Further, the disciples documented that their world was turned upside down when Jesus allowed himself to be captured, tortured, and crucified. None knew how to process the fact that Jesus had come to free us from sin's bondage rather than from the oppression of our fellow man, and it was especially difficult to accept that his death was necessary to procure our freedom. Naturally, when Jesus died on the cross, his closest followers were paralyzed. Peter, one of Jesus's inner three, denied even knowing Jesus out of fear that exposure of their relationship would forfeit his own life. The disciples scattered, lost and broken, their faith crushed.

In a powerful and sudden turn of events, the remaining disciples were transformed. Jesus's tomb was found empty the Sunday after his death. Jesus then appeared, raised from the grave, to his disciples, mother, closest friends, and hundreds of Jews. Upon witnessing the miracles that Jesus had prophesized, his disciples, including Matthew, Mark, Luke, and John, reacted with renewed hope, devotion, and dedication to Jesus's commission. They acted without regard for their mortal interests. Their leader had been killed but overcame the grave. Fortified upon seeing and touching their resurrected leader, they risked life, limb, and all worldly interests to profess the good news that Jesus was indeed the risen Messiah, come not to save us from one another but to save us from our sins. Greenleaf noted the great truths declared by Jesus's apostles, "that Christ had risen from the dead, and that only through repentance from sin, and faith in him, could men hope for salvation." Despite their differences and in spite of persecution, the disciples declared this good news uniformly and in the words of Greenleaf "with one voice, everywhere, not only under the greatest discouragements, but in the face of the most appalling terrors that can be presented to the mind of man...The laws of every country were against the teaching of [Jesus's] disciples...The fashion of the world was against them." Still they persisted to peacefully and inoffensively propagate the news of Jesus's sacrifice, and despite persecution, they rejoiced with every convert. Greenleaf was amazed by their devotion and enthusiasm. He wrote, "They could expect nothing but contempt, opposition, revilings, bitter persecutions, stripes [to be whipped], imprisonments, torments and cruel deaths. Yet this faith they zealously did propagate; and all these miseries they endured undismayed, nay, rejoicing. As one after another was put to a miserable death, the survivors only prosecuted their work with increased vigor and resolution." We should not fail to recognize the courage and heroism of these men. They faced certain persecution and probable death but did not sway from their faith. They had all the reason in the world to carefully consider their position and how they would represent what they had seen and heard. They had every chance to deny these truths and safe themselves from physical pain and torture. Yet they prevailed and remained steadfast in profession of their faith.

> The annals of military warfare afford scarcely an example of the like heroic constancy, patience and unblenching courage. They had every possible motive to review carefully the grounds of their faith, and the evidences of the great facts and truths which they asserted; and these motives were pressed upon their attention with the most melancholy and terrific frequency. It was therefore impossible that they could have persisted in affirming the truths they have narrated, had not Jesus actually rose from the dead, and

had they not known this fact as certainly as they knew any other fact...From these absurdities there is no escape, but in the perfect conviction and admission that they were good men, testifying to that which they had carefully observed and considered, and well knew to be true. (Greenleaf 1846)

Greenleaf concluded beyond a shadow of a doubt that these authors and other followers of Jesus had converted from frightened and broken men to men of extraordinary faith, courage, and conviction. Furthermore, it is inconceivable for any to suppose that these disciples willingly exposed themselves to torment, torture, and even death for something they knew to be a deception. No, without a doubt, they were certain that Jesus had died, risen, and then ascended into heaven. They believed honestly, vigorously, and wholly that they had walked the earth with the Son of God.

Ability: The ability of a witness to speak the truth is dependent on the witness's opportunity to interpret circumstances and interactions, on the accuracy of his or her powers of observation, and on the soundness of his or her memory. Regarding the latter, we must consider the context and culture of the first century. Before writing was prolific and the printing press was invented, cultures relied heavily on oral tradition to pass along historical records and vital knowledge. In fact, it was not uncommon for the rabbis of Jesus's time to commit the entire Torah to memory. Craig Bloomberg stated, "We have to put ourselves into the ancient world without modern media, without even a print-based culture, in which the only, and the standard, way of preserving information was through oral tradition, most of which was memorized" (Strobel 2007). Note also that the witnesses' ministries were public and filled with the opportunity for correction, if necessary, by contemporaries and other eyewitnesses both for and against the propagation of this "good news." Greenleaf asserts that not only are the legal requirements met by each author to establish sufficient ability, but the testimonies themselves establish additional evidence as to their specialized powers to observe and communicate facts.

No lawyer is permitted to argue in disparagement of the intelligence or integrity of a witness, against whom the case itself afforded no particle of testimony...This is sufficient for our purpose, in regard to these witnesses. But more than this is evident, from the minuteness of their narratives, and from their history. Matthew was trained, by his calling, to habits of severe investigation and suspicious scrutiny; and Luke's profession demanded an exactness of observation equally close and searching. The other two evangelists, it has been well remarked, were as much too unlearned to forge the story of their Master's Life, as these were too learned and acute to be deceived by any imposture.

Consistency and conformity: Strobel's and Greenleaf's conclusions are remarkably similar: sufficient consistency and discrepancy exist to suggest the witnesses were independent observers without previous collaboration or collusion. Greenleaf's evaluation of the conformity of the witnessed events to the actual truth was largely focused on miracles professedly performed by Jesus. Opponents suggest miracles do not happen (see "What's the Probability of That?"), but we have found that the occurrence of a miracle may indeed be more probable than the occurrence of a single a random event for a significantly complex interaction and outcome.

Miracles, say the objectors, are impossible; and therefore the evangelists were either deceivers or deceived; and in either case their narratives against the possibility of miracles, was founded on the broad and bold assumption that all things are governed by immutable laws, or fixed modes of motion and relation, termed by the laws of nature, by which God himself is of necessity bound. This erroneous assumption is the tortoise, on which stands the elephant which upholds his system of atheism. He does not inform us who made these immutable laws, nor whence they derive their binding force and irresistible operation. The argument supposes that the creator of all things first made a code of laws, and then put it out of his own power to change them. (Greenleaf 1846)

The argument against miracles suggests that we confine our data to that which we have personally experienced and thus deny our instincts to infer and extrapolate beyond immediate experience. A request for us to accept the argument against miracles is a request that we deny our feelings, intuition, and compassion, which we have found is a mistake that can often lead to poor decisions (refer to "Manage Thought" in *VerAegis—Relationships*). Simon Greenleaf's quest was life changing; his beliefs and his foundational principles were changing, and despite his intention to prove otherwise, he became convinced that these were honest and sincere men. He began to believe in their god as the everlasting creator and ultimate savior of man and earth. He began to believe in miracles.

> But if we may infer, from what we see and know, that there is a Supreme Being, by whom this world was created, we may certainly, and with equal reason, believe him capable of works which we have never yet known him to perform. We may fairly conclude that the power which was originally put forth to create the world is still constantly and without ceasing exerted to sustain it; and that the experienced connection between cause and effect is but the uniform and constantly active operation of the finger of God. "A miracle is improbable, when we can perceive no sufficient cause, in reference to his creatures, why the Deity should not vary his modes of operation; it ceases to be so, when such cause is assigned." But the full discussion of the subject of miracles forms no part of the present design. Their credibility has been fully established, and the objections of skeptics most satisfactorily met and overthrown. (Greenleaf 1846)

Delving into the facts of the Gospels, we find that in each case of healing or a similar miracle, the afflicted were known within the communities to have been afflicted for years, and the miracles were not only proclaimed by the newly cured but through the testimony of family, friends, and the community at large. Such broad and conforming testimonies serve to cement these miracles as real. These remarkable incidents were acknowledged within the communities where the cured people lived; how could claims be made that the blind could see, the lame could walk, the lepers had become whole, and the mentally afflicted had become sane if it were not true? Jesus and his followers would have been run out of town if they were charlatans, for the deception could not have been preserved. Even opponents of Jesus acknowledged his miracles, and though the results were good, they tried to twist the facts, accusing Jesus of using evil forces to produce good and noble results. After one such accusation from a group of Pharisees, Jesus responded, "Every kingdom divided against itself will be ruined, and every city or household divided against itself will not stand. If Satan drives out Satan, he is divided against himself. How then can his kingdom stand? And if I drive out demons by Beelzebul, by whom do your people drive them out? So then, they will be your judges. But if it is by the Spirit of God that I drive out demons, then the kingdom of God has come upon you." (Matt. 12:25-28 [NIV]) Regarding the veracity of Jesus's miracles, Greenleaf noted, "All these [miracles]...were facts, plain and simple in their nature, easily seen and fully comprehended by persons of common capacity and observation. If they were separately testified to, by different witnesses of ordinary intelligence and integrity, in any court of justice, the jury would be bound to believe them; and a verdict, rendered contrary to the uncontradicted testimony of credible witnesses to any of these plain facts, separately taken, would be liable to be set aside, as a verdict against evidence." In a court of law, if one credible witness testified to a fact, the fact is considered to be proved. So when a witness confirmed a family member to be lame or blind and then subsequently healed by Jesus, we too must consider the fact to be proved. In the case of Bartimeus, who was known to be blind and then healed by faith in Jesus Greenleaf wrote, "that Bartimeus was blind, according to the uniform course of administering justice, this fact would be taken as satisfactorily proved. So also, if his subsequent restoration to sight were the sole fact in question, this also would be deemed established, by the like evidence. Nor would the rule of evidence be at all different, if the fact to be proved were the declaration of Jesus, immediately preceding his restoration to sight, that his faith had made him whole." Greenleaf included a dramatic declaration and summary of his findings regarding the evidence that Jesus did indeed perform miracles:

> In each of these cases, each isolated fact was capable of being accurately observed, and certainly known; and the evidence demands our assent, precisely as the like evidence upon any other indifferent subject. The connection of the word or the act of Jesus with the restoration of the blind, lame and dead, to sight, and health, and life, as cause and effect, is a conclusion which our reason is compelled to admit, from the uniformity of their concurrence, in such a multitude of instances, as well as from the universal conviction of all, whether friends or foes, who beheld the miracles which he wrought. Indeed, if the truth of one of the miracles is satisfactorily established, our belief cannot reasonably be withheld from them all.

The New Testament Gospels record at least forty separate miracles performed by Jesus and witnessed by many during the course of his ministry and our belief cannot reasonably be withheld from them. They include the following:

- Walking on water
- Mastery over nature and weather
- Turning water to wine
- Healing the sick
- Returning sight to the blind
- Making the lame walk
- Exercising (driving demons from) the possessed
- Raising the dead

These miracles are clear indications that Jesus possessed the attributes we found were necessary for the creator of the universe:

unlimited power and complete and total knowledge. Interestingly, even Jesus's critics were amazed by his powers, though they argued that the source of his power was not the living God of Abraham. William Lane Craig, a research professor at Biola University, commented, "Jesus's contemporaries, that is, people who liked him, people who were indifferent, neutral, and people who opposed him, all acknowledged he did extraordinary things. Now, of course the people who liked Jesus, and believed in him and followed him, said Jesus did these powerful works because of the Spirit of God. People who opposed him would say, 'Well, I admit he does these amazing things, but it's because the devil is helping him'" (Strobel 2007).

However, Jesus's miracles were not so easily dismissed. The reason is twofold: First, Jesus did so much good that it is not conceivable that his good would flow from a source of evil. Second, he stood apart from the magicians and sorcerers of his time who did not produce timeless results that withstood the test of community. He did not produce tricks that amused but produced miraculous results that amazed. Mark Straus relayed to Strobel, "[Other] miracle workers that we find occasionally in the first century are magicians, they use incantations, they use spells, they try to coerce gods or divine figures to work on their behalf. That's very different from Jesus's miracles. Jesus's miracles were to demonstrate the power of the kingdom of God. When he healed the sick he pointed back to Isaiah's prophecies that when God's Kingdom would come, when God's salvation would come, the lame would walk, the blind would see. This was the demonstration that God's Kingdom was arriving" (Strobel 2007).

Agreement of Gospels with contemporary facts and circumstances: Greenleaf was and perhaps remains the utmost authority regarding attributes of testimony from true and false witnesses and the power of circumstantial evidence. He asserts that increased numbers of witnesses and circumstances in turn increase the probability of detecting a false witness, because there are an increasing number of points to find either collusion or major discrepancy. He contends, "The more largely the narrative partakes of these characters [intricate details, a great number of steps, numerous witnesses] the further it will be found removed from all suspicion of contrivance or design, and the more profoundly the mind will repose on the conviction of its truth."

Greenleaf then concludes that the Gospels are filled with circumstantial evidence that points to authenticity and accuracy:

> The narratives of the sacred writers, both Jewish and Christian, abound in examples of this kind of evidence, the value of which is hardly capable of being properly estimated...In all human transactions, the highest degree of assurance to which we can arrive, short of the evidence of our own senses, is that of probability. The most that can be asserted is, that the narrative is more likely to be true than false; and it may be in the highest degree more likely, but still be short of absolute mathematical certainty. Yet this very probability may be so great as to satisfy the mind of the most cautious, and enforce the assent of the most reluctant and unbelieving. If it is such as usually satisfies reasonable men, in matters of ordinary transaction, it is all which the greatest skeptic has a right to require; for it is by such evidence alone that our rights are determined, in the civil tribunals; and on no other evidence do they proceed, even in capital case.

Greenleaf suggests that Christians ask only that non-Christians open-mindedly evaluate the evidence for Christ and the resurrection as they would the evidence for any other trial of phenomena. In fact, this is what Greenleaf did: he evaluated the evidence, tested the integrity of each witness, and compared one with another as if they were testifying in a court of law. Not only did he conclude that the resurrection was no hoax, but he confidently professed that any who bravely and honestly undertook the same examination of the evidence would come to the same conclusion: "The result, it is confidently believed, will be an undoubting conviction of their integrity, ability, and truth" (Greenleaf 1846).

Both Strobel and Greenleaf concluded that the Gospels are based on capable and truthful eyewitness testimony, and early church leaders took further pains to ensure not only the authorship but also the authenticity of these documents. Strobel next tackled the question of preservation: was the New Testament passed down through time without distortion?

Recall that Jesus lived and preached in an oral culture before writing was prolific. His contemporaries relied heavily on oral tradition to pass along historical records and vital knowledge, and it was not uncommon for the rabbis to commit the entire Torah to memory. Today, with television, computers, and the Internet, we are skeptical of oral traditions, but in ancient times, stories were passed on reliably, because they were passed on in community, and any mistakes were addressed on the spot, with open discussion, to ensure accuracy. Historical records were verbally passed down by individuals to people who were already familiar with them. So mistakes were not tolerated; the process was self-correcting. According to JP Moreland, "We now have scholarly studies that have been done of oral cultures and we know that through several generations oral traditions could be passed on without changing a thing" (Strobel 2007).

Given the short period between the time of Jesus's death, ascension, and the writing of the Gospels, combined with the exceptional reliability of oral tradition in this ancient culture, we can easily conclude that the New Testament is an accurate record of history. Furthermore, based on comparisons of modern text and ancient manuscripts, we find that the writings have remained largely unchanged (note that there are many versions of the Bible in existence today, with only minor changes among them to accommodate more modern vernacular). According to world-class scholar Bruce Metzger, professor emeritus at Princeton Theological Seminary, there exist an unprecedented (relative to other ancient manuscripts) number of New Testament manuscripts that can be dated incredibly close to the original writings. With the abundance of manuscripts, scholars have been able to show that the modern New Testament is 99.5 percent free of textual discrepancies, with no major Christian doctrine in doubt (Strobel 2000). Likewise, Mark Straus, a professor of the New Testament at Bethel Seminary, told Strobel, "We have better manuscript attestation for the New Testament than any other ancient document. For example, the bible of the Greeks, Homer's Iliad, is preserved in maybe 600 manuscripts, the oldest of them a thousand years after the document was originally written. The New Testament, we have something like 5,000 Greek manuscripts; so everyone agrees, whether liberal or conservative, we have an incredibly reliable New Testament." Further, church historians have preserved the entire New Testament via quotations from early church leaders over the first four centuries. In other words, if needed, the entire New Testament could be reconstructed by using the historical documentation of these quotations.

Jesus Existed! Performed Miracles! Who Was He?

Was Jesus a great man, a god, or both? Take a leap of faith or seek to understand; evaluate the evidence and come to your own conclusion, as did both Greenleaf and Strobel. Arrive at an answer. Complacency is not an option for something of this import. Non-Christians friends of mine have asserted to me in personal discussions that Jesus was a great man and a wonderful philosopher—maybe even a prophet—but surely not the Son of God. One of my favorite quotes from C. S. Lewis is a concise philosophical response to such a debate: should we accept Jesus Christ as merely a good man and a prophet or as the Son of God, who lived as a man and died for us so that we may eventually be released from sin's oppressive grip?

> I [C. S Lewis] am trying here to prevent anyone saying the really foolish thing that people often say about Him [Jesus]: "I'm ready to accept Jesus as a great moral teacher, but I don't accept his claim to be God." That is the one thing we must not say. A man who was merely a man and said the sort of things Jesus said would not be a great moral teacher. He would either be a lunatic—on the

level with the man who says he is a poached egg—or else he would be the Devil of Hell. You must make your choice. Either this man was, and is, the Son of God, or else a madman or something worse. You can shut him up for a fool, you can spit at him and kill him as a demon or you can fall at his feet and call him Lord and God, but let us not come with any patronizing nonsense about his being a great human teacher. He has not left that open to us. He did not intend to. (Wiley 2011)

Indeed, Jesus claimed to be the Son of God. No sane, honest, and good man would make such a claim if it were not true. Close your eyes and imagine the scene: Jesus is chained and surrounded by angry Jewish leaders and abusive soldiers. He has been beaten, ridiculed and spat upon since being captured in the garden of Gethsemane. The high priest Caiaphas and members of the Sanhedrin have gathered to review incriminating evidence and testimony, but they find that the evidence by itself is not compelling, they need a confession. Caiaphas points his crooked finger and, trembling in anger, finally orders Jesus to tell them plainly—is he the Messiah? Jesus answers that not only is he the Messiah but he will be seated at the right hand of the Father, and all will witness him coming again in glory.

> The high priest said to him, "I charge you under oath by the living God: Tell us if you are the Messiah, the Son of God."
>
> "You have said so," Jesus replied. "But I say to all of you: From now on you will see the Son of Man sitting at the right hand of the Mighty One and coming on the clouds of heaven."
>
> Then the high priest tore his clothes and said, "He has spoken blasphemy! Why do we need any more witnesses? Look, now you have heard the blasphemy. What do you think?"
>
> "He is worthy of death," they answered.
>
> Then they spit in his face and struck him with their fists. Others slapped him and said, "Prophesy to us, Messiah. Who hit you?" (Matt. 26:63–68 [NIV])

Jesus knew well that if he denied his claim to deity, he would walk away for lack of evidence, whereas professing himself the Son of God would lead to torture and an excruciating death on the cross (a death that only hours before he had prayed to his father, "Father, if it is Your will, take this cup away from Me; nevertheless not My will, but Yours, be done." Luke 22:42 (NKJV)); yet he claimed without fear or pause that he was the Son of God, the Son of man.

Jesus is referred to as the Son of man more than eighty times in the New Testament. The human connotations of this term may be somewhat obvious, but for full understanding, one must refer to Old Testament scripture written circa 100 BC by the Jewish prophet Daniel:

> In my vision at night I looked, and there before me was one like a son of man, coming with the clouds of heaven. He approached the Ancient of Days and was led into his presence. He was given authority, glory and sovereign power; all nations and peoples of every language worshiped him. His dominion is an everlasting dominion that will not pass away, and his kingdom is one that will never be destroyed. (Dan. 7:13–14 [NIV])

Some believe that the term "Son of God" refers to Jesus's deity and "Son of man," to his humanity, which is true in part, but Daniel 7:13 clearly refers to the Son of man as a messiah who was led into the presence of God (the Ancient of Days) and is bestowed with everlasting authority, glory, and power. It is this portrait of an everlasting messiah in possession of an everlasting dominion that Jesus identifies himself with when he claims to be the Son of man. Ben Witherington III, professor of New Testament interpretation at Asbury Seminary, enthusiastically discussed Jesus's character with Strobel.

> Now this is one of the things I love about Jesus and it says something to us. His identity is complex, he can't be pigeon holed, he fits no one formula; there are a lot of aspects to who he is. But always, he presents himself as the challenge to the status quo, to preconditioned thinking about what the Son of God, what the

Messiah must be. He's carving out his own niche. He's doing his own thing like a great and creative artist. He is not simply replicating anything from the past. He is taking bits and pieces of prophecies and ideas, and wisdom literature, and law, and you name it, and he's made a whole new gumbo; he's serving it up and people don't know what to think. He goes into a synagogue and says some of this stuff and they go, "Wow! A new teaching...and with authority; shazam!" (Strobel 2007)

Greenleaf and Strobel found that Matthew, Mark, Luke, and John, as well as other disciples and early church leaders, believed wholeheartedly that Jesus was the Son of God. Strobel wanted to delve more deeply into the physical evidence, however, because he knew that direct evidence, such as fingerprints and DNA, is the icing on the cake when striving to establish "guilt" beyond a shadow of a doubt, and he wanted to determine if any similar evidence existed to prove beyond a shadow of a doubt that Jesus was the Messiah referred to in the Old Testament. How could he find such "fingerprint" evidence?

The Old Testament contained many major and minor prophecies predicting the coming of the Messiah and the acts he was destined to perform while on earth. During his quest, Strobel asked, "Do these prophecies create a fingerprint that in all of history only Jesus Christ manages to match?" Scholars have determined that Jesus fulfilled a minimum of forty-eight major prophecies, each written a minimum of three centuries before his birth. These major prophecies and hundreds more, when lesser prophecies are considered, indicated where he would be born, where his ministry would start, that he would be called Immanuel, that he would be a prophet, that his mother would be a virgin, and that he would die a violent death. In Psalm 22, David wrote of the Messiah's death, "they have pierced my hands and my feet." David wrote Psalm 22 about three hundred years before crucifixion was established as corporal punishment.

Dr. Peter Stoner, professor emeritus of mathematics and science at Westmont University, set out to determine the odds of one person fulfilling these prophecies. His study was undertaken by approximately six hundred students and is included in his book *Science Speaks*, published in 1969. He and his students evaluated the odds of each prophecy and then combined them to determine the collective probability. For example, they considered the prophecy that the Messiah would be born in the city of Bethlehem. Stoner and his students calculated the average population of Bethlehem from the times of Micah the prophet to the present day and then divided it by the average population of earth during the same period to determine that the chance of any one person being born in Bethlehem was approximately 1 in 280,000. Stoner submitted his methodology and calculations to a review committee of American Scientific Affiliation, who, upon examination, verified the soundness, dependability, and accuracy of the process.

The calculations show that fulfilling only eight of the prophecies has a chance of 1 in 10^{17}, and fulfilling the forty-eight major prophecies that Jesus alone fulfilled has an inconceivable chance of 1 in 10^{157}. Consider the enormity of this number: hydrogen is one of the most abundant elements in the universe and has a radius of approximately 25 x 10^{-12} meters, which is ten thousand times the radius of a single electron. To understand the improbability of any human ever fulfilling forty-eight prophecies of the Old Testament, imagine the volume of 10^{157} electrons (not hydrogen, the smallest element, but electrons); it would be equivalent to the volume of 2.6 billion trillion trillion universes, or 2.6 x 10^{33} universes (Assuming the radius of the observable universe is approximately forty-six billion light-years [Helpern 2012].). Now imagine that one electron is marked and then mixed randomly among the others. Imagine blindfolding an atomic-level spacewalker and requesting that he or she find that one electron. It is simply inconceivable.

Perhaps another more tangible example will help. Imagine the volume of the planet Earth. Assuming that a grain of sand has an average diameter of two millimeters, it would only require less than 10^{15} grains to create a mass with similar volume to that of Earth. Now imagine the odds of finding one black grain of sand mixed among all others that are white. The odds of 1 in 10^{157} are far worse.

We have historically validated documents that testify to the fact that Jesus and Jesus alone fulfilled a minimum of the forty-eight major prophecies against staggering odds. This is the fingerprint data that validates Jesus alone as the Messiah. He is part of a much greater, intelligent plan. Neither he nor we exist due to accidents; we are not merely the results of a series of random, unguided events but the architecture of a deliberate and loving creator.

Did Jesus Defeat Death?

If true, the resurrection of Jesus Christ is the single most pivotal event in the history of mankind. Fulfilling all the other prophecies, despite the improbability, pales in comparison to rising alive from the grave and ascending to heaven. Anyone can claim to be the Son of God and allege the ability to perform miracles or even the ability to overcome death itself, but how many can back it up? Michael Licona, director of apologetics at the North American Mission Board, Southern Baptist Convention, spoke to a group of students on the topic.

> While Jesus was on earth, he made some really radical claims. He claimed to be the uniquely divine servant of God, and he claimed that the only way that we could get to God would be through him. Now, I submit to you that if one of your professors made some claims like that you would think that he or she was a few French fries short of a Happy Meal. Those are some really audacious claims. Well, a lot of Jesus's critics responded to him the same way that you or I would respond to someone making those claims today. "Oh yeah, pal? You really think that's who you are? Well, tell you what; why don't you show it to us? Why don't you give us

a sign? Show us a miracle or something." And Jesus said, "Well, I'll give you [a] miracle, [a] sign: My resurrection from the dead." (Strobel 2007)

In order to understand the validity of Jesus's resurrection, we need to confirm that Jesus did not survive the crucifixion, that his body was actually missing from the tomb, and that he did indeed appear alive after rising from the grave.

Did Jesus Survive the Crucifixion?

The chances of surviving crucifixion were unheard of in Jesus's day; in fact, I have found reference to only one person who supposedly survived Roman crucifixion, and that was only after intervention. In his self-titled book *The Works of Flavius Josephus*, the Roman Jewish historian writes of many crucifixions that he witnessed: "I saw many captives crucified, and remembered three of them as my former acquaintances. I was very sorry at this in my mind, and went with tears in my eyes to Titus, and told him of them; so he immediately commanded them to be taken down, and to have the greatest care taken of them, in order to aid their recovery; yet two of them died under the physician's hands, while the third recovered." We cannot ascertain from this note how long they had been on the cross or the extent of their injuries prior to crucifixion—only that the crucifixion was interrupted, the best care possible administered, and yet two of the three perished.

Consider for a moment the training and motivation of Jesus's Roman executors. The Romans were experts at killing. They were trained professionals who devised crucifixion as not only a punishment but a real and horrific deterrent to all in their conquered domains. Crucifixion was designed to be long, excruciating, and deadly. Michael Licona discussed crucifixion in Strobel's documentary: "Crucifixion and the tortures that normally preceded it was the worst way to die in antiquity. A person was scourged to the point usually that their intestines, arteries and veins were laid bare. And then after that, a person was dragged out where they were impaled to a cross or a tree, and then left hanging there in excruciating pain. In fact, the word 'excruciating' comes from the Latin, 'out of the cross.'" If you have not already seen Mel Gibson's *The Passion of the Christ*, you will find it to be a powerfully realistic depiction of the flogging and crucifixion of Jesus, though it is not recommended for those who are squeamish.

Roman soldiers were charged with killing their prisoners, and failure to do so would result in their own deaths. And Jesus was not just any prisoner; he was a rebel leader. No, the soldiers charged with the flogging and crucifixion of Jesus had no reason to let him survive.

As we learned earlier, John followed Jesus to Calgary Hill and later documented the event as corroborated by another eyewitness.

> Because the Jewish leaders did not want the bodies left on the crosses during the Sabbath, they asked Pilate to have the legs broken and the bodies taken down. The soldiers therefore came and broke the legs of the first man who had been crucified with Jesus, and then those of the other. But when they came to Jesus and found that he was already dead, they did not break his legs. Instead, one of the soldiers pierced Jesus's side with a spear, bringing a sudden flow of blood and water. The man who saw it has given testimony, and his testimony is true. He knows that he tells the truth, and he testifies so that you also may believe. These things happened so that the scripture would be fulfilled: "Not one of his bones will be broken," and, as another scripture says, "They will look on the one they have pierced." (John 19:31–37 [NIV])

In fact, it was common for soldiers to break the legs of their charges near the end of the crucifixion process in order to hasten suffocation (when hanging by one's arms with no support from below, soon the ability to inhale is lost due to pressure on the lungs and diaphragm) if they had not already expired due to blood loss and shock. Seeing that Jesus was dead, they did not break his legs. Instead, they pierced his side with a spear to confirm that he indeed had expired.

Crucifixion resulted in death by one of two ways. The first was asphyxiation, which means simply that the person lost the ability to breathe. Crucifixion victims had to pull themselves up with their arms, causing the nails through their wrists to press on the nerves of the carpal tunnel, inducing great pain, while simultaneously pushing up with their legs that had nails driven through the ankles and heels. Over time, the prisoner would succumb to fatigue, pain, and loss of blood, unable to push up enough to breathe, resulting in the buildup of fluid around the heart and lungs; ultimately, gasping for air, the crucified would die of suffocation. The second way people died during crucifixion was through severe blood loss and shock. Often the victim's heart rate would accelerate, striving to deliver blood to oxygen-starved vital organs. The prolonged rapid heart rate would again cause fluid to gather around the heart and lungs. Finally, unable to deliver or receive enough oxygen, the heart would fail, perhaps even rupturing in its final attempt to deliver life's blood. John's account of the scourging and crucifixion of Jesus is consistent with other historical documentation of these methods of execution, as well as with modern-day medical understanding:

> There is evidence from Scripture that Jesus experienced hypovolemic shock as a result of being flogged. As Jesus carried His own cross to Golgotha (John 19:17), He collapsed, and a man named Simon was forced to either carry the cross or help Jesus carry the cross the rest of way to the hill (Matthew 27:32–33; Mark 15:21–22; Luke 23:26). This collapse indicates Jesus had low blood pressure. Another indicator that Jesus suffered from hypovolemic shock was that He declared He was thirsty as He hung on the cross (John 19:28), indicating His body's desire to replenish fluids.

> Prior to death, the sustained rapid heartbeat caused by hypovolemic shock also causes fluid to gather in the sack around the heart and around the lungs. This gathering of fluid in the membrane around the heart is called pericardial effusion, and the fluid gathering around the lungs is called pleural effusion. This

explains why, after Jesus died and a Roman soldier thrust a spear through Jesus's side (probably His right side, piercing both the lungs and the heart), blood and water came from His side just as John recorded in his Gospel (John 19:34). (Houdmann)

Clearly, Jesus could not have survived the flogging and crucifixion. Even when his executioners believed he had died, they thrust a spear deep into his side to confirm beyond doubt that they had achieved their goal and were not at risk of punishment. Blood and water-like fluid poured from his final wound. Satisfied, they roughly dropped the cross, ripped the nails from Jesus's hands and feet, and tossed Jesus's unquestionably dead body to the ground. He did not move, moan, or breathe. They had accomplished their task with exacting cruelty and efficiency. Jesus was dead. He had taken our sins upon himself and died so that we could be saved: "So when Jesus had received the sour wine, He said, 'It is finished!' And bowing His head, He gave up His spirit" (John 19:30 [NKJV]).

The words Jesus uttered, "It is finished," have been found on pottery unearthed during archaeological digs. This phrase in Hebrew indicates that the pottery was paid for in full. So Jesus was in fact stating that he had died to pay in full for our sins.

Was Jesus's Tomb Found Empty?

If Jesus did not rise from the dead, there would be no Christianity. It is to the advantage of the non-Christian to debunk the claims that Jesus did in fact rise. The authors of the Gospels document both Jesus's burial and his rise, and they clearly state that Jesus was buried in a tomb owned by Joseph of Arimathea, a member of the Jewish Sanhedrin council (the supreme council or court in Ancient Israel comprised of 70 men and a high priest who oversaw proceedings) that condemned Jesus. Joseph was rich and famous, so if the burial account of the Gospels were fabricated, Jesus's followers would have been labeled liars and the entirety of their Gospels thrown in question—but that was not the case. Hundreds and thousands of Jews converted to Christianity after Jesus's Resurrection and did not call into question the fact that Joseph donated his tomb for Jesus's burial. Considering that the followers of Christ had been devoted and claimed to love Jesus, the fact that they went passive and allowed Joseph (not one of Jesus's followers but a member of the council which accused him of blasphemy) to assume the responsibility to ensure that Jesus had a decent and honorable burial was then and remains an embarrassment, emphasizing the extent to which his followers were shocked, scattered, and lost upon Jesus's death. The Jewish leadership was motivated to ensure that Jesus did not falsely rise from the grave. Jesus's followers should have been motivated to witness his resurrection. The Jewish leaders were compelled to know and have access to where Jesus was buried in order to control the situation and adequately ensure that his body remained in the tomb. These leaders feared that his body would be stolen to fake his resurrection; they were committed to making certain that did not happen.

We have learned that the men who followed Jesus, by their own admission as documented in the New Testament, scattered and lost faith at his capture and crucifixion. Humbling oneself in front of others is a difficult task, and it would have been more self-serving for them to profess that they had remained steadfast and true. Instead they professed their fear, confusion and desertion. Greenleaf and Strobel concluded that the Four Evangelists sang the song of their disgrace not because it was self-serving but because it was simply the truth.

Likewise, it was a disgrace to them that Jesus's empty tomb was discovered not by one of the remaining eleven closest followers of Jesus but by women. Because Jesus was buried on the Sabbath, his body was not properly prepared. A group of women who loved Jesus returned the morning after the Sabbath to the tomb with spices and perfumes in order to prepare Jesus's body. It would have been more believable in their ancient society if someone of importance had found and then professed the empty tomb. At a minimum, the story would be afforded more credence had the empty tomb been discovered by men, as in the ancient Israeli-Palestinian world, even more so than now, women were not held in high esteem; they were considered second-class citizens.

Given the status of women in that society, it is important to note that potential conspirators were not likely to have chosen women to discover an empty tomb if they were indeed attempting to fake Jesus's resurrection. Women were not viewed as credible witnesses, especially Mary Magdalene, who like many of Jesus's followers, had a questionable past. In fact, the disciples' first response to news of the empty tomb was one of disbelief. Yet the authors of the Gospels documented that women indeed discovered the empty tomb, not because it was self-serving but because it was true. These women could not have overpowered the armed guards or moved the massive stone that enclosed the tomb, and they could not have removed Jesus's body without detection and capture by the guards tasked with ensuring that Jesus's body not be removed. Clearly, the Jewish leaders knew that Jesus claimed that he would rise. They were highly motivated to wipe out the "rebel" movement and took extreme caution to ensure that no one was able to covertly remove Jesus's body, but they were not prepared to prevent Jesus from leaving of his own accord.

> Now there was a man named Joseph, a member of the Council, a good and upright man, who had not consented to their decision and action. He came from the Judean town of Arimathea, and he himself was waiting for the kingdom of God. Going to Pilate, he asked for Jesus's body. Then he took it down, wrapped it in linen cloth and placed it in a tomb cut in the rock, one in which no one had yet been laid. It was Preparation Day, and the Sabbath was about to begin. The women who had come with Jesus from Galilee followed Joseph and saw the tomb and how his body was laid in it. Then they went home and prepared spices and perfumes. But they rested on the Sabbath in obedience to the commandment. (Luke 23:50–56 [NIV])

On the first day of the week, very early in the morning, the women took the spices they had prepared and went to the tomb. They found the stone rolled away from the tomb, but when they entered, they did not find the body of the Lord Jesus...When they came back from the tomb, they told all these things to the Eleven and to all the others. It was Mary Magdalene, Joanna, Mary the mother of James, and the others with them who told this to the apostles. But they did not believe the women, because their words seemed to them like nonsense. Peter, however, got up and ran to the tomb. Bending over, he saw the strips of linen lying by themselves, and he went away, wondering to himself what had happened. (Luke 24:1–12 [NIV])

Licona responded to the conspiracy theory, "If you were going to invent an account about an empty tomb, then why on earth would you invent witnesses, primary witnesses, whom no one would believe? In fact they would scoff at that later on." Bishop Wright likewise expounded, "In fact, early Christians were bombarded by japes by the 'pagans' that Jesus's resurrection was just based on the testimony of hysterical women, but they did not sway" (Strobel 2007).

Matthew reported that Jewish leaders, upon learning that Jesus's body was missing, conspired to "frame" the disciples: "When the chief priests had met with the elders and devised a plan, they gave the soldiers a large sum of money, telling them, 'You are to say, "His disciples came during the night and stole him away while we were asleep"'" (Matt. 28:12–13 [NIV]). Justin Martyr and Quintus Tertullianus, also known as Tertullian, two early converts to Christianity renowned for their ability and discipline to support a position through a systematic use of information (apologetics when applied to Christianity), corroborated Matthew's assertion. This presented a conundrum for Jewish leaders. They could not claim Jesus's body stolen without admitting the tomb was empty, and they could not prove the body stolen. If the body were not stolen, and Jesus did not rise, the Jewish leaders needed the populace to believe that

Jesus's body remained in the tomb. Licona explained this dilemma: "Matthew reports that the Jewish authorities were claiming that the disciples of Jesus had stolen his corpse. And this is verified by Justin and Tertullian a little bit later on, saying that the Jewish leaders were still saying the same thing in their day. Now here's the question: if the body is still in the tomb, why are you saying that the disciples had stolen it?" (Strobel 2007).

Eventually, both Jesus's opponents and followers acknowledged that his tomb was empty early that Sunday morning. Clearly, if the tomb had not been empty, Jewish leaders would have produced the body to refute the claims of his resurrection. The tomb was guarded, but no one saw Jesus's body removed. So, despite the leadership's attempts to dishonor the disciples and their mandate (strong desire) to keep Jesus in the tomb, we must conclude that Jesus's tomb was empty and his followers, honest and true.

Was Jesus Seen Alive after His Crucifixion?

Saul was Jewish, born a Roman citizen in Tarsus of Cilicia. He studied under the famous and well-respected rabbi, Gamaliel, and was thoroughly trained in Jewish law and tradition. He was a zealous follower of Yahweh and was relentless in the duties assigned to him by Jewish leaders: he was responsible for identifying, finding, arresting, and even persecuting to death the followers of the rebel Jesus. In fact, Saul supervised the stoning of Stephen, the first Christian to be martyred for his assertion to Jewish leaders that Christ is standing in the place of honor at God's right hand. One day, upon intercepting the letters of Christian correspondents, Saul's pursuit led him down the road to Damascus, where he and his colleagues planned to capture Christians and return them as prisoners to Jerusalem. Saul was confident that Jesus was a false messiah and thus believed that Christians were blasphemers deserving of death.

It was about noon. Saul's group neared the city of Damascus when suddenly, a blinding light flashed from the heavens before them. Disoriented and shocked, Saul fell to his knees and heard a voice asking loudly, "Saul! Saul! Why do you persecute me?" (Acts 22:7 [NIV]). Frightened and confused, Saul asked the voice to identify himself. "I am Jesus of Nazareth," the voice responded, "whom you are persecuting" (Acts 22:8 [NIV]). "The men with Saul stood speechless, for they heard the sound of someone's voice but saw no one!" (Acts 9:7 [NLT]). Jesus then instructed Saul to continue on to Damascus, where he would learn all he had been assigned. Saul, still blinded by the bright light that flashed when Jesus appeared, was led to Damascus by his companions. Saul was physically blinded yet was now beginning to see the error of his ways. Ironically, his colleagues, in the midst of a miracle, had their vision, but still could not see the truth.

In Damascus, Saul met a man named Ananias, a devout Jew and strict follower of the law, highly respected in the Jewish community. By the power of Jesus, Ananias restored Saul's sight and then instructed him, "The God of our ancestors has chosen you to know his will and to see the Righteous One and to hear words from his mouth. You will be his witness to all people of what you have seen and heard. And now what are you waiting for? Get up, be baptized and wash your sins away, calling on his name." (Acts 22:14–16 [NIV]) The risen Jesus commissioned Saul, the Christian killer, to not only abandon his persecution of Christians but become an advocate. Thus, Saul became Paul the convert, instantaneously transfigured from devout Jew and persecutor of Christians to zealous follower and evangelist for Jesus's cause.

Upon returning to Jerusalem, Paul (Saul) professed to his fellow Jews all that had happened. There was uproar in the streets due to his testimony. The Roman commander, seeing Paul as the cause of the commotion, ordered that Paul be taken to the barracks to be flogged and interrogated. Paul then asked the Roman centurion if it was legal to flog a Roman citizen who had not been found guilty; the centurion returned Paul to his commander, alarmed that he had shackled a Roman citizen, perhaps without just cause. The commander, in order to understand the accusations against him, brought Paul before the chief priests and all the members of the Sanhedrin (the judicial court system in Israel). Paul professed that he had done no ill and had fulfilled his duty to God in all good conscience. The high priest ordered that Paul be struck in the mouth, and Paul responded by accusing the priest of failure to follow precisely the same laws Paul was accused of breaking. The tension escalated; the Jewish leaders, waving their fists, shouted that Paul had insulted God's high priest.

Then Paul, knowing that some of them were Sadducees and the others Pharisees, called out in the Sanhedrin, "My brothers, I am a Pharisee, descended from Pharisees. I stand on trial because of the hope of the resurrection of the dead." When he said this, a dispute broke out between the Pharisees and the Sadducees, and the assembly was divided. (The Sadducees say that there is no resurrection, and that there are neither angels nor spirits, but the Pharisees believe all these things.) There was a great uproar, and some of the teachers of the law who were Pharisees stood up and argued vigorously. "We find nothing wrong with this man," they said. "What if a spirit or an angel has spoken to him?" (Acts 23:6–9 [NIV])

The dispute between the Pharisees and Sadducees became so violent that, fearing Paul would be torn to pieces, the commander ordered the troops to go into the fervor, remove Paul by force, and return him into the barracks. The next night, Jesus appeared to Paul again, saying, "Take courage! As you have testified about me in Jerusalem, so you must also testify in Rome." (Acts 23:11 [NIV])

Before Paul's next hearing, the commander learned of a plot by many Jews to ambush and kill Paul. To avoid the conflict, the commander transferred Paul under guard of two hundred soldiers, two hundred spearmen, and seventy horsemen to Governor Felix of Caesarea that very night.

Paul pled his case, and Felix found in him no guilt. Several days later, Felix, along with his Jewish wife, Drusilla, sent for Paul and listened to him as he spoke of his newfound faith in Jesus. Worried by Paul's story, Felix kept him prisoner rather than set him free, but he frequently sent for Paul for conversation. Felix was succeeded after two years by Porcius Festus, who, as a favor to the Jewish leaders, maintained Paul's incarceration. Jewish leaders appealed to Festus regarding Paul's fate, requesting again that Paul be punished and that he again review their case. The Jews were unable to prove any of their charges when the case was heard by Festus, and so it was requested that Paul be returned to Jerusalem to be tried there. Festus presented the request to Paul, who in turn stated that he had been found without fault, that the charges were not true, and that, though he was not afraid to die, no one had the right to turn him over to the Jews. Paul then appealed to Caesar. Festus consulted with his council and granted Paul's request.

A few days later, King Herod Agrippa, known simply as Agrippa, brother of Drusilla (Governor Felix's wife), arrived with his sister Bernice to welcome Festus to his new post. Seizing the opportunity, Festus discussed Paul's case with the king. Festus relayed that he had expected the Jewish leaders to charge Paul with crimes, but that they only raised points of difference regarding their religion, mainly concerning whether or not a man named Jesus was alive or dead. Festus desired to better understand the charges against Paul prior to sending him to Caesar in Italy. King Agrippa agreed to hear Paul. The next day, Paul was brought before Agrippa, Bernice, and Festus. Agrippa granted Paul permission to talk. Paul was thankful to speak to King Agrippa, whom he felt was well acquainted with Jewish customs and controversies. Paul explained his own background as follows:

> The Jewish people all know the way I have lived ever since I was a child, from the beginning of my life in my own country, and also in Jerusalem. They have known me for a long time and can testify, if they are willing, that I conformed to the strictest sect of our religion, living as a Pharisee. And now it is because of my hope in what God has promised our ancestors that I am on trial today. This

is the promise our twelve tribes are hoping to see fulfilled as they earnestly serve God day and night. King Agrippa, it is because of this hope that these Jews are accusing me. Why should any of you consider it incredible that God raises the dead? I too was convinced that I ought to do all that was possible to oppose the name of Jesus of Nazareth. And that is just what I did in Jerusalem. On the authority of the chief priests I put many of the Lord's people in prison, and when they were put to death, I cast my vote against them. Many a time I went from one synagogue to another to have them punished, and I tried to force them to blaspheme. I was so obsessed with persecuting them that I even hunted them down in foreign cities. (Acts 26:4–11 [NIV])

Paul testified that Jesus had appeared to him on the road to Damascus and instructed, "I am sending you to them to open their eyes and turn them from darkness to light, and from the power of Satan to God, so that they may receive forgiveness of sins and a place among those who are sanctified by faith in me" (Acts 26:17–18 [NIV]).

Paul continued in his testimony as follows:

So then, King Agrippa, I was not disobedient to the vision from heaven. First to those in Damascus, then to those in Jerusalem and in all Judea, and then to the Gentiles, I preached that they should repent and turn to God and demonstrate their repentance by their deeds. That is why some Jews seized me in the temple courts and tried to kill me. But God has helped me to this very day; so I stand here and testify to small and great alike. I am saying nothing beyond what the prophets and Moses said would happen—that the Messiah would suffer and, as the first to rise from the dead, would bring the message of light to his own people and to the Gentiles. (Acts 26:18–19 [NIV])

Festus interrupted and declared Paul insane. Paul professed not only that was he sane but that all that he said was truthful. He called upon Agrippa's knowledge of the prophets.

Then Agrippa said to Paul, "Do you think that in such a short time you can persuade me to be a Christian?"

Paul replied, "Short time or long—I pray to God that not only you but all who are listening to me today may become what I am, except for these chains."

The king rose, and with him the governor and Bernice and those sitting with them. After they left the room, they began saying to one another, "This man is not doing anything that deserves death or imprisonment." Agrippa said to Festus, "This man could have been set free if he had not appealed to Caesar." (Acts 26:28–32 [NIV])

Thus began Paul's amazing ministry—one of hardship and imprisonment, but unwavering in the knowledge that he had seen a dead man alive as a raised god. Paul's honesty and integrity meet the standards set forth by Greenleaf. In his letter to the Church of Corinth, Paul wrote of the most important doctrines of Christian belief:

For what I received I passed on to you as of first importance: that Christ died for our sins according to the Scriptures, that he was buried, that he was raised on the third day according to the Scriptures, and that he appeared to Cephas, and then to the Twelve. After that, he appeared to more than five hundred of the brothers and sisters at the same time, most of whom are still living, though some have fallen asleep. Then he appeared to James [Jesus's half brother who did not believe Jesus was the Son of God until seeing him risen], then to all the apostles, and last of all he appeared to me also. (1 Cor. 15:3–8 [NIV])

Paul's testimony to the new Church of Corinth is quite significant. First, Paul provides eyewitness testimony of Jesus's resurrection. Second, he establishes that the news of and belief in Jesus's resurrection has begun to spread quickly shortly after Jesus's crucifixion, while eye witnesses still lived—long before legends and myths could have warped the truth. The vim and vigor of Jesus's followers to return to him with complete devotion, after having scattered at his death but prior to his resurrection; their subsequent willingness to be persecuted and even killed for their belief; and the dramatic growth of the faith despite widespread persecution stand as strong circumstantial evidence that Jesus did indeed rise from the grave.

Cornelius Tacitus, Roman historian, wrote in AD 104, "Nero...inflicted the most exquisite tortures on a class hated for their abominations, called Christians by the populace. Christus, from whom the name had its origin, suffered the extreme penalty at the hands of one of our procurators, Pontius Pilatus, and a most mischievous superstition, thus checked for the moment, again broke out not only in Judea, but even in Rome." Even the most critical skeptic must concede that the eleven remaining disciples and other early Christians must at least have believed that Jesus had risen, because they were not likely to have subjected themselves to pain, torture, and at times death for something they knew to be a lie. Mark Strauss of Bethel Seminary conversed with Strobel.

> Other Messianic figures had risen in the past, had claimed to be somebody, and had been suppressed and killed by the Romans. Yet, no movement arose around those dead messiahs. But these disciples of Jesus were willing to go to the ends of the earth proclaiming the gospel message, were willing to suffer and die for that. The transformation from a bunch of defeated cowards to boldly, fearlessly proclaiming the Gospel even to the point of death to me confirms that something happened on that First Easter morning. (Strobel 2007)

Jesus's followers denied him when he died. They were confused and scattered, still persecuted by Jewish Pharisees such as Saul (Paul). But something dramatic happened to change all of that; they found amazing strength and courage. Jesus's own brother, James, who had not accepted Jesus as the Messiah while he lived, converted to Christianity and later died a martyr rather than recant. He had seen his half brother, Jesus, raised from the grave; he had learned the truth. He believed. He loved. He was resolved, faithful, and unwavering. Likewise, Saul, on his journey to imprison and punish more Christians, was converted by the risen Jesus. Saul began his journey to Damascus thinking that all Christians would be eradicated. Instead, he returned as Paul the Evangelist, professing his faith—even while imprisoned, to soldiers, guards, governors, kings, priests, Jews, and gentiles alike.

Few people are willing to die for something they believe in—fewer still for something they are unsure of, and vastly fewer (if any) for something they know to be a lie! We are compelled to conclude that Jesus's tomb was empty because Jesus defeated death. His body was not to be found by Jewish leaders nor the guards who were charged with ensuring he was not removed. The risen Jesus walked among and conversed with hundreds of Jews following his resurrection. He continued to preach and carried out the noblest act in the history of humanity: he died for us so that our sins would be forgiven and we need not live eternity separated from God, our Father and Creator.

If Jesus Is God, Then Why…?

I've been asked, "How can you believe in a god of mercy with all the violence, pain, and suffering that exist in our world?" and "Why should anyone believe in a god who sends to hell all those who do not believe in him, even if they have never heard of him?" Another common line of thinking suggests, "If I need only to believe in Jesus to enter heaven, why should I be good?" At times, these questions are posed by someone who feels that my faith in Jesus is misplaced and thus attempts to save me from my ignorance. Most often, however, the questions are asked with genuine concern and interest. In either case, they deserve respectful and carefully considered responses. Jesus provided the answers; we need only listen with the intent to understand.

Sheep, Goats, Grace, and Mercy

God's mercy and grace give me hope—for myself, and for our world.

Billy Graham

It is true that Christians believe, as a result of Jesus's ministry, that all who enter God's Kingdom will enter through Jesus Christ. But what does this mean? What did Jesus teach of righteousness, grace, and mercy? We need only look to Jesus's parables of the good shepherd and his sheep and of the sheep and the goats to find the answers to these questions.

The Good Shepherd and His Sheep

> Therefore Jesus said again, "Very truly I tell you, I am the gate for the sheep. All who have come before me are thieves and robbers, but the sheep have not listened to them. I am the gate; whoever enters through me will be saved. They will come in and go out, and find pasture. The thief comes only to steal and kill and destroy; I have come that they may have life, and have it to the full." (John 10:7–10 [NIV])

Jesus referred to other false messiahs who sought in vain to deceive his sheep, and he clearly proclaims that those who enter through him will be saved. He answered more directly in his response to Thomas ("doubting Thomas," who needed to feel Jesus's wrists and feet before believing that Jesus had risen from the grave), one of his disciples who asked how they could know the way: "Jesus said to him, 'I am the way, and the truth, and the life; no one comes to the Father but through me'" (John 14:6 [NASB]).

In these two statements, Jesus refrains from a discussion of worthiness; instead he implies that it is not by merit that the sheep are saved but that they (we) in fact gain entrance through him. Paul taught in his letter to the Ephesians that we were created to do good works, but it is only by grace that we will be saved:

For it is by grace you have been saved, through faith—and this is not from yourselves, it is the gift of God—not by works, so that no one can boast. For we are God's handiwork, created in Christ Jesus to do good works, which God prepared in advance for us to do. (Eph. 2:8–10 [NIV])

We were put here to do good things, to contribute; yet we all have our "issues" and fall short of earning salvation. Many struggle with the concept of grace and thus question, "If we cannot earn our way into heaven, why be good at all? Why not do whatever we desire and then seek forgiveness?" The answer is simple and threefold. First, as answered by Paul, we were put here to do good works—it is our calling. Second, God the Father knows our true heart. He we cannot fool. Third, Jesus teaches that he, the Son of man, will come again in glory to be our judge. In his parable of the sheep and goats, Jesus describes how we will be judged as righteous (aligned in spirit with God's will) or unrighteous (not aligned in spirit with God's will) based on our true hearts and actions.

The Sheep and the Goats

When the Son of Man comes in his glory, and all the angels with him, he will sit on his glorious throne. All the nations will be gathered before him, and he will separate the people one from another as a shepherd separates the sheep from the goats. He will put the sheep on his right and the goats on his left.

Then the King will say to those on his right, "Come, you who are blessed by my Father; take your inheritance, the kingdom prepared for you since the creation of the world. For I was hungry and you gave me something to eat, I was thirsty and you gave me something to drink, I was a stranger and you invited me in, I needed clothes and you clothed me, I was sick and you looked after me, I was in prison and you came to visit me."

Then the righteous will answer him, "Lord, when did we see you hungry and feed you, or thirsty and give you something to drink?

When did we see you a stranger and invite you in, or needing clothes and clothe you? When did we see you sick or in prison and go to visit you?"

The King will reply, "Truly I tell you, whatever you did for one of the least of these brothers and sisters of mine, you did for me."

Then he will say to those on his left, "Depart from me, you who are cursed, into the eternal fire prepared for the devil and his angels. For I was hungry and you gave me nothing to eat, I was thirsty and you gave me nothing to drink, I was a stranger and you did not invite me in, I needed clothes and you did not clothe me, I was sick and in prison and you did not look after me." (Matt. 25:31–41 [NIV])

Pastor Matt Hannan of New Heights Church in Vancouver, Washington, teaches that grace is God giving to us what we don't deserve (passage to heaven through Jesus's sacrifice), and mercy is God not giving to us what we do deserve (punishment and separation from God for choosing to sin).

I have always found that mercy bears richer fruits than strict justice.

Abraham Lincoln

Jesus teaches in the parable of the good shepherd that he is the "mechanism," or gate through which we enter to be saved (by his grace). Then he describes in the parable of The Sheep and the Goats how he, the Son of man, will divide the righteous from those who are not righteous: the righteous will be invited (out of mercy, because by merit, we all fall short) to enter through him and live with him in eternity (a gift given by grace); the remainder will live in eternity isolated from his goodness. It is this isolation from God that is hell. His love for us is so great that He gifted to us free will; He gave the freedom to choose Him and the freedom to choose to do good or ill. Humanity's choice to do that which is unrighteous has opened Pandora's box, releasing both the ills of man and nature. Make no mistake: the problems we face today are not due to God's great love but due to humanity's misuse of free will. We find it inconvenient and undesirable to live according to Christian standards. His wrath is fueled by our application of free will and our subsequent refusal of his invitation to accept his gift of mercy. He does not consign us to hell. Hell is our choice. When we choose poorly, when we choose a self-destructive path, God is angered. His wrath is fueled by love, not hate. Love is God's driving force. We turn our backs on Him, refuse to believe in Him, deny His creation, and blame the ills of this earth on Him, thus labeling Him unloving. Is his anger really so different from ours?

> Think how we feel when we see someone we love [especially our child] ravaged by unwise actions or relationships. Do we respond with benign tolerance as we might toward strangers? Far from it...Anger isn't the opposite of love. Hate is, and the final form of hate is indifference...God's wrath is not a cranky explosion, but his settled opposition to the cancer...which is eating out the insides of the human race he loves with his whole being. (Pippert 1990)

We have miscalculated! God is reacting to our behavior as a loving parent reacts to a child who is on a path of self-destruction—though perhaps with more compassion than many. He did not choose evil; we did. He simply gave us the power to choose.

Is God just in His dealing with us? Will professed believers go to heaven even when they are ill spirited and don't strive to be good? Will Jesus consign to hell someone who has never heard of him, even if that person strives to be good and is righteous?

In C. S. Lewis's last book of The Chronicles of Narnia, *The Last Battle*, there is a scene where a warrior named Emeth, a Calormene, enemy of Narnia and servant of the god Tash, enters a stable with the hope of laying eyes upon his god. Upon entering, however, Emeth finds only deception as weaved by his fellow Calormenes and is forced to slay one of his own comrades or die by "friendly" hands. After felling his unrighteous comrade-in-arms, Emeth finds in the stable a beautiful world like no other. New hope swells within him—hope that this is indeed Tash's land, where he might have the opportunity to gaze upon the face of his god. Moments later, however, he comes face-to-face with the great lion Aslan, who in The Chronicles of Narnia symbolizes the risen Jesus. Emeth falls at Aslan's feet, realizing immediately that he faces the true god and believing it is surely the hour of his death, ready to deservingly forfeit his life as punishment for following the evil Tash (who he now realizes is a false god or devil). Emeth feels in his heart, however, that it will be better to have laid eyes on the greatness of the true god (Aslan) and die than to be king of the world and have lived without knowing the truth.

But to Emeth's great surprise, Aslan bends down, licks Emeth's forehead, and welcomes him. Aslan knows Emeth's true heart. Emeth feels a terrible burden and confesses that he is regretfully a follower of Tash and thus unworthy of Aslan's love. Aslan does not waver, lovingly asserting that all the good and noble acts performed by Emeth throughout his life are acceptable in the name of Aslan.

> "Child, all the service thou has done to Tash, I account as service done to me."
>
> Emeth queried, "Is it then true...that thou and Tash are one?"
>
> With consternation laced with love Aslan bellowed, "It is false. Not because he and I are one, but because we are opposites...I take to me the services which thou hast done to him, for I and he are of such different kinds that no service which is vile can be done to me and none which is not vile can be done to him. Therefore, if any man swear by Tash and keep his oath for the oath's sake, it is by me that he has truly sworn, though he know it not, and it is I who reward him. And if any man do a cruelty in my name...it is Tash whom he serves and by Tash his deed is accepted." (Lewis 1956)

Aslan's acceptance of Emeth, a nonbeliever, ruffled a few feathers in the Christian community. Many Christians felt that C. S. Lewis was wrong. Lewis responded to the ill feelings in one of his letters:

I think that every prayer which is sincerely made even to a false god or to a very imperfectly conceived true God, is accepted by the true God and that Christ saves many who do not think they know Him. For He is (dimly) present in the good side of the inferior teachers they follow. In the parable of *The Sheep and the Goats*...those who are saved do not seem to know that they have served Christ. But of course our anxiety about unbelievers is most usefully employed when it leads us not to speculation but to earnest prayer for them and the attempt to be in our own lives such good advertisements for Christianity as will make it attractive.

In the parable of the sheep and the goats, Jesus implies that those who perform good deeds do so in Jesus's name, even when they do not personally "know" Jesus. Jesus separates the righteous whose spirits are aligned with God's spirit and who have performed good deeds from those who have not performed those good deeds, clearly professing that what we do and how we do it matters. Remember that being righteous does not mean we have lived up to the standard and character of God; it means we desire to be good and strive to follow God's ways.

The word "righteous" (including "righteousness") appears 493 times in the New International Version Bible, the first time in Genesis 6:9: "Noah was a righteous man." Noah served God the Father, but in his time, Jesus had not yet walked the earth and would not do so for thousands more years. In fact, all humans who lived before Christ had no chance (while living) to accept Jesus specifically as their savior; yet he is the gate to heaven through which we must enter. King David of the Israelites prophesized the savior's fate in Psalm 22, hundreds of years before crucifixion was devised, noting that he would be surrounded by a pack of villains who would pierce his hands and feet, divide his clothes, cast lots for his garments, dislocate his bones, and flog him so badly that his bones would be on display. King David, his descendants, contemporaries and ancestors sacrificed animals to God, symbolizing Jesus's eventual sacrifice. Ultimately, King David—like all others—sinned and fell short of God's commandments, but he was a man of God's heart, and though he did not specifically know Jesus, who had not yet walked the earth, Jesus found a way to enter David's heart. Noah's and King David's first revelations revealed a general understanding of an all-powerful God rather than a specific relationship with Jesus Christ. They embraced the God of Creation and longed to know Him better. David prophesized of Jesus and through his relationship with God the Father, was led to a specific revelation of the coming savior, and thus embraced Jesus who (David foresaw) would come, suffer, and die for us.

Many people (Christians and non-Christians) struggle with this concept today: how can people be damned to hell if they are good people who have not had a chance to know Jesus? Jesus answered this in part in the parable of the sheep and the goats. The righteous are righteous because of their deeds and their hearts. Those deeds may be simple rather than extensive. Jesus did not state that the righteous helped all those in need—just that they helped. Jesus did not state that they recited the Gospel or evangelized—only that they cared for those in need and visited those who were lonely. It is implied that these sheep were not fully aware that they were serving Jesus, just as Emeth did not know he was serving Aslan. But God knew their hearts as He knows ours (and as Aslan knew Emeth's). He knows each person's level of learning and the extent of his or her revelation. All sheep are exposed to God's world, though some are born into much more difficult situations and are not privy to many of His great wonders. God understands to what extent each has received messages of the general revelation that there is a creator—and it is the creator we should worship, not his creation. God also knows if we have been exposed to specific revelation—specific knowledge of Jesus, whether gained from an inner "feeling," like David had before he prophesized about the Savior's crucifixion, or gained through study or interaction with other Christians. God knows intimately our gifts of revelation regarding Jesus and will hold us accordingly accountable.

In the parable of the good shepherd, Jesus stated, "I am the good shepherd; I know my sheep and my sheep know me" (John 10:14 [NIV]). Consider the statement "my sheep know me" along with the implication that some of the righteous sheep did not seem to specifically know Jesus. Jesus continued, "I have other sheep that are not of this sheep pen. I must bring them also. They too will listen to my voice, and there shall be one flock and one shepherd" (John 10:16 [NIV]).

Jesus taught that sheep are righteous and that he has sheep who know him and others who are not of the same sheep pen who do not, though they too will listen to his voice. Theirs is perhaps a general rather than a specific revelation. Specific revelation happens when we each have an opportunity to "listen" to his voice, whether from an internal or external source.

Jesus asserts that he must bring all his sheep together into one flock and pen. Further, he indicates that all sheep will enter his kingdom through him, strongly suggesting that even those who performed good deeds without specific revelation will have a chance to accept, follow, and "come to the Father"; all righteous sheep will have an opportunity to accept Jesus via specific revelation.

Howard Storm was a thirty-eight-year-old college professor of art on a field trip in Europe with a group of students and his wife. One morning while in Paris, he experienced a sudden and excruciating pain in his abdomen. "The pain was the most excruciating I had experienced in my life, it just dropped me right down to the ground" (Storm 2011). Howard's stomach had perforated. He was fortunate that a doctor was nearby, who was able to diagnose what had happened. They called the paramedics, and Howard was rushed to the emergency room at a general hospital, where he was seen by two more doctors who "knew exactly what was wrong" but were unable to treat his perforation. So Howard was transferred to the surgery hospital a few blocks away, where he was "parked," because there were no surgeons available to operate. "There I lay for eight to ten hours…with no medication…no attention whatsoever." The nurse came into his room at around eighty thirty in the evening to inform him that there would not be a surgeon available until the next day: "Well, when she said that, I knew that it was over for me. I knew that I was dead. The only thing that was keeping me alive was that I didn't want to die. I was scared to death of dying, because, as far as I knew (I was an atheist, a non-believer, a person who lived for the gratification you could get out of the moment)...next to the pain, dying was the worst thing that could happen to you...it [dying] was the end of life and there was no more, there wasn't anything else" (Storm 2011).

Howard could no longer bear the pain, so he said good-bye to his wife. They declared their love for each other. They both knew it was over, and he shut his eyes. It seemed like only moments later, he was standing next to his bed, next to his wife. He felt great. He called to his wife, but she did not respond. Then he noticed the body in the bed— it looked like him. He became agitated and upset, but then he heard soft, gentle voices calling to him from outside his room. He followed them. The voices belonged to men and women, and they understood what Howard needed. He thought they were with the hospital. He left the bright room and entered the dim hallway. As he followed them, the hallway became darker. The light faded gradually, and their gentle, inviting voices became increasingly bossy. Howard became wary; sensing this, they urged him on with increasing hostility.

Howard stopped. He was no longer willing to follow. Hands reached for him to push him farther. These men and women clambered over him. They yelled, screeched, screamed, and pushed, hit, bit, and clawed Howard. He fought back, trying to free himself. It seemed to Howard that they derived satisfaction from his pain. Eventually he was lying on the floor, ripped up and in pain, mental and physical. He felt the pain was unjust. Howard heard his own voice order him to pray to God. He thought to himself, "I don't believe in God." He tried to remember—how do you pray? Howard struggled to pray. He did not know how, but he noticed that every time he mentioned God's name, the people around him seemed to feel pain. They moved away. Howard continued, and as his prayers grew stronger, the people receded. They disappeared.

Howard now found himself alone. It seemed he was in a place that had no time. He lay there pondering his life. He realized he had been selfish. The only god in his adult life was himself. The people who had just attacked him were people just like him—people who had lived godless, selfish, materialistic lives, doomed to inflict pain on one another for eternity. Howard realized he was now one of them, and though he did not want to be there, he came to the stark realization that it was just—it was what he sowed—what he deserved. He had not served God, only himself, and these were his just desserts.

Howard lay there for what seemed like an eternity, contemplating his fate, when in the back of his mind, a faint image began to appear. The image was that of himself as a child, sitting at a piano and singing a song: "Jesus loves me...la, la, la. Jesus loves me...la, la." This reminded him that there was a time in his life, when he was young and innocent, when he believed in something good, something powerful, something greater than himself, and now he longed for that—he wanted that back: "I didn't know Jesus, but I wanted to know Jesus. I didn't know His love, but I wanted to know His love. I didn't know if He was real, but I wanted him to be real." Howard called out, "Jesus, please save me!" And he came. Howard recalled that far off in the darkness, he saw a speck of light. The speck grew until it was so bright that it seemed as though it would consume him, but the light was not hot or dangerous.

Howard recounted, "He was in this light, and He reached down out of this light and gently started to pick me up and in His light I could see that I was [covered by] gore, and filth and wounds all over; I looked like roadkill....As He is touching me, everything just goes away, all the wounds, all the pain, all the dirt...I am whole, healed, and inside I am filled with His Love...it's the best thing that ever happened to me...to know that love."

Jesus carried Howard away. Howard felt wonderful, yet, like Emeth, unworthy. He felt shame. Jesus stopped and said to Howard, "We don't make mistakes; you belong here." Jesus summoned angels who proceeded to show Howard his life from beginning to end. Howard shared what they taught him regarding what throughout his life he had done well and what he had done poorly:

> It was real simple. When I had been a loving, kind person—considerate of other people, it made the angels happy, it made Jesus happy, and they let me know that it made God happy. And when I had been selfish and manipulative, it made the angels unhappy, it made Jesus unhappy, and they let me know that it made God unhappy. What they were trying to convey to me, in a nutshell, was my whole purpose of my existence had been to love God, love my neighbors, [and love] myself.

Howard realized he had failed. Yet they told him that it was not his time to go: he needed to go back to his life and try to do it better. Howard feared that after knowing Jesus's great love, he could not bear to reenter the world without it. Laughing with him, they said he had never been alone. Howard had left God; God had never left Howard. They sent Howard back, forever changed by his near-death experience and assured by faith that he would never walk alone.

It was now around nine thirty. Howard awoke suddenly. The nurse who had earlier informed them that there was no doctor available to operate returned with news that a doctor had arrived. Howard longed to tell his wife what had happened. "The strange thing about this experience is that the memory has not faded at all, it has stayed intense, and the reason, I believe, that God gave me this experience is so that I would have the opportunity to share it with somebody...so it could be of help to them." God, Jesus, and the angels knew Howard's heart. Though he had lived without Jesus, Jesus did not live without Howard. He brought Howard, a sheep of another pen, into the fold. Howard was given the opportunity to accept Jesus as evil was clawing at his mortal soul. Fortunately for Howard, Jesus prevailed.

There is yet another conundrum: if being good is sufficient to be called righteous, then why should we strive to know Christ sooner rather than later? I believe the answer, once again, is threefold. First, with the strength of Jesus, we have a much better chance of being righteous and successfully combatting the temptations of evil. Recall that Howard could not fight off the lost and evil spirits until he called upon God. Recall, also, step 5 in the process to resist temptation: take time to ask God for help. He will often provide an escape route that leads to doing something good. Second, more people will come to Jesus through positive, loving examples from good Christians than from private revelation (dreams, visions, etc., as happened with King David). Jesus will reach more people through social media and social interaction with Christians: iron sharpens iron. Third, he is the gate: we each need to accept Jesus as our bridge to God the Father, and it is far better to commit sooner rather than later in order to avoid encounters such as that experienced by Howard Storm.

Without the grace of God and the sacrifice of Jesus, we all fall short, and though we try, we cannot be truly righteous. Jesus taught and led by example. He lived without sin. He knew we could not do the same, so he commissioned the sheep who know him to teach the good news to those who have not had the opportunity to know him.

> All authority in heaven and on earth has been given to me. Therefore go and make disciples of all nations, baptizing them in the name of the Father and of the Son and of the Holy Spirit, and teaching them to obey everything I have commanded you. And surely I am with you always, to the very end of the age. (Matt. 28:18–20 [NIV])

Christian (Religious) Conundrums

And so the Lord says, "These people say they are mine. They honor me with their lips, but their hearts are far from me. And their worship of me is nothing but man-made rules learned by rote.

Isaiah 29:13 (NLT)

Unfortunately, many who claim to be followers of Christ have alienated non- Christians by acting in a manner that is not appealing. Jesus suggests that those who claim to be men of God but are not righteous are not sheep, but goats. In Jesus's time, there was a group of strict Jewish leaders known as the Pharisees (recall Saul). The Pharisees promoted strict observance of religious ceremonies and adherence to oral laws and traditions. They believed in an afterlife and the coming of a messiah. Some Pharisees overheard Jesus teaching his disciples that one could not serve two masters; they could not serve both God and money. The Pharisees, who loved money, heard all this and were sneering at Jesus. He said to them, "You are the ones who justify yourselves in the eyes of others, **but God knows your hearts.**" (Luke 16:14–15 [NIV])

It is clear that Jesus considered the hypocritical Pharisees to be goats, though they considered themselves devout men of God. In Revelation, we learn more of the plight of the goats who falsely claim to be godly and of the rewards for the sheep who are called righteous by Jesus (Figure 6).

> I will make those who are of the synagogue of Satan, who claim to be Jews though they are not, but are liars—I will make them come and fall down at your feet and acknowledge that I have loved you. Since you have kept my command to endure patiently, I will also keep you from the hour of trial that is going to come on the whole world to test the inhabitants of the earth. (Rev. 3:9–10 [NIV])

Figure 6: The flock of sheep to the right and the herd of goats to the left. The goats have chosen to separate themselves from Jesus and thus are cursed. The sheep have chosen to do good deeds and through general, then specific revelation accept the voice of Jesus and become one flock in Christ.

The flock of sheep consists of good-spirited, righteous people, both who know Jesus through specific revelation and who have not yet come to know him but have had a general revelation. The herd of goats consists of ill-spirited people, some who claim to be righteous but are not and others who claim to be godly but are not, and still others who openly embrace evil. This can be confusing; on one hand, we learn that we cannot "earn" our way into heaven, and on the other, we learn that we will be called sheep because of our "works"—feeding the hungry, providing shelter to the homeless, and caring for those in need.

One way to look at this is that being of good spirit, being righteous, is necessary yet not sufficient to receive our final reward. Try as we may, there is only one man who has walked the earth and been judged worthy to enter the realm of heaven. That man was with God in the beginning. He was sent by his father, God the Father, and is part of the Holy Trinity. That man is Jesus. Before he was man, he was wholly God. He took on human flesh to know our temptations. He passed all tests despite the weakness of that flesh. All others have fallen and will fall short. In ancient times people performed sacrifices to atone for their sins, yet these sacrifices, in reality, were only symbolic of the ultimate sacrifice which was paid in full by Jesus and it is only by Jesus's sacrifice on the cross that our sins are cleansed. Only once our sins are cleansed can we enter heaven and be in the presence of God. In other words, the sins we hold within our spirit are evil, and evil cannot exist in the presence of God, just as an acid cannot exist in the presence of a base. Either the solution becomes basic, acidic, or neutral; it cannot be basic and acidic at the same time. When judged righteous, we become his sheep, and by then accepting Jesus as our savior, we are cleansed and receive passage through the gate into his one kingdom; without this cleansing, we cannot enter.

Another conundrum shared by many Christians, especially those who are early in their journey, is frustration over their prayers going unanswered. They lament, "I've accepted Jesus in my heart, but I don't feel his presence. He doesn't answer my prayers. I thought it said in the Bible, 'Ask and you shall receive.' I ask, I pray, and it seems that much of the time, my prayers fall on deaf ears." What does Jesus's promise mean?

> I tell you the truth, anyone who believes in me will do the same works I have done, and even greater works, because I am going to be with the Father. You can ask for anything in my name, and I will do it, so that the Son can bring glory to the Father. Yes, ask me for anything in my name, and I will do it! (John 14:12–14 [NLT])

Shortly before his last day, Jesus warned the disciples that though his teachings were meant to keep them from stumbling, they would soon be tested and have doubts, and they would be cast out of synagogues by the many Jewish leaders who did not accept Jesus, truly not knowing the Son or the Father. Jesus then introduced the Holy Spirit, stating that when he left to be with his father in heaven, he would send the Holy Spirit to guide his followers on his behalf. Jesus stated that he and the Father would hear our prayers, and the Holy Spirit would be a conduit through which he communicated with his followers. Jesus prophesized about his death, his resurrection, and finally, his intent and promise to answer our prayers. He realized they were confused and wanted to ask more. He explained as follows:

> Are you asking yourselves what I meant? I said in a little while you won't see me, but a little while after that you will see me again. I tell you the truth, you will weep and mourn over what is going to happen to me, but the world will rejoice. You will grieve, but your grief [caused by my death] will suddenly turn to wonderful joy [because of my resurrection]. It will be like a woman suffering the pains of labor. When her child is born, her anguish gives way to joy because she has brought a new baby into the world. So you have sorrow now, but I will see you again; then you will rejoice, and no one can rob you of that joy. At that time you won't need to ask me for anything. I tell you the truth, you will ask the Father directly, and he will grant your request because you use my name. You haven't done this before. Ask, using my name, and you will receive, and you will have abundant joy. (John 16:19–24 [NLT])

John expounded on Jesus's promise to answer prayers in a formal instructional letter to early Christians: "Now, this is the confidence that we have in Him, that if we ask anything *according to His will*, He hears us. And if we know that He hears us, whatever we ask, we know that we have the petitions that we have asked of Him" (1 John 5:14 [NKJV]). With what you have learned about God, the Father, and the Son, do you think it reasonable to interpret these statements or promises to mean that Jesus will be like our Santa, giving anything we desire? These verses must be examined in the context of the time and place in which they were written and in the context of God's character as evident in His worldly creation and His word, the Bible. Common themes will then surface that shed light on the manner in which we should interpret this text. In chapter 14 of his Gospel, John quotes Jesus as saying, "He who believes in Me, the works that I do, he will do also…Whatever you ask in My name, that will I do, so that the Father may be glorified in the Son." And in John 16, he writes, "If you ask the

Father for anything in My name, He will give it to you," clarifying in 1 John 5, "If we ask anything **according to His will**, He hears us."

Jesus defines in these statements several important qualifiers for the requests His father will grant. Ask in Jesus's name and the Father will grant your request for help and guidance with the following:

- Works we carry on in His name
- Works consistent with His character
- Works similar to what He performed during his ministry
- Works that glorify the Father through the accomplishments of His son's team
- Works that align with His will and plan

God is on a Journey, and He has invited us to join Him. When our prayers are consistent with His plan, they will be granted.

Consider for a moment the thought "God's will, not ours be done." At first glance, this may seem offensive, but take pause and think more deeply. God is our creator, our Father, and similar to our children's behavior toward us, we may make requests of God that he knows are not good for us or others. It is an important role of any parent to refuse when a child's requests are excessive, illogical, potentially hurtful to others, or just plain dangerous. Is it too farfetched to believe that God, the ultimate good parent, will maintain healthy barriers and not succumb to our negotiations and pleas? Further, some of our prayers may be aligned with God's will but not His schedule. Our prayers may be granted according to His timing but perhaps not even during our life on earth; for instance, if we pray that His will be done on earth as it is in heaven, we know that this will not happen until Jesus comes again.

Imagine a futuristic vehicle that will automatically navigate and drive to your desired location. You need to maintain the vehicle, enter addresses, and participate in the journey. Imagine God as the perfect navigator: if you listen perfectly, He will identify for you each location you need to visit and provide the proper coordinates. However, He has provided us free will in our actions and our prayers—the ability to choose to follow His plan. As a consequence of our free will, human desires, and imperfect hearing, we don't always enter the correct coordinates, and God won't help us get to a place He knows we should not go, just as He will not grant a prayer for that which we or others should not have. Even when we request the correct destination, at times we stray from the chosen path either because we don't properly hear the directions due to "background noise" (the radio, passengers talking, or a phone call) or because we simply decide to take another route. The result for our navigation system is the same in either case: constant messages of "recalculating...recalculating" in attempts to steer us back to His intended course. During our times of trials and tribulations, we often feel we are traveling alone, but God will never leave us, even if we leave Him. In fact, trials and tribulations are often God's message "recalculating" in hopes that He can motivate us to rejoin him on His path. Mary Stevenson captures this concept beautifully in the following poem:

Footprints in the Sand

One night I dreamed I was walking along the beach with the Lord.

Many scenes from my life flashed across the sky.

In each scene I noticed footprints in the sand.

Sometimes there were two sets of footprints,

Other times there were one set of footprints.

This bothered me because I noticed

That during the low periods of my life,

When I was suffering from

Anguish, sorrow or defeat,

I could see only one set of footprints.

So I said to the Lord,

"You promised me Lord,

That if I followed you,

You would walk with me always.

But I have noticed that during

The most trying periods of my life

There have only been one

Set of footprints in the sand.

Why, when I needed you most,

You have not been there for me?"

The Lord replied,

"The times when you have

Seen only one set of footprints,

Is when I carried you."

God is on a journey. He has invited us to join Him. Some follow without question. Some (like me) follow but need to continually check the path to stay on course. Others join but expect God to change His direction due to their participation. Some merely feign participation in God's journey to achieve their own devious ends, and still others flaunt that they won't join. God will follow His plan in any case, and like a caring and loving Father, He longs for us to do the same.

Imagine following His plan: establishing lasting and meaningful relationships; loving our neighbors, ourselves, and our god; striving at work, home, and within our communities to make worthwhile and lasting contributions; helping others with a glad spirit; and accepting Jesus within our hearts—all the time knowing that, no matter how we try, we will stray. We wonder, "Will we still be judged for our sins?"

The Book of Life

When Jesus was teaching at the Mount of Olives, with a crowd all around him, teachers of law and the Pharisees brought to him an adulterous woman. They stood her before the crowd and stated her crime, dictating her punishment according to the Law of Moses: she was to be stoned until dead. They were trying to trap Jesus by leaving him only two options: defy the Law of Moses and be guilty of heresy, or condemn the women to death by stoning, which would be a violation of Roman rule (the death sentence could be proclaimed only by the Roman ruler). Jesus bent down to write with his finger in the dirt. Their questions persisted:

> When they kept on questioning him, he straightened up and said to them, "Let any one of you who is without sin be the first to throw a stone at her." Again he stooped down and wrote on the ground.
>
> At this, those who heard began to go away one at a time, the older ones first, until only Jesus was left, with the woman still standing there. Jesus straightened up and asked her, "Woman, where are they? Has no one condemned you?"
>
> "No one, sir," she said.
>
> "Then neither do I condemn you," Jesus declared. "Go now and leave your life of sin." (John 8:7–11 [NIV])

What did Jesus write that dispersed the crowd? John does not tell us the answer to this question, but I was once asked to consider the following as a potential explanation: Jesus bent slowly down. He gazed into the crowd. He noticed many men of prominence and scratched in the dirt their names in a row. As they kept questioning him, Jesus straightened and said, "Let any one of you who is without sin be the first to throw a stone at her." As people in the crowd pondered Jesus's challenge, Jesus bent again and began to write transgressions under each name, starting with the most senior leader. When this leader realized what was happening, he bowed his head and departed before

137

more could be written. Jesus moved to the next name, writing with the same result. Soon the leaders and followers were leaving before their sins were published for all to see. Finally no one was left, for no one was without sin. John did not document what Jesus wrote in the dirt, so we can only guess, but imagining Jesus writing sins in the sand helps us to understand what is meant by the hour of trial, which is also known as the judgment of the dead.

In the book of Revelation, the final book of the New Testament, John refers to the different books that will be used during the hour of trial. In the time of judgment, those who are goats are considered to be "dead to Christ," and those dead to Christ will be judged according to what they have done. Ultimately, because of their choice to be separated from God, they will be consigned to hell, confined to living an eternity separated from His goodness (symbolized by a "lake of fire"). Those whose names are found in the Book of Life (a.k.a. the book of the living) are those who have accepted Jesus and, thus, are considered to be alive in Christ. These sheep are spared from being judged by what they have done. Their sins are washed away; they are spared the judgment of the dead as they receive the rewards of heaven.

> I saw the dead, great and small, standing before the throne, and books were opened. Another book was opened, which is the book of life. The dead were judged according to what they had done as recorded in the books. The sea gave up the dead that were in it, and death and Hades gave up the dead that were in them, and each person was judged according to what they had done. Then death and Hades were thrown into the lake of fire. The lake of fire is the second death. Anyone whose name was not found written in the book of life was thrown into the lake of fire. (Rev. 20:12–15 [NIV])

John continues to describe his vision of the reward awaiting those who have accepted Jesus as their savior.

Then I saw "a new heaven and a new earth"...And I heard a loud voice from the throne saying, "Look! God's dwelling place is now among the people, and he will dwell with them. They will be his people, and God himself will be with them and be their God. He will wipe every tear from their eyes. There will be no more death or mourning or crying or pain, for the old order of things has passed away."

He who was seated on the throne said, "I am making everything new!" Then he said, "Write this down, for these words are trustworthy and true."

He said to me: "It is done. I am the Alpha and the Omega, the Beginning and the End. To the thirsty I will give water without cost from the spring of the water of life. Those who are victorious will inherit all this, and I will be their God and they will be my children. But the cowardly, the unbelieving, the vile, the murderers, the sexually immoral, those who practice magic arts, the idolaters and all liars—they will be consigned to the fiery lake of burning sulfur. This is the second death." (Rev. 21:1–8 [NIV])

All have sinned. Some will choose grace and mercy; some will choose to pay for their sins. Each of our earthly bodies will suffer death, some will experience the second death. God knows our hearts. Rejecting our creator or feigning love with ill spirit results in separation from God and finally the second death. Embracing our creator (general revelation) and being of good spirit opens the door to opportunity. Ultimately, it is our specific revelation (realization) that it is only through Jesus, the Son of God who was born man yet wholly God—subjected to torture and crucifixion only to rise again so that our sins will be forgiven, that the reward of grace can be received. It is only through Jesus that our sins are cleansed and we are made ready to enter heaven to spend eternity with God the Father. When we die, our souls separate from our physical bodies. Those souls who have chosen to remain separated from God will be judged and suffer a second death consigned to the fiery lake; those who accept Jesus will be cleansed and spend eternity with God and all His glory.

Does hope exist for someone who has been unrighteous? Is there forgiveness? Can someone find his or her way from the goats to the sheep, from nonbeliever to believer? God knows our hearts. With a true change of heart, can we find forgiveness? Billy Moore humbled himself and accepted Jesus, who was able to navigate Billy's way off death row. In his story of Emeth, C. S. Lewis depicts a man who lived what he thought was a righteous life for a false god. When faced with the true god, Emeth knew immediately of his mistake, humbled himself, and accepted Aslan as the true god. Lewis asserts in this story that the lost can be found, but more importantly, Jesus taught through his parables that not only can the lost be found, but there will be rejoicing in heaven for all who are. Former atheist Howard Storm, in his near-death experience, learned personally of Jesus's love. He is a modern-day Emeth. Howard felt unworthy. He felt lost. When given a second chance, he accepted Jesus.

According to Luke, Jesus was often surrounded by tax collectors and sinners. The Pharisees and scribes complained, "This man receives sinners and eats with them." Jesus responded to the complaint with two short parables, the first telling of a lost sheep who wondered off, the shepherd left ninety-nine sheep to find the single lost sheep and the second of a woman who lost one of ten silver coins. Each parable had a twist that in itself was surprising. In the first, we are surprised that the shepherd left the ninety-nine sheep to find the one, and in the second we are surprised to learn that upon finding the one lost coin, the woman called out to her friends and neighbors to rejoice that she had found the coin. In both parables, when the lost are found, Jesus proclaims there will be joy in heaven just as when the lost is found...when a sinner repents. He then told the parable of the lost (or prodigal) son.

There was a man who had two sons. The younger one said to his father, "Father, give me my share of the estate." So he divided his property between them.

Not long after that, the younger son got together all he had, set off for a distant country and there squandered his wealth in wild living. After he had spent everything, there was a severe famine in that whole country, and he began to be in need. So he went and hired himself out to a citizen of that country, who sent him to his fields to feed pigs. He longed to fill his stomach with the pods that the pigs were eating, but no one gave him anything.

When he came to his senses, he said, "How many of my father's hired servants have food to spare, and here I am starving to death! I will set out and go back to my father and say to him: Father, I have sinned against heaven and against you. I am no longer worthy to be called your son; make me like one of your hired servants." So he got up and went to his father.

But while he was still a long way off, his father saw him and was filled with compassion for him; he ran to his son, threw his arms around him and kissed him.

The son said to him, "Father, I have sinned against heaven and against you. I am no longer worthy to be called your son."

But the father said to his servants, "Quick! Bring the best robe and put it on him. Put a ring on his finger and sandals on his feet. Bring the fattened calf and kill it. Let's have a feast and celebrate. For this son of mine was dead and is alive again; he was lost and is found." So they began to celebrate.

Meanwhile, the older son was in the field. When he came near the house, he heard music and dancing. So he called one of the servants and asked him what was going on. "Your brother has come," he replied, "and your father has killed the fattened calf because he has him back safe and sound."

The older brother became angry and refused to go in. So his father went out and pled with him. But he answered his father, "Look! All these years I've been slaving for you and never disobeyed your orders. Yet you never gave me even a young goat so I could celebrate with my friends. But when this son of yours who has squandered your property with prostitutes comes home, you kill the fattened calf for him!"

"My son," the father said, "you are always with me, and everything I have is yours. But we had to celebrate and be glad, because this brother of yours was dead and is alive again; he was lost and is found." (Luke 15:11–31 [NIV])

In his parables of the lost sheep and the lost coin, Jesus appealed to the crowd with types of loss that they would easily understand—a sheep that had wandered off and a coin that had been misplaced. In each case, great happiness followed the finding of the lost. In the story of the father and his sons, however, Jesus wove a more intricate story. Most of our attention in this story is drawn to the first son who wanders off and suffers loss through his own poor choices. These poor choices are kindred to those that kindle our anger when we see a loved one wander down a path of self-destruction; his father is sorrowed and perhaps angered by those choices, but he yields to his son's free will. The father, however, does not withdraw his love and longs for his son to return. When the day comes that the son finally returns, the father rejoices; he throws a party to end all parties. Jesus is again teaching that there will be rejoicing in heaven when a lost sinner has a change of heart, repents, and returns to the Father. Just as the father in the story knows that his lost son has undergone a change of heart, so too Jesus knows when we have a change of heart. This change of heart transfigures us from an ill-spirited to a good-spirited person, and in turn triggers the party in heaven.

Jesus does not end with the story of the younger brother; he continues to describe the response of the older brother, who had remained at home serving his father righteously. When the older brother learned of the party for his returned brother, he was angered and became jealous and sullen. His prideful heart hardened toward both his brother and his father. The second son was then lost to pride and self-righteousness, and his change of heart prevented him from joining the celebration. Recall *Figure* 6: The flock of sheep to the right and the herd of goats to the left. The second son believed he was a righteous, godly man, but his hardened heart prevented him from being so. His anger and pride isolated him from the true love of his father and from bestowing grace upon his younger brother. The older son did not feel that it was fair that the younger son, who had abandoned his father, should be so loved and in anger, shunned his father's true love. The younger brother, like the lost sheep, was dynamically lost (lost due to his spirit and behavior) before being found. The older son, like the coin, was statically lost. His separation was solely due to spirit and attitude. Many of his actions we righteous, but his spirt was not. God knows our hearts and he knew the hearts of the complaining Pharisees!

Some struggle with the fact that someone like Billy Moore, a confessed murderer might receive the same grace as Mother Teresa. Jesus addresses the concept of fairness in his parable of the workers in the vineyard, as described by Matthew. In this parable, we find a kind of fairness that is profoundly contradictory to our worldly view.

> For the kingdom of heaven is like a landowner who went out early in the morning to hire workers for his vineyard. He agreed to pay them a denarius for the day and sent them into his vineyard. About nine in the morning he went out and saw others standing in the marketplace doing nothing. He told them, "You also go and work in my vineyard, and I will pay you whatever is right." So they went. He went out again about noon and about three in the afternoon and did the same thing. About five in the afternoon he went out and found still others standing around. He asked them, "Why have you been standing here all day long doing nothing?"

"Because no one has hired us," they answered. He said to them, "You also go and work in my vineyard."

When evening came, the owner of the vineyard said to his foreman, "Call the workers and pay them their wages, beginning with the last ones hired and going on to the first." The workers who were hired about five in the afternoon came and each received a denarius. So when those came who were hired first, they expected to receive more. But each one of them also received a denarius. When they received it, they began to grumble against the landowner. "These who were hired last worked only one hour," they said, "and you have made them equal to us who have borne the burden of the work and the heat of the day."

But he answered one of them, "I am not being unfair to you, friend. Didn't you agree to work for a denarius? Take your pay and go. I want to give the one who was hired last the same as I gave you. Don't I have the right to do what I want with my own money? Or are you envious because I am generous?" So the last will be first, and the first will be last. (Matt. 20:1–16 [NIV])

In this story, Jesus challenges his audience's sensibilities of fairness. It is generally believed that pay is proportional to contribution and that those who satisfactorily perform the same job for ten hours should be paid tenfold the earnings of those who have performed for only one hour. How does the landowner respond to accusations that he is not fair? He answers in two parts: first, he reminds the workers that he is paying the agreed wage, and second, he points out that he has the right to be generous. Think back to the righteous sheep and the unrighteous goats. In truth, none is worthy to enter the realm of heaven. Only Jesus, who was both man and god, has walked the earth and been worthy of heaven. It is only by his generosity that we are afforded the opportunity go to heaven, and though Jesus would love for us to be of his heart for all our lives, he knows that some will join early, some will join late, some will be posers, some will leave, and some will never join. Regardless of when we come to Christ, the ultimate reward is spending eternity in heaven. There is hope for all in Jesus: hope for Billy Moore, for Mother Teresa, for you and for me.

Some of the misunderstanding by Jesus's audience stems from a misunderstanding of his generous and loving character. *The Shack*, a controversial novel by author William P. Young, is the story of Mackenzie Philips, a father of five, who, after the death of his youngest daughter, finds himself trapped in what he calls the "Great Sadness." During Mackenzie's greatest hour of need, God presents Himself in forms that are most appealing to Mackenzie. God the Father first presents Himself as a mother figure in order to reach Mackenzie, who had an abusive father. Only after God has helped Mackenzie reconcile with the spirit of his deceased earthly father (i.e., restore their relationship but not resolve that past behaviors were acceptable) does He then present himself as a father figure.

Put on your green thinking caps. Suppose that God personally plants the seed of hunger to know Him in each of us and then presents Himself somewhat differently to each. His fundamental character remains constant from the beginning of times to the end of times: He is "compassionate, generous, and gracious, slow to anger, abounding in love and faithfulness." But just suppose He appears to us as we need Him based on our personal relationship with Him rather than based on a strict definition of any culture or religion. In other words, God is defined by God rather than by Pharisees, Catholics, Protestants, or any other religion. Is it possible that our understanding is limited—that we, individually and collectively, do not fully understand God?

Ravi Zacharias was born in Madras, India, in 1946, and is now a leading authority in apologetics, traveling the world defending Christian principles through a logical and systematic use of philosophy and data. I encourage you to search YouTube to view many of his interesting talks. He was born into a family who was "nominally" Christian. Ravi stated in an interview for Lee Strobel's Book *The Case for Faith*, "In fact, the reason they [his parents] were Christian was simply because they were not Buddhists, Muslims or Hindus." He continued describing his path to faith.

I came to believe in Jesus in two stages. The first stage was when I heard the gospel publicly proclaimed in an auditorium when I was seventeen. I said to myself, "Something about this is true and I want it." I went forward and was counseled, but I did not really understand. The baggage was too much. At the time, I was under a lot of pressure in a culture where academic performance was of supreme importance. I couldn't cope with it. I also had a particularly strict father, and I struggled with that. I took a lot of punishment physically.

So a few months later, I decided to end my own life. I was not depressed; my friends would have been shocked to hear suicide was on my mind. But for me, Life had no meaning or purpose. I went to school one day and used the keys to the science lab to check out some poisons. I put them into a glass of water, gobbled it up, and collapsed on my knees.

My servant in the house rushed me to the hospital; if he were not there, I would be dead. They emptied the poisons out of me. As I lay in bed, a friend walked in with a New Testament and showed me John chapter 14. I couldn't hold the book; my body was too dehydrated. My mother had to read it to me.

There she was reading where Jesus was talking to Thomas and saying, "I am the way, the truth, and the life. No one comes to the Father except through me." Then she came to verse 18, where Jesus tells his disciples, "Because I live, you also will live."

That verse touched my soul. I said in a prayer, "Jesus, I don't know much about who you are, but you are telling me you're the author of true life." I didn't understand the concept of sin. In that culture, I couldn't have. But what I did know was that he was offering himself to me to give me life. So, I said, "If you take me out of this hospital room, I will leave no stone unturned in my pursuit of truth." And I walked out of the room five days later an absolutely brand new man. I began to study the Bible, and it dramatically changed my life. My brothers then came to follow Jesus, as did my parents before they died.

But it was in that hospital room where Christ told me—through nobody explaining it to me—that he could give me what life was really meant to be. And I've never looked back. Years of study have only confirmed my decision to follow him. I took some philosophy course at Cambridge under a renowned atheist, and I remember thinking in astonishment, "These are the best arguments atheists have?" It merely confirmed the truth of Scripture.

I have traveled the world. I have searched high and low. I have found nothing that satisfies my mind, my heart, and the deepest longings of my soul like Jesus does. He is not only the way, the truth and the life; He is personal to me. He is my way, and my life—just as He can be for anyone who reaches out to Him. (Strobel 2000)

Jesus presented himself to Ravi in a hospital room in India. Ravi was lucky to know Jesus and find his way. But in others, the seed grows in different ways and with incomplete or imperfect understanding of our God-shaped hole, we arrive at an imperfect understanding of who—and what—God is. Perhaps there are common themes that transcend the differences among all the incomplete or imperfect understandings in this world. Is it too far of a leap to consider that those common themes might include the golden rule, which has found its way into so many religions and beliefs (see "What Lies within You?")?

Trust in the Lord with all your heart; do not depend on your own understanding. Seek his will in all you do, and he will show you which path to take.

Proverbs 3:5–6 (NLT)

If one believes there is a god who created heaven and earth, then there is reason to believe He has a plan and a desire for a personal relationship with each of us, despite our differing worldly beliefs.

Imagine how different the world might be if, after quietly pondering the possibilities, all agreed that God is only fully understood by God despite our differing denominations, (or "abominations," in the words of Ravi Zacharias), and as a consequence, we cease our futile feuding over claims of knowing absolute truth. To me it seems illogical for any human to believe that we are capable, with our acutely limited mental capacity, to completely grasp the intricacies of our creator...the creator of our universe and life itself. We are free to choose. He gave us that freedom, so why then do we feel it is our right to strip the gift of free will from others?

God gifted us free will: the ability to choose whether or not we follow Him. He prefers we follow His plan rather than our own, but He does not mandate it. He has left bread crumbs for us to follow. He has charged us with helping and teaching one another. His signature is all over the natural world, present in the natural laws, which He has written, present in the grandeur of our greatest mountains and the elegance of the simplest cells. He has implanted desires in our souls, and as we have discussed, it is not good but evil that attempts to warp even our noblest desires. Is it really so difficult to believe that in the midst of all worldly turmoil, we each have an incomplete view of His desired path for us and an incomplete understanding of His plan? Do we really think that our limited minds, which struggle with the mysteries of this world, are capable of fully encompassing the mysteries of God's kingdom? It follows, then, that the gaps in our understanding have left room for shades of gray, rather than the black-and-white dogmatic theologies espoused by many religious and political leaders to divide humanity into groups that satisfy their purpose. The apostle Paul warned in his letter to the Colossians, "Be wise in the way you act toward outsiders; make the most of every opportunity" (Col. 4:5 [NIV]).

Is it God's purpose to divide us into factions, both religious and nonreligious? If yes, then why should we be wise in the way we act toward those who differ from our beliefs? Clearly, He will divide us when our time comes (the sheep and the goats); do we really need to divide ourselves in advance? What are the motives and underlying principles that would lead to such divisions? There is a story of a town-hall meeting that took place in a "typical" Irish town. Protestants, Catholics, and atheists all debated. When the atheist had finished, a woman stood and asked, "Yes, but is it the Catholic God or the Protestant God in whom you do not believe?"

We need to be wiser in the way we act. We need not push others away by professing to know the absolute truth that is reserved wholly by God himself. We can present God's word to the best of our capability while striving to remain humble. The American actor and director Clint Eastwood identified one of the root causes of extreme positions as insecurity: "I'm interested in the fact that the less secure a man is, the more likely he is to have extreme prejudice."

Not until we overcome insecurity, become confident in the notion that we cannot possibly know all; not until we encourage open minds and open hearts, yet maintain the courage of our convictions while embracing a good spirit, acting with consideration and kindness, love and respect; not until then will we reach the maturity level necessary to become a world more united—a world void of "extreme prejudice." Only then will our eyes and hearts be truly opened to the call of our shepherd. We will never have the capacity to know all that is known by our creator, but with His strength and wisdom, we can find the capacity to treat others with courage and consideration while here on earth. Perhaps by leaning on his wisdom and love, we will better understand His purpose; perhaps we can understand why a loving god allows some to choose separation from Him and thus consign themselves, whom He still loves, to hell. Perhaps we can better understand how it is humankind's application of His gift of free will that allows so much evil to exist in this world.

Perhaps we can better understand the irony: we have learned that it is because He loves us so much that we may become the victim of evil or end up in hell. Out of love, God gifted to all of humankind free will and by doing so gave us the power to choose Him or not. Thus we are gifted a power that God himself does not have—just as an acid cannot exist within a base, evil cannot exist in God, and God cannot do that which is evil. By gifting free will to humans, He has afforded us the power to do evil, and in choosing so, we separate ourselves from Him. If we allow evil to grow in us like a cancer, it then becomes our hell; separating us from God. Thus, it is not a lack of or withholding of God's love that has made our world difficult; it is our application of free will that is responsible for opening the world to evil and heartache. Make no mistake: God wants us to choose Him and he is angered when we close our hearts and consign ourselves to hell; it is our choice. He knows it is the wrong choice and is angered when we stray. He taught that we each are to love Him with all our heart, soul and mind and that we are to love our neighbor as we love our self. This is true of non-Christians and Christians alike. We require God's grace, and we need to shine so others may find His grace through our lives. C. S. Lewis suggested we live a life that makes our beliefs and values attractive to others. I suggest that by treating others with dignity and respect in good times and bad, in joy, sorrow, or anger, by kindling our own spirit, we may ignite another!

What Is the Conclusion? Is Jesus a God or a Man?

Like Simon Greenleaf and Dr. Peter Stoner, upon reviewing the facts, Lee Strobel concluded that Jesus was, beyond a shadow of a doubt, who he claimed to be—not merely a good man but the Son of God who had conquered death to save all who accept him.

> The evidence accumulated over time until November 8, 1981, which is sort of when I reached a critical mass. I remember going alone in my room and I took a yellow legal pad and put a line down the middle and on one side I started to list all evidence I had encountered for Jesus Christ being the Son of God, and on the other side, all the negative evidence against that. And I wrote and I wrote page after page, and finally, I put my pen down, I said, "Wait a minute, in light of this avalanche of evidence pointing

toward the truth of Christianity, it would require more faith for me to maintain my atheism than to become a follower of Jesus Christ." And so that's the moment that I decided, consistent with the evidence, the most logical, the most rational step I could take was a step of faith in the same direction the evidence was pointing, and put my trust in Jesus.

For Lee, the data had illuminated a clear path forward and he closed his *Case for Christ* documentary by professing his conversion from avid atheist to passionate believer. He challenged his viewers to do four things:

1. Make it a priority to investigate the evidence.
2. Resolve to have an open mind.
3. Go where the evidence takes you.
4. Resolve to reach your own verdict in the case of Christ.

After accepting Jesus as his savior, Lee thought, "You know, maybe Leslie would like to hear about this." Leslie was ecstatic, thinking Lee's conversion too good to be true. Even their five-year-old daughter was amazed at the transformation that took place when her daddy accepted Jesus. Leslie explained, "When Lee became a Christian, his whole life started to change to the extent that our five-year-old daughter, who also saw those changes, went to her Sunday school teacher and told her that she wanted Jesus to do in her life what he had done in her daddy's life" (Strobel 2007).

Billy Moore's and Howard Storms's conversions to Christ were more experiential and faith felt than cerebral, but no more or less miracles. There was rejoicing in heaven.

Kindle your spirit; ignite another.

Answer Your Calling-Live Outside Your Comfort Zone

I didn't go to religion to make me happy. I always knew a bottle of Port would do that. If you want a religion to make you feel really comfortable, I certainly don't recommend Christianity.

C. S. Lewis

There is no greater calling than to serve your fellow men. There is no greater contribution than to help the weak. There is no greater satisfaction than to have done it well.

Walter Reuther

I have a calling in my soul, if you like, to try to make my life in some way worthwhile. What is the value of my existence?

Annie Lennox

To laugh often and much; To win the respect of intelligent people and the affection of children; To earn the appreciation of honest critics and endure the betrayal of false friends; To appreciate beauty, to find the best in others; To leave the world a bit better, whether by a healthy child, a garden patch, or a redeemed social condition; To know even one life has breathed easier because you have lived. This is to have succeeded.

Ralph Waldo Emerson

To Answer Correctly, First You Must Hear Correctly

At some point in our lives, we experience a yearning, a desire, for something we cannot quite comprehend. We feel perhaps a bit empty or restless. We become unsettled, not unlike Arthur Gordon. We question our contribution, our "jobs," and our relationships. Often we are left grasping at straws, unable to pinpoint the root cause of our angst. We have become ill in spirit—ill spirited. The hole in our spirit bleeds through, staining our relationships, causing pain for others as well as ourselves. We long to know our destined paths.

We all have strayed and faltered during our lives. As children, our parents were responsible for guiding us. But as we matured, we assumed the responsibility for our own paths. We have made decisions big and small, and where we stand today is a culmination of the outcomes of those decisions. Some enjoy a beacon or lighthouse forever shining in the distance, leading to their destination. Others float aimlessly, grasping at the latest fad, idol, or fancy, grappling to find a temporary port in the storm—perhaps even experimenting with each new drug to find temporary escape.

Regardless of our situation, at one time or another, we will face the feeling that we may be on the wrong path. Some may face this challenge repeatedly, as if trapped on a merry-go-round, while for others, it is a rare experience. It is during these times of uncertainty that we are most vulnerable. Will we choose the path of righteousness or fall prey to temptation? Recall the steps that evil will take to seize, hold, and lead us astray, and beware—evil assumes many unsuspecting forms (a new job, staying in an unsatisfying yet secure position, a new love that ultimately will destroy relationships, a new drug, etc.).

> **Step 1**: Evil identifies a desire from within our hearts.

> **Step 2**: Evil plants a seed of doubt; uncertainty grows.

> **Step 3**: Evil seeks to deceive using lies of commission, omission, or half truths. Evil tempts us.

Step 4: Evil leads us to disobedience. We give in to temptation.

Step 5: Evil abandons us to face the consequences of our actions, certain only to return and exploit yet another desire.

But we are not called to follow evil. We each are called to do good for others. We are called to serve. In order to follow your true calling, you must learn to hear and interpret what you are being called to do, you must learn to recognize temptations that lead down a wayward path; and must find extraordinary strength to resist. Finally, you must acknowledge that your strength alone may be insufficient to resist these repeated temptations. Recall the steps for rejecting invitations to do evil:

Step 1: Recognize the pattern of temptation. It starts with your inner desires or wanting.

Step 2: Examine the motives behind your desires; if they are wrong, nothing can be right. "Love the Lord your God with all your heart and with all your soul and with all your mind" and "love your neighbor as yourself."

Step 3: Do not be intimidated or feel weak just because you are tempted. We all are tempted. You are no different. Being tempted is not wrong, responding poorly is the problem.

Step 4: Be prepared to do good. "For we are God's handiwork, created in Christ Jesus to do good works, which God prepared in advance for us to do." (Eph. 2:10 [NIV]) Be strong for yourself and others. Identify, in advance of temptations, acts of service to which you will devote your time when temptations arise. Put your temptation behind you...do that which is good, right and just.

Step 5: Take time to ask God for help. Timothy (1 Timothy 5) explained that those in need and left all alone need to place their hope in God and continue, night and day, to pray and ask God for help. Be prepared to hear His answer;

it is His extraordinary strength that will free you from your bonds. His strength—not yours. If you feel uncomfortable seeking God alone, seek Him through a trusted friend whom you know has faith.

It can be difficult to parse the voice of good from all the worldly influences we face each day. At times during my life, I was quite confident that I heard His plans; at others, I was not so certain. For instance, at fourteen, I was preparing for my confirmation (confirmation is one of seven sacraments through which Catholics pass on their religious journey), and while I prayed about my life, I received a message that I would remain single until my late twenties, at which time I would marry and soon after have two children, a girl and then a boy. The message was clear and provided focus for me as a teenager and young adult. If pressured to become "more serious" than I thought was necessary for someone who would not marry for over a decade, I was open and honest about not committing myself to a long-term relationship. On the other hand, I have often struggled to understand God's desires for me concerning my career choices.

Through my experiences and struggles, I have found there are keys to help discover and hear the voice of good—the voice of God. Find a quiet place to be alone; stop, think, listen, and examine your motives. Write your thoughts in a journal. Refer to your journal often. Read and discuss the meanings contained in the Bible, not just in your time of need, but regularly, so that the concepts become part of your spirit and are in your mind when tempted. Seek the counsel of others—mentors, pastors, priests, and trusted friends. Recognize which messages are not the voice of good; evil seeks to deceive and misery loves company. Being able to clearly identify that which is not God is vital. In technical terms, one needs to develop a high signal-to-noise (good-to-evil) ratio by maximizing good (maximizing God), then identifying and eliminating the voice of evil as much as possible...minimizing stress. Finally, evaluate your circumstances, collect data, then document and evaluate your options. Pray. Once your analysis is complete, listen carefully to how you feel about your decision. Pray. Listen some more.

Stop, Think, and Listen

While alone in your "quiet place," evaluate your motivations. Evaluate the voices in your head. Do these voices support the easy way out? Are you coveting something that you do not need and should not have? If acted on, would your motivations violate fundamental principles of the golden rule or put the health, safety, and welfare of you and others at undue risk? Are you worried that if all your friends and family members learn of your decisions and contemplated actions they would by disappointed? If you listen and answer yes to any of these questions, then you are not hearing the voice of good.

If, on the other hand, these voices are telling you to consider and act on the needs of others; if the advised direction brings discomfort due to difficulty rather than lack of morality; and if it becomes clear that the value of your existence will be increased to others, and that if acted on, your actions are righteous and loving, then you are likely hearing the voice of good.

Read and Discuss the Bible

Do not offer any part of yourself to sin as an instrument of wickedness, but rather offer yourselves to God as those who have been brought from death to life; and offer every part of yourself to him as an instrument of righteousness.

Romans 6:13 (NIV)

If still confused, ask for God's help. He will illuminate a path forward, and the meaning of His words will (over time) become apparent. I have been reading the Bible off and on for many decades. I first started when my eighth-grade catechism teacher gifted me my first Bible (prior to that I used an abridged version for my Catechism classes). Admittedly, there was more that I did not understand than I understood at that time, but truths that the Lord revealed to me at His timing were what I needed when I needed them. Slowly, through years of reading the bible and attending teaching churches, my understanding has increased, but only with the help of others who have guided me. Further, in order to better understand His word, it was necessary that I learn more about the times during which the texts were written. A better understanding of history allows one to discern His meaning within the context of the times. We can collaborate with others to determine how His words translate in today's world. Through this understanding, we are better armed to face today's temptations. We are armed to follow a more righteous path, the path of sheep rather than goats.

I have struggled for a long time with Christians who state that the Bible is the word of God and then choose to take an "à la carte" view, choosing the verse to best support their case without considering the context in which the verse was written. The lessons of life have taught me that to better interpret the Bible (New and Old Testaments), it is important to extrapolate from the context of the times during which the texts were written to the context of our times today. By doing so, I believe you will find two types of inspired statements in the Bible.

Category one consists of inspired words based on unchanging principles set forth by God. These principles are timeless and unchanging. His Ten Commandments, the golden rule, the Great Commandment, and instructions to "perform according to your gifts" stand as examples of unchanging principles.

"Teacher, which is the greatest commandment in the Law?"

Jesus replied: "'Love the Lord your God with all your heart and with all your soul and with all your mind.' This is the first and greatest commandment. And the second is like it: 'Love your neighbor as yourself.' All

the Law and the Prophets hang on these two commandments."
Matt. 22:36–40 (NIV)

Category two consists of inspired words based on society's values during the times in which they were written. These are tricky and require thought before arriving at conclusions regarding God's intent. Jesus's instruction to pay back to Caesar what is owed (taxes); stoning as a penalty for blasphemy, murder, and other offenses; Paul's instruction to "let your women keep silent in the churches, for they are not permitted to speak"; and Moses's assertion that the world was created in seven days stand as examples of inspired words chosen to facilitate the understanding of those who lived during the authors' lifetime and in the same society.

It is difficult to argue the opposite of many of the Ten Commandments and create sound arguments that would be accepted by most moral, competent, and sane individuals. However, it is not difficult at all to suggest that we not pay taxes to Caesar and find unanimous agreement. Thus, we must conclude that we should not take the comment to pay tax to Caesar literally. Rather, we conclude that Jesus desires for us to live within the laws of our society as long as doing so does not violate one of his directly inspired words (those in category one).

In another similar example, Jesus loved and spoke directly to women, so it is difficult to conceive that we should not benefit in our churches from the wisdom and love of our fellow female Christians. However, if we examine the society at the time Paul sent his letter to the leaders in Corinth, nearly two thousand years ago, we find that in the Middle East and Greece (where Corinth was located) women were not prominent in society. Though women could testify, they could not sit on juries or be litigants. Women were represented in court by their fathers or husbands. They were not allowed to inherit property and in general were absent from central public life and from the core of political, judicial, economic, and cultural life—substantially different from our society in America but perhaps not so different from that in parts of modern day Middle East. So how should we interpret the instruction to "let your women keep silent in the churches" in today's world? My belief is that this instruction is intimately linked to the instruction to "be careful how you act among nonbelievers," and since by definition, Jesus's great commission is to "find lost sheep," our churches need to cater to nonbelievers and thus honor many of society's "values" as long as they do not violate God's unchanging principles (again from category one). Thus, I interpret that in America, Jesus would say it is perfectly fine to have women speak in our churches but that he would recommend women speaking at churches be avoided in cultures that would reject God's word if presented by a woman. By adhering to society's standards without violating principles, the probability of "finding lost sheep" is increased, and each lost sheep that is found brings opportunities to change those standards over time. Slowly and continuously, His principles take hold. (Recall a time in the United States when women did not possess the rights they enjoy today.)

Once while eating lunch in a conference room at work, I spoke with a Christian man who was adamant that if one considered Moses's interpretation of God's message in the book of Genesis regarding the creation of earth, it could be surmised that the earth and the universe were approximately six thousand years old. (Recall that the big bang theory suggests that the universe came suddenly into existence approximately fourteen billion years ago.) Moses wrote that in the beginning, the earth was without form, in a void of darkness, when God spoke into existence light to create night and day. Moses called this the first day of creation. Moses continued, documenting that on the second day, God created the firmament (a.k.a. heavens) in the "midst of the waters" and divided the waters above and below. On the third day, God spoke into existence lands and seas, and grasses, plants, herbs, and fruits. On the fourth, God added to the skies stars, the sun, and the moon to control the seasons as well as night and day. On the fifth day, God filled the seas and lands with living creatures. And finally, on the sixth day, He created humankind in His own image. On the seventh day, He rested.

My friend suggested that we take Moses's story literally, and that by taking into account Jesus's lineage, we could infer that four thousand years passed between creation and Jesus's birth, which was just over two thousand years ago. This man was an engineer. I asked him about the fossil record, carbon dating, and so forth. He disregarded the scientific data, stating that the processes were flawed. Another colleague overheard our discussion and pulled me aside later, noting that such dogmatic Christian doctrine, which seemed to suggest that to be a Christian is to close one's mind to scientific data, was the reason he could not accept Christianity. I suggested that not all Christians close their minds to science.

Rather than try to resolve the debate, I suggested that Moses's understanding of Earth's history and the intricate mysteries of the universe was extremely limited relative to our own, and that given his understanding, it is conceivable that he interpreted God's message to the best of his ability and faithfully recorded the history of creation in a manner that was understandable to his contemporaries. I ask now that you imagine that God requests that you (his newly appointed program manager) create a project plan that is divided into several major phases, some of which will occur in parallel, while others need happen in series. You convey to Moses that there were seven major phases for creation, and Moses interprets each phase as a day. Today we have more data and should interpret the phases differently, perhaps to span a period of approximately fourteen billion years (Figure 7).

ID	Task Name	Task Notes	Phase (day)							
			1	2	3	4	5	6	7	8
1	Big Bang: Create the universe (from 14B years ago).	Let there be light! End phase (day) 1								
2	Create the heavens (Solar system from 14B to 4.5B years ago)	Start with Big Bang. Complete in 9.5B years. End phase (day) 2								
3	Create dry land add first living cells on earth 10B years after big bang (from 4.5 to 4B years ago).	Start after phase (day) 2 is complete.								
4	Add complex cells, microscopic animals and plants to earth (from 4B to 500 million years ago).	Complete after ~13.5B years. End phase (day) 3.								
5	Fine tune day, night, and tides to establish the seasons (from 14B to 530 million years ago).	Start with Big Bang. Complete in 13.5B years. End phase (day) 4								
6	Add and remove living creatures: insects, reptiles, fish, and birds (from 530 M to 150M years ago).	Start the biological big bang and complete in 380M years (end day 5)								
7	Add and remove various creatures (from 150M to 250,000 years ago)	Final preparation of earth for man, nearly 150M years								
8	Create humans in my image (from 250,000 to 14,000 years ago).	13.8-14B years after Big Bang, 136k years. End phase (day) 6								
9	Celebrate with my son, Jesus, and rest (from 14,000 to 1 BC).	Start after task 8. Duration ~12,000 years. End phase (day) 7								
10	Send my son, Jesus, to save a fallen world. Rejoice each time a 'lamb' is saved.	Start after task 9. Prepare for rejection. (Begin the end of days)								

Figure 7: Potential correlation between modern-day and biblical understanding of creation

Read and discuss the Bible. Offer yourself, mind and spirit, to good. Avoid assuming absolute understanding of God's intentions and plans. Open your heart to the possibilities—let information illuminate your path. Reject the invitation to do evil. Feel the God-shaped hole in your heart being filled with His energy and warmth. This energy and warmth will overflow your being; in turn, you will begin to treat others with more respect and kindness. A healthier spirit will bring with it healthier relationships and help you to love others and love yourself.

Seek the Counsel of Others

Two are better than one, because they have a good return for their labor: If either of them falls down, one can help the other up. But pity anyone who falls and has no one to help them up. Also, if two lie down together, they will keep warm. But how can one keep warm alone? Though one may be overpowered, two

can defend themselves. A cord of three strands is not quickly broken.

Ecclesiastes 4:9–12 (NIV)

As iron sharpens iron, so a man sharpens the countenance of his friend.

Proverbs 27:17 (NKJV)

For where two or three are gathered together in My name, I am there in the midst of them.

Matthew 18:20 (NKJV)

Just as it is vital to seek the counsel of others to facilitate the acquisition of knowledge, the importance of collaboration in the application of knowledge is tenfold. Recall the definition of synergy—the whole is greater than the sum of the parts. We are social beings. We can learn from the mistakes of others, take strength in their encouragement, and receive guidance from their criticisms. A key to success is to seek the counsel of those known to speak truthfully even when it is difficult. It is too often easy, but not fruitful, to find someone who agrees with us rather than someone who challenges our paradigm. For example, if we are faced with divorce, we may be tempted to seek the advice of our still-bitter recently divorced friend, knowing he or she will support our decision rather than probe our motives. We may enjoy the validation and relish talking poorly of our spouse, but in doing so we do not improve our circumstances. Though it is tempting to seek this "bad mud" to bind us with others, it will be more fruitful to seek the counsel of those who will tell it like it is. Yes, we can read books, learn from others' advice and behavior, but when left unapplied, knowledge remains something only to fill the space between our ears. We need to act and often require others to keep us on task.

Seek the counsel of pastors, priests, trusted mentors, or friends who have a tendency to tell you what you need to hear, rather than what you want to hear. Then be willing to act. Seek a person of sound morals

162

and faith then follow the example they set. Professor Bradley Wright, a sociologist at the University of Connecticut, explains with data why it is important to team with others of faith and then to act accordingly. He analyzed divorce rates of Christians who attended church regularly versus those who rarely attended. His analysis showed that people who identified as Christians but rarely attended church suffered a 60 percent divorce rate, whereas those who attended church regularly suffered a still high (but lower) 38 percent divorce rate (Stanton 2011). Churchgoers who interact regularly are nearly 40 percent less likely to divorce than believers who are not held accountable by like-minded peers. Jesus will never abandon us, but solo faith is not nearly as fortified against evil as faith rooted in fellowship with others, for when we gather in Jesus's name, he is there with each of us to lend each his strength, compassion, and wisdom...a rope of three strands is not easily broken.

Recognize That Evil Seeks to Deceive

Recall that evil uses a pattern, consistent throughout the Bible and our lives, and has the potential to grow like a cancer from within, forever blocking us from our true calling. Once it has identified our inner desire and planted a seed of doubt, evil seeks to deceive using lies of commission, omission, or half-truths. The deceit identifies for us the "path of least resistance," which in reality leads only to a rough road of sorrow and self-destruction. Our true calling is for good; we were not created to do evil things. Yet we have been deceived and try to convince ourselves that a loving creator would not judge us but accept us as we are, despite all the wrong we do. True, He loves us unconditionally, but it is that love that kindles His anger when we are deceived and turn our backs to Him, just as most parents are angered when their children succumb to the peer pressure of their misguided friends. He does not turn His back on us; He cries in anguish when we turn from Him. He suffers much with this pain. He sent His only son to die for us; I admit I am too weak to send my son to die for others, but God is stronger. God's love for us is great, and so too His anger is great when we turn our backs, but His mercy and forgiveness are infinite when we return; he accepts us.

Evil leads us to disobedience as we proclaim, "If it feels right, do it!" What we should cry out is, "This feels right, but is it?" What are our inner motives? Are we helping or hurting others? Will our actions lead to results that improve the world for our loved ones, family, friends, church, and community or are they simply motivated by self-indulgence? Will God rejoice in heaven? Will our actions embarrass or enrage our loved ones? Tough words, difficult decisions—but the consequences of succumbing to evil in the near term will lead to our fall in the long run. Evil abandons us to face the consequences of our actions. God carries us when we falter.

Evaluate, Listen, and Feel

Evaluate your circumstances. How are you doing? How are your friends and family? Do they enjoy your company? Do they trust you? Do they trust that you are someone to whom they can bring both good and bad news without fearing your response? Do they believe you when you commit to do something for them? Are you always tired, fraught with stress and worry, or well rested, energized, and ready to attack each day? Be truthful. If you are following God's rather than your own plans, then nothing can stand in your way.

Joni Eareckson Tada is a quadriplegic who has prayed each day for God's strength, and despite being paralyzed as a teenager from the neck down, she has made amazing contributions as an artist, an author and as a mentor to others who are physically impaired (see "Anger Management Summary"). Joni could have easily succumbed to evil's nasty grip, but she called upon the strength of God and became a blessing to others. When you are tired, weary, and confused—pray. When you are motivated, energetic, and feel as though nothing can stop you—pray. Once the analysis of your circumstances is complete, listen carefully to how you feel about your decision. Pray. Listen more. God will touch your inner feelings. Listen. Initially you may not perceive a difference, but over time, you will recognize when you are aligned with or askew of God's plans.

Called from the Killing Fields of Sudan

Six-year-old Lopepe Lomong's eyes were closed as he prayed. The morning sun shone down on his face; he felt warm and secure at his modest outdoor church in the small South Sudanese village of Kimotong. He prayed peacefully together with his parents and his congregation. Without warning, rhyme, or reason, his peace and serenity were shattered.

> I heard them before I saw them. When I looked up, I saw soldiers pouring out of the back of the trucks. "Everybody down! Now!" they shouted as they ran into the middle of the congregation. I knew our country was at war. About once a month my mother and father grabbed me and my brothers and sister and ran for shelter as bombs fell in the distance from airplanes that flew far overhead. But I had never seen a soldier until this bright, summer Sunday, and I had never expected to see soldiers invade an outdoor church service. (Lomong 2012)

His mother wrapped Lopepe tightly in her arms, as if to hide and protect him as they dropped to the ground. The soldiers screamed that they had come to steal the children. Lopepe was frightened, yet thankful that his brothers and sister had planned to attend a different service on that day. Screams erupted from all around. Lopepe cried. His mother held him so tightly his ribs hurt. She tried to calm him, but she too was full of fear, and it showed.

> Suddenly I felt a hand on my back. I looked up and saw a giant man standing over me. When you are a little boy, every adult looks like a giant. His gun was slung behind his back. A chain of bullets hung across his chest. My mother pled with him, "No, no, no! Don't take my boy!" The soldier did not reply. With one hand he yanked my mother's arm off me while picking me up with the other. He

dragged me past the giant tree at the front of our church and toward the trucks. (Lomong 2012)

Lopepe's unarmed parents chased after the soldiers, as did most of the other parents. The children were being tossed into the back of the military transport when one of the soldiers swung back toward the crying parents, aimed his weapon, and threatened to open fire. Lopepe bounced off another boy and then slammed into the dirty, hot metal truck bed. When all the children were deposited, the tailgate slammed shut, and the green canopy closed tightly around the sides and back; no child could escape, and no daring parent could enter. The truck sped off. The summer sun beat down on the canopy. The hot, dusty air made it hard to breathe, and the hot metal bed hurt bare feet, arms, and legs.

Eventually the truck screeched to a stop. Lopepe did not know where he was, and though he did not know it at the time, his childhood had ended. The canopy flew open. Blindfolds were wrapped securely over the children's eyes, so tightly that Lopepe could feel his pulse beating in his temples. He was thrown from the truck and caught by another pair of hands before he hit the ground. His hand was placed on the shoulder of a child in front of him, and seconds later, he felt a hand on his back. They marched blindly for what seemed to be an unnervingly long time. They stopped. Suddenly the shoulder under his hand disappeared; Lopepe feared he would be beaten for breaking the chain. He was pushed from behind. The blindfold was suddenly ripped from his eyes. He braced himself to face the blinding sun, but instead, he opened his eyes to a dark, one-room thatched hut crammed with male children and teenagers.

Six-year-old Lopepe had never felt more alone. Perhaps if he had been older, he may have recognized some of his fellow villagers, but his life revolved around his family, and now they were gone. He thought of his mom and dad, his older brother, Abraham, and his younger siblings, John and Grace. He missed them already but was glad they had not been kidnapped. His survival instincts kicked in, and he studied his surroundings. There were soldiers at the door. Some seemed like giants, but many seemed to be mere teens. One of the older boys in the hut declared the soldiers were rebels. A small debate erupted. They pondered, if rebels were fighting to protect south Sudan, then why kidnap the children? Lopepe heard a voice explain that they were not kidnapped but rather recruited by force to become soldiers. Lopepe was confused: he was not big enough to carry a gun. What would they want with him? His thoughts were interrupted.

"You're Lopepe, aren't you? From Kimotong, right? When I saw them shove you through the door, I thought that was you," the young teenage boy said. "We're from Kimotong too. We know your family. You have an older brother named Abraham, right?"

"Yes."

"Is he here too?"

"No. He and my other brother and sister were coming to a later church service. I was the only one taken."

"Don't worry," said the boy as he introduced his two friends. "You stick close to us and you will be all right."

"Really? Why would you want to look out for me?"

"We're from the same village, which makes us family."

"Okay," I said. "Thank you." For the first time since my nightmare began, I felt like I was not alone. God had sent three angels to watch over me. Soon they would do much, much more. (Lomong 2012)

When night came, the boys remained packed in the hut, with barely room to lie down on the cold, hard ground. Lopepe blew on his hands to warm them as he shivered in the cold, dark African night; he could not get warm. He hugged the boy next to him for warmth, and the boy hugged him back. They were family. Boys cried throughout the night for their families, and gradually they began to quietly discuss why they had been taken. They needed to use the restroom and were famished;

they had not eaten breakfast before church. Yet they tried to sleep, too afraid to request food or restroom. Slept came begrudgingly. Lopepe awoke to what sounded to him like angry cows. Confused and disoriented, he opened his eyes. Then he remembered what had happened and realized he was far from his family and home.

The boys were fed from a community bucket that contained cooked sorghum (a type of grass that is raised for grain), water, and sand—barely edible. The astute boys ate slowly, separating the grain from the sand. The less fortunate paid the price. Finally, one boy requested to be allowed to use the restroom. The guard yanked him from the room, beat him for "attempting to escape," and led him at gunpoint to the woods, where he did his business and was then escorted back, beaten again, and thrown back in the hut. The boys decided it was better to relieve bowels and bladders in the crowded hut rather than bear the beatings.

Days passed, and the routine remained unchanged: they sat, too crowded, never allowed to leave, eating only sorghum from the bucket once daily. One bitter dawn, the routine changed: not all the boys awoke from their sleep.

By the third or fourth day I noticed something new: not everyone got up when it was time to eat our one meal. At first I thought these boys were sleeping in, which surprised me because it was so hard to sleep in these conditions. Looking closer I noticed these sleepy boys did not stir at all. They were dead. I'd never seen a dead boy before. I wanted to cry, but I did not dare. Instead I sat and stared at the dead boys, horrified; wondering if that would be me soon.

After a few days of boys dying, I heard shouting outside. The room became quiet..."Why are we keeping these boys if they're dying on us like this?" a man yelled.

"We thought we needed more time to break their wills before we start the training," someone replied.

"If you wait much longer, they'll all be dead. Get it started. Now!"

"But some of them are too small."

"How is that my problem?" the man shouted back. "Pull out the ones strong enough to hold a rifle and start training them."

"What about the rest?"

"What about them?" the man snapped back. "The way things are going in there, we won't have to worry about them much longer anyway." (Lomong 2012)

The older boys, including Lopepe's three angels, were being transformed into soldiers, but Lopepe was left in the "reject" pile, too small to be trained. He was ripped from his family and left without a purpose, without hope of ever seeing his home or family again. He would either grow big enough to be trained or fail to awaken one cold morning. Yet Lopepe refused to give in. With a strong spirit, he forced himself to have purpose. Each day when the older boys left to be trained, he cleaned his corner of the hut, sweeping the dirt floor and removing garbage and debris. Still with each passing day, the stench grew worse. Lopepe's group of boys dwindled as death became a prominent part of life in this prison camp. As his group became weaker, the older boys became stronger and more like soldiers. Lopepe feared what would happen when the transformation was complete. What would become of his angels? What would become of him?

"You're going to see your mom again."

"What?" I nearly shouted.

"Shh, not so loud," one of my three teenage friends said. "You can't tell anyone." He looked around the room. Most of the boys had settled down for the night, although one or two were up walking around. "This is our secret, okay, Lopepe?"

"I won't say a word." My friend gave me a look. "No, really. I know I talk a lot, but I won't say anything. I promise."

"Good. You won't have to keep the secret for long," he said with a grin. "Come here." He motioned for me to come between the three of them. "Sleep over here between us tonight."

"Okay," I said. Since we slept on the floor, one spot was about the same as any other. By now, I was used to sleeping on the cold floor. However, on this night, I was so excited I could hardly go to sleep. "I'm going to see my mom again!" (Lomong 2012)

That night, Lopepe followed his three teenage angels as they quietly slipped from the hut. They crept stealthily on their bellies across the camp, while soldiers huddled around fires, until they escaped through a small hole in the fence. Lopepe was barefoot and much smaller than the others, but with them he ran. They ran by night and the early morning light and slept by day, dreaming of home and always taking care to face the direction they must run once they awoke. Each time they crossed a dirt road, they brushed their footprints away. Each day, they miraculously stumbled upon fruit and water and avoided being caught. Lopepe later reflected that God was watching over them. Exhausted after a few nights of running, the fields of savannah grass gave way to open fields with no cover to be had. They could not turn back; they had no choice but to cross. Suddenly they came upon a tin-roofed building with a couple of trucks and a car parked nearby. They heard men's voices, but the voices were not speaking Buya, the native language of Kimotong. Where were they?

They dropped to the ground to avoid being seen, but it was too late. One of the soldiers had spotted them. They were caught. After three nights and days of running to freedom, they were caught. The soldiers questioned the boys, but without a common language, they could not communicate.

They had been arrested, but these soldiers were not threatening; they were not Sudanese rebels or army. In fact, they were Kenyan border guards. The guards gave them water and fed them corn—corn without sand. It wasn't home, but they were safe. The four were loaded into a truck and taken away—to where they did not know, but they felt safe. They arrived in the Kakuma United Nations refugee camp, poor and hungry. Lopepe wondered if this was the Kenyan school to which his father had dreamed of sending his kids. Though they did have classes and church, he soon became aware that a school, it was not.

> Kakuma was a tent city filled primarily with boys like me, boys from Sudan who'd been separated from their families by civil war. Some had been turned into soldiers. Others came here because their villages had been destroyed in the fighting. None of us belonged here. Yet here we were, far from home, in a country to which we did not belong. I am grateful that Kenya gave boys like me a place to escape war. The border guards who arrested me and my three angels could well have forced us to walk back to where we came from. Even worse, they could have handed us over to the rebels. Instead, they let us stay in their country. (Lomong 2012)

It took three weeks for Lopepe's feet to heal from his barefooted trek through the African wilderness, and once he was able to walk, he found his three angels had disappeared, never to be seen again.

> The three teenage boys who saved my life were never heard from again. I've tried to find them on the trips I have taken back to Sudan over the past few years. No one in my village or the surrounding area has any idea who they were. It is as if they simply appeared in the prison camp, took care of me, led me to freedom, and then disappeared, just like angels in the Bible. (Lomong 2012)

Without his three friends, Lopepe needed to find a new family, which he did rather easily. He lived in a tent of ten boys in Kakuma's section fifty-eight, the equatorial Sudanese section of the camp, where he and his roommates had first arrived. Lopepe had a roof over his head. He had chores. He had a home. He had a new family. He started school not long after his arrival, but it was not the school of which his father had dreamed. He wrote his letters and numbers in dirt with a stick and sang most of his lessons. Most days, they sang for two or more hours.

If Lopepe answered a question correctly, the teacher questioned the next boy. Incorrect answers earned a swat with a switch. When he was not singing, he played soccer or ran around the camp. The older boys had made a rule that before you could play, a lap must be run. It sounds easy, but the perimeter of the camp was eighteen miles long! He wanted to play every day, so every day, he ran.

Six days a week, they ate only one meal, but Tuesdays were different. Every Tuesday around noon, workers from the fenced UN compound pushed wheelbarrows through the camp to the dump. The first time Lopepe heard the squeak of the wheels, he did not know what was happening. He followed as his friends ran excitedly through the camp. Chaos ensued as the UN workers emptied the wheelbarrows into the dump.

> Boys went after the garbage like hungry hyenas fighting over a gazelle carcass. One of the boys from my tent popped up from the pit, handed me a half-eaten banana, and said, "Get it back to the tent and don't let anything happen to it." I did what I was told. That was part of life in my camp family. We all had chores to do, roles to play, and we all did them. I guarded that banana like it was the crown jewels of England. Yes, Tuesdays were the high point of our week; the one day we ate well—the day we ate garbage.

> Life may have been hard, but we were happy. Yes, boys died and food was difficult to come by, but at least no one was shooting at us. We only ate one meal a day, but for me, coming into the camp at the age of six, I accepted this as normal. I never thought that life was unfair because I had to eat garbage. Instead, I looked at the scraps of food from the dump as a blessing. Not all the boys in the camp could do this. I knew some who chose to feel sorry for themselves, who complained constantly about their lot in life. What is the point of such complaining? After all the whining and complaining is over, you still live in a refugee camp. All the complaining in the world will not make your life any better. Instead, you must choose to make the best of whatever the

situation in which you find yourself, even in a place like Kakuma. (Lomong 2012)

Lopepe lived in dire conditions but remained pragmatically optimistic. He had a strong spirit and continued to attend church, where he sang praises to God. Lopepe found strength in his faith and never doubted for a moment that God was there with him. Lopepe's new family dubbed him Lopez, and the Catholic priests of Kakuma named him Joseph when he completed his confirmation. By this time, he had assumed additional responsibilities in the camp, and he was ready for a deeper relationship with God.

> Over the three or four weeks leading up to Christmas, the priest taught us many Bible stories. More than that, He taught us how to be close to God. That's what I wanted. I did not have an earthly mother or father any longer. I wanted to have that Father relationship with God. (Lomong 2012)

Unbeknown to Lopez, two major events were about to occur in his life. The first was on his daily eighteen-mile trek around Kakuma, when he proposed that he work for a farmer who lived just outside the camp. The farmer was rich by Kakuma standards and agreed to pay only if the job was performed to his satisfaction, which it was. So Lopez started to earn some money. This same farmer had a small television powered by a car battery, and it was on that television that Lopez watched Michael Johnson win the gold metal running for the United States in the Olympics. Lopez had a new dream—to run in the Olympics with the letters *USA* across his chest. This dream was less than two months old when the second event occurred: the priest announced one Sunday in October that the United States had decided to allow a limited number of the Kakuma lost boys to come to America.

> The priest might as well have said Jesus had thrown open the doors of heaven to us. From where I lived, the only difference between America and heaven was that I had to die to go to heaven. I knew all about America—at least I thought I did. The boys in the camp

talked about America..."Everyone eats as much food as they want," boys said. "Anyone in America can get any job they want," I heard. "That's the place where all your dreams come true." (Lomong 2012)

There was a catch. Up to thirty-five hundred boys would be allowed to move permanently to the United States, a visiting American announced in English, pausing for the Swahili translation, and anyone could apply by submitting an essay over the next three weeks—but the essay needed to be written in English. The essays were to be dropped off at church and then delivered by the priests to the US embassy. Lopez was in. He could neither speak nor read English, but that would not stop him. He wrote the story of his abduction, escape, and life in Kakuma. He wrote his essay in Swahili as a prayer to God, confident that God would deliver him to the United States. His family of friends assisted as best they could in the translation.

For ten years, Lopez had lived in Kakuma, eating one meal a day except for on garbage Tuesdays, running his eighteen miles a day so that he could play soccer, and completing his lessons in the dirt with a stick. He submitted his story (prayer), and it was accepted. After waiting for what seemed an eternity, Lopez boarded a plane bound for Nairobi for interviews, tests, and a crash course on life in America. Again, it seemed like an eternity before his American parents (Rob and Barbara Rogers) were identified and approved; he was the last of his Kakuma family to leave Nairobi.

A worker called me in for my fourth and final interview. This time, the interviewer was not only an American, but an American who had just flown in from the United States itself. He worked for Immigration and Naturalization Services (INS). I knew this interview was very important. "Are you still in touch with your family back in Sudan?" he asked. "No. I have not seen or heard from them since I was kidnapped when I was six."

174

"Okay, then. Uh…Why aren't Juja and Kakuma places you can call home?"

"As a Sudanese, I cannot call them home. The rules prevent me from being anything besides a refugee there."

"Why is that not enough for you?"

"I want to do more with my life than survive in a camp." I looked him in the eye. "That is not the kind of life anyone wants."

"What do you want to do in America?"

I broke out in a huge grin. "I want to work hard! I love to work." The American did not smile back. He looked down at his piece of paper.

"Okay. I think that's all I need." (Lomong 2012)

Sixteen-year-old Lopepe Lopez Joseph Lomong arrived in New Jersey, jet-lagged and without any worldly belongings but strong in faith and ready for adventure. Despite ten years of schooling in Kakuma, he read, wrote, and performed math at a second-grade level. His American mom was determined to help him graduate high school by his eighteenth year and Lopez still harbored his dream of running in the Olympics. The odds were stacked against him, but he had faith that God was on his side.

Lopez Lomong achieved those goals and more. He graduated from high school, ran track in college, and met President George Bush as US flag bearer in the 2008 Olympics. He won his first national title in 2009, when he finished first in the US Outdoor Championships, and repeated the feat in June of 2010. Lopez graduated from college on December 16, 2011, and represented the United States again in the 2012 Olympics. He has been a powerful voice for the lost boys of Sudan. As a member of Team Darfur, an international association of athletes devoted to raising awareness of the travesties related to the war in Darfur, he has used his international status as a platform to inform the public, while taking care not to politicize the Olympics. He has since established the Lopez Lomong Foundation and 4 South Sudan project, through which he works to change lives and bring healing to the African nation.

If you truly desire to understand what it means to hear and answer your calling, I encourage you to read *Running for My Life: One Lost Boy's Journey from the Killing Fields of Sudan to the Olympic Games*, by Lopez Lomong with Mark Tabb. Lopez's story is inspiring. He has a good spirit and a strong sense of family, having contributed greatly to the world around him. When faced with hardships most can only imagine (or read about), he has never left God, and God never left him.

> Jeremiah 29:11 says, "For I know the plans I have for you," says the LORD. "They are plans for good and not for disaster, to give you a future and a hope." These words sound like God wrote them specifically for me. I lived through disaster. I lived through hardship and death. Yet God never left me. He changed me from Lopez the lost boy to Joseph. And just like Joseph in the Bible, He took what was once intended for evil and transformed it into good. (Lomong 2012)

You Hear Your Calling—Now What?

So you see, faith by itself isn't enough. Unless it produces good deeds, it is dead and useless.
James 2:17 (NLT)

Being of good spirit is not enough. Having great relationships is not enough. Simply hearing your calling is not enough. We are called to act. Our faith, our love, and our compassion must be balanced with action. Pastor Rick Warren began his book *The Purpose Driven Life* with the decidedly simple statement, "It's not about you" (Warren 2002). He continues to explain that we are each put here on earth to achieve a higher purpose than our own self-centered satisfaction. He proposes five higher purposes. We are all (1) planned for God's pleasure, (2) formed to be part of God's family, (3) created to become like Christ, (4) shaped for serving God, and (5) made for a mission.

These five purposes align with the three dimensions of our lives we seek to balance (Figure 8).

Relationships	Formed for God's family
Contribution	Shaped for serving God
	Made for a mission
Spirit	Planned for God's pleasure
	Created to become like Christ

Figure 8: A purpose-driven, balanced life

Consider young Lopepe. Though ripped away from his parents and stolen from church, never once did he leave God's family for which he was formed. Never once did he feel forsaken. He formed relationships with others; like-minded, good people became his friends. He helped his friends and his friends helped him. At some point during his first weeks at Kakuma, Lopepe began to fear the worst; he felt the only thing that could have kept his parents from finding him was death. But as James Stockdale did for many in the Vietnamese concentration camp, Lopepe's new friends did for him: they stopped him from dying of a broken heart by helping him to abandon false hopes and face his brutal reality.

"Why don't they come?" I asked over and over to anyone who would listen during my first weeks in the camp. Tears flowed. "If they are looking for me, why can't they find me?"

"You can't think like that, Lopepe," a friend finally answered. I tried to look away and ignore him, but he got right in my face. "Stop it, Lopepe. Stop! You see that boy over there?" He pointed to a boy we all knew about. Like me, he was one of the younger ones. Unlike me, he was not going to survive much longer. He rarely left his tent. All day every day he sat in his tent rocking, rocking, rocking, his mind slowly slipping away. "You cannot sit and wish for something that is never going to happen, or you will lose your mind. No, you must focus on here and now. Do your chores. Go to school. Keep

177

your mind busy. The past is gone. It will not come back. You must live in this day."

"But..." I said, tears welling up in my eyes.

"No buts," he said. "This is the life you now have. You must accept it and go forward or you will end up like that other boy." He then smiled at me, which seemed oddly out of place. "You can do this, my friend. I know you can. You are strong."

My friend patted me on the back and left to go play soccer. I sat and stared at the rocking boy...What will it be, Lopepe? I asked myself. The answer was easy. I jumped up, ran out of the tent, and chased after my friend to the soccer field. My homesickness did not immediately stop, but it changed. The moment I ran over to the soccer field, I knew my parents were never going to come and rescue me. (Lomong 2012)

Lopepe was shaped to serve. He continued to attend church and learn scripture. He learned about Jesus, and with Jesus in his heart, everything Lopepe did, he did to serve God; he served God by serving others. As Lopepe grew older, he continued developing as a Christian and a "man," becoming Lopez and eventually Joseph. Lopez was driven to work and driven to serve. Even when he wrote his essay to gain entry to the United States, he considered his essay a prayer to God. He prayed and desired to follow the path God laid before him, and his path was to thrive and to serve.

By my fifth or sixth year in the camp...I was in charge of the ration cards for all the boys in our tent. To make sure no one lost his card, I kept them all together in a safe place. I also calculated our daily rations...If I miscalculated, we would go hungry. I made sure I never miscalculated. Every Christmas and Easter the UN also gave us a chicken, one for each tent. One chicken is not very much meat for ten hungry boys. Therefore, to make it stretch, we cooked it in a soup. Not everyone actually got a piece of meat. But by making it into a soup, we all got a taste of chicken...The more responsibilities

I took on, the more I wanted. I loved to work. I enjoyed taking care of the younger boys. We had to look out for one another to survive, and survival was the name of the game in the camp. But I wanted to thrive, not just survive. I looked for ways to do more for my family of boys…I helped plant a garden next to our house, and I carried the water to each little plant to keep it from dying in the desert sun. Slowly but surely, I was becoming a different boy. The way I saw life in the camp evolved, as did the way I viewed church and my relationship with God. (Lomong 2012)

Lopez was created to become like Christ, and he was made for a mission. He prayed often. He learned scriptures. He heard his calling and he acted. He sang and worshiped God with all of his heart. He played soccer. He ran; he was born to run. In his native tongue, the name Lopepe means "fast." When he arrived in the United States, he used his God-given speed to win races through which he gained public recognition. His calling, though, was deeper than just running. He knew he had to give back, so he used his fame to raise awareness of the travesties committed in Sudan, and he created the Lopez Lomong Foundation to take God's healing to the children of Sudan.

> **The master was full of praise. "Well done, my good and faithful servant. You have been faithful in handling this small amount, so now I will give you many more responsibilities. Let's celebrate together!"**
> Matthew 25:21 (NLT)

The spirit with which Lopez approaches life is amazing! He garnered God's strength and not only endured severe hardships, but thrived and became an Olympic athlete. I cannot presume to speak for God, but the Bible does. The Bible tells stories of men like Noah, Moses, Abraham, and King David, all of whom pleased God. These men prayed often. They prayed to hear God's plan, and they obeyed. Though they were not perfect, they strove to follow God's laws. Overall, the actions they took brought God pleasure; He called them men of His heart. In reading Lopez Lomong's story, I am left with the strong impression that he too is a man of God's heart and has brought pleasure to God.

So when questioning whether or not you are adhering to God's plan, consider your answers to the following questions:

1. Are your closest friends among Christ's sheep?

2. Better yet, do they know Christ as Christ knows them?

3. Do your friends hold you accountable rather than simply placate your wayward desires?

4. Do you believe there is a bigger purpose to be served than simply finding material pleasure during your life on this earth?

5. Do you approach life with the desire to serve others rather than be served?

6. When you "go to work," do you feel in your heart that God gains pleasure through your actions?

7. It is easy to be loving and respectful when others are loving and respectful, but when you respond in trying situations, do you believe you respond as Jesus would?

8. Do you live by the golden rule?

If your faithful answer to each of these questions is yes, there is a good chance you are walking with God. If any answer is no or "I don't know," then in the words of the great Star Wars Jedi and philosopher Obi-Wan Kenobi, "You want to go home and rethink your life." It is time or past time to evaluate your environment. Paul included a call to action to church members in Philipia:

> Therefore if you have any encouragement from being united with Christ, if any comfort from His love, if any common sharing in the Spirit, if any tenderness and compassion, then make my joy complete by being like-minded, having the same love, being one in spirit and of one mind. Do nothing out of selfish ambition or vain conceit. Rather, in humility value others above yourselves, not

looking to your own interests but each of you to the interests of the others.

In your relationships with one another, have the same mind-set as Christ Jesus:

> Who, being in very nature God, did not consider equality with God something to be used to his own advantage; rather, he made himself nothing by taking the very nature of a servant, being made in human likeness. And being found in appearance as a man, he humbled himself by becoming obedient to death—even death on a cross!

> Therefore God exalted him to the highest place and gave him the name that is above every name, that at the name of Jesus every knee should bow, in heaven and on earth and under the earth, and every tongue acknowledge that Jesus Christ is Lord, to the glory of God the Father.

Therefore, my dear friends, as you have always obeyed—not only in my presence, but now much more in my absence—continue to work out your salvation with fear and trembling, for it is God who works in you to will and to act in order to fulfill his good purpose. (Phil. 2:1–13 [NIV])

Hear your calling. Align yourself with His plan. The world is His and will be yours. Forge strong, lasting relationships. With His power you will rejoice, overcome obstacles, and be quick to listen and slow to anger. Out of His love, your healthy spirit and good deeds will flow.

Half the lies they tell about me aren't true.

Yogi Berra

Anger is an acid that can do more harm to the vessel in which it is stored than to anything on which it is poured.

Mark Twain

Anybody can become angry—that is easy, but to be angry with the right person and to the right degree and at the right time and for the right purpose, and in the right way—is not easy.

Aristotle

Usually when people are sad, they don't do anything. They just cry over their condition. But when they get angry, they bring about a change.

James Russell Lowell

I was just finishing a meeting at work and getting ready for lunch. My cell phone rang. It was my wife, Sheri. "Jim, I need your help," she started in an exasperated voice. "Jimmy's anger has been getting worse, and I don't know how to deal with him when he is like this." Jimmy was fully entrenched in his "terrible twos." His older sister, Teagan, was in kindergarten and at a notably different maturity level, but even when in her twos, she had handled her anger quite differently. Jimmy often lashed out, and he needed to learn quickly how to deal with his strong emotions. Sheri filled me in on the details of Jimmy's offenses—not too unlike many two-year-olds but new to us! I agreed to get home early to give her a break, and then to work with him so that he could better express his anger. Knowing that I had the same innate issues that were plaguing Jimmy, I immediately sought help. I found several books to review and purchased a couple of books that were simple, targeted children, and were quite helpful for Jimmy, Teagan, and me. (You are never too old to learn!) From the several books I read, while sharing stories and learnings with both children, we agreed on the following set of anger guidelines—helpful rules to help us benefit from and manager our anger:

1. It is *okay* to be angry.

2. It is *okay* to talk about what makes you angry and how you feel when you are angry. Recall from VerAegis—Relationships calling upon the FBI (feelings, behavior, impact).

3. It is *not okay* to hurt people physically or with your words when you are angry.

4. It is *not okay* to damage property (yours or others') when you are angry.

After a surprisingly short time, Jimmy did get a better handle on his anger; he at least got his biting and hitting under control. I like to think that both kids were able to internalize these rules and use them routinely. More pragmatically, I think they did anything to avoid the conversations (a.k.a. lectures) that followed inappropriate displays of anger: "We understand you are angry. What are the rules of anger? What is okay? What is not okay? Let's talk about this. Did you express your anger in manner that was okay? Did you hurt somebody with your words? Did you hurt anybody's body or property? Did you say anything mean? What happened to trigger your anger? Did you feel hurt? Did you expect one thing and get another? What will you do differently next time?"

It is clear to me that both Jimmy and Teagan have continued to mature and now handle their anger exceedingly well. Teagan is more apt to either quietly deal with her anger or perhaps openly discuss her feelings. Jimmy, on the other hand, needs time to ponder the situation, and only after considerable thought does he share concisely both his feelings and expectations. For many people (myself included), anger management presents itself as a lifelong and ripe opportunity for self-improvement. Whether we have an abundance of courage but at times lack the appropriate discipline to act considerately, or if we at times lack the courage to openly and honestly stand up for our feelings and convictions, there is room for improvement. I often wonder, however, if it is indeed readily apparent that anger is a good opportunity for self-improvement, why, then, is it so difficult for many of us to learn from our "angry" mistakes?

Recall that certain situations require different methods of thought (refer to "Manage Thought" in *VerAegis—Relationships* and "Making Good Decisions Is Key to Being Effective" in *VerAegis—Contribution*). Emotions or feelings should be applied during time-sensitive situations with somewhat predictable patterns—though at times, emotions can deceive us due to our loss aversion or the allure of an improbable win. Reason is best applied in new situations where creative solutions are required, but even the most mundane decisions can be paralyzing if we lose connection with our inner feelings and preferences. We all have emotional triggers that kindle our anger. Often the randomness of events that trigger our anger makes it difficult for our subconscious minds to decipher a pattern. Yet when we step back and review, we may find common themes. We don't have a reliable "game film" to review, so retrospective analysis depends entirely on memory (which while angry and mono-focused may be impaired) and on the discipline required to contemplate our anger.

As a consequence, our mistakes, which are often obvious to others, are not readily apparent to ourselves. Often we "cover up" our actions or inactions, justifying them as appropriate, because we either have not learned healthy methods for dealing with anger and so cannot distinguish between appropriate or inappropriate responses, or we have been taught that anger is wrong and so justify our responses as not being rooted in anger. In the face of this emotional complexity, one fact is abundantly clear: anger is natural, and it is important to acknowledge that anger is an emotion we all experience. Anger is a God-given gift with purpose—self-preservation and the preservation of those we love and preservation of our convictions. Anger is an important and precious gift...don't lose it!

So God created mankind in his own image, in the image of God he created them; male and female he created them.

(Gen. 1:27 [NIV])

If we were indeed created in God's image, it is helpful to compose a picture God's image. There are many clues throughout the Bible. A few are included here.

And he passed in front of Moses, proclaiming, "The LORD, the LORD, the compassionate and gracious God, slow to anger, abounding in love and faithfulness." (Exod. 34:6 [NIV])

The LORD is slow to anger, abounding in love and forgiving sin and rebellion. (Num. 14:18 [NIV])

But you are a forgiving God, gracious and compassionate; slow to anger and abounding in love. Therefore you did not desert them. (Neh. 9:17 [NIV])

But you, O Lord, are a compassionate and gracious God, slow to anger, abounding in love and faithfulness. (Ps. 86:15 [NIV])

When Jesus saw what was happening, he was angry with his disciples. He said to them, "Let the children come to me. Don't stop them! For the Kingdom of God belongs to those who are like these children. (Mark 10:14 [NLT])

The LORD is gracious and compassionate; slow to anger and rich in love. (Ps. 145:8 [NIV])

"So he [Jesus] made a whip out of cords, and drove all from the temple courts, both sheep and cattle; he scattered the coins of the money changers and overturned their tables." (John 2:15 [NIV])

Whether one embraces or refutes the existence of God, we can learn from these biblical teachings that have withstood the test of over four thousand years. We can paint a picture of how we should respond to our anger: be slow to anger, compassionate, gracious, loving, faithful, and forgiving. God is not represented as being devoid of anger; we should not expect that we should not feel anger. Anger is not wrong. We are designed to feel anger, and sometimes it is deeply appropriate—decidedly human—to feel it. But we are to balance our anger with compassion, love, and grace. Our anger is designed to help us protect convictions that are based on principles just as Jesus did when he protected children and drove sinners from his Father's house!

Many struggle with the idea of an angry god, mistakenly thinking that an angry god is not a loving god, but notice that in all the passages above, He is described as being slow to anger and abounding in love. Anger is not the opposite of love; hate is the opposite of love. Think about those whom you love most deeply: are they not precisely the same people who can drive you to anger more often and easily than any others?

When you are emotionally vested and believe someone you love is doing wrong (not fulfilling your expectations), you become angry—sometimes very angry. We are not so different from God in this regard;

it is because He loves us that He becomes angry when we do wrong, and He takes pleasure in us when we do well. His anger is displeasure. Our anger too is most often displeasure—not dislike. The key to being effective is responding to our anger in the right way.

> **Be angry, and do not sin. Meditate within your heart on your bed, and be still.**
> Psalm 4:4 (NKJV)

Love and anger are linked as the most powerful of human emotions. Love is more highly regarded than anger, but anger, when used effectively, can positively alter the course of the world. Because of anger:

- The United States and its allies stopped Hitler and his allies.

- Gandhi and his followers pioneered the use of nonviolent civil disobedience to fight for civil rights and freedom.

- Martin Luther King and his followers were able to advance the rights of African Americans employing peaceful measures, engaging in nonviolent civil disobedience.

- Suffragettes successfully lobbied to increase women's rights in Britain and the United States.

However, when channeled incorrectly, anger can threaten the fabric of society. Anger played a powerful role in Hitler's, Stalin's, and Mao's ability to drive millions of people to embrace atrocious behaviors that defy the most basic of human logic. Likewise, the strength of marriage, the health of families, and the futures of our children are threatened by an inability to correctly channel anger.

> **Darkness cannot drive out darkness; only light can do that. Hate cannot drive our hate; only love can do that.**
> Martin Luther King Jr

Anger is a positively natural and necessary emotion. As Dr. Les Carter puts it, "Anger can be defined as 'the emotion of self-preservation.' Angry people wish to preserve personal worth, perceived needs and heartfelt convictions." Like countries at war, angry people try to protect their borders (personal boundaries).

All people feel they have significance, and they often become frustrated in situations where they pessimistically assume others will not or cannot treat them in a manner they feel is consistent with their significance. However, when angered, many people respond so distastefully that the receiver of that anger cannot possibly appreciate either their message or their worth! In other words, it is not anger itself but our response to anger that is often inappropriate. We are not defined by our mistakes, but by how we respond to them; likewise, we need not be defined by anger but by how we respond to it.

> **The ultimate measure of a man is not where he stands in moment of comfort and convenience, but where he stands at times of challenge and controversy.**
> Marin Luther King Jr.

Do you know where you stand in times of challenge and controversy? Do others know? Are you satisfied with your anger management, or do you have the room and desire to improve? Pursuing opportunities for self-improvement through anger management is not fundamentally different from striving to improve other areas of our lives. We need to do the following:

- Admit we can and need to improve.
- Learn to identify behavioral mistakes made while angry, and acknowledge inappropriate responses to anger as opportunities to improve.
- Learn that we are capable to control ourselves, and influence others. Understand the difference.
- Learn to avoid repeating mistakes by creating game plans.
- Work with and learn from others.

- Pray.

Plans and change processes are necessary to help us learn from our mistakes. Recall the see-plan-do-get process from "Embrace Change" in *VerAegis—Relationships*. See Figure 9 for an example of the change cycle applied to anger response.

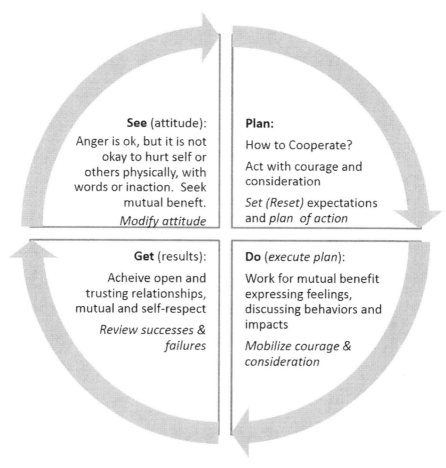

See (attitude):
Anger is ok, but it is not okay to hurt self or others physically, with words or inaction. Seek mutual beneft.
Modify attitude

Plan:
How to Cooperate?
Act with courage and consideration
Set (Reset) expectations and *plan of action*

Get (results):
Acheive open and trusting relationships, mutual and self-respect
Review successes & failures

Do (*execute plan*):
Work for mutual benefit expressing feelings, discussing behaviors and impacts
Mobilize courage & consideration

Figure 9: Anger-management change cycle

We need to see the results of our actions and change our attitude accordingly. Our attitude should be one of mutual benefit where we acknowledge that anger is natural and acceptable but that it is not okay to hurt ourselves or others physically or mentally, nor to damage property, whether ours or others'. We also need to determine in advance how we will cooperate in times of challenge and controversy. When your spouse treats you like a child, what will you do? Will you have an established plan so that you can diffuse rather than escalate? When your child or employee rebels, what will you do? How will you invoke the courage to stand for convictions with consideration and respect for others involved? In the continuous cycle, you must review and modify your plan based on successes and failures. Most importantly, you must recognize the need to put forth the effort to improve. Any plan without execution is doomed to fail. Inappropriate responses to anger manifest through both action and inaction. Failure to respond is as inappropriate as acting impulsively; without resolution, problems lie dormant like ticking time bombs waiting to destroy relationships.

Resolving controversy always involves more than one party, and all must work for mutual benefit, focusing on feelings and behaviors, discussing and understanding their impact, and seeking reconciliation. There will be times when others refuse to pull their weight, but the execution of your corrective action plan requires your mobilized courage and kindness. The fruit of your plan will be open and trusting relationships (but not over night) and increased mutual and self-respect. When the trend in your relationships is positive, your plan is working; when nerves are frayed and relationships strained, your attitude, plan, and execution require refinement. Always seek help and guidance from others whom you trust to be honest and open. Churches are great resources where one can find both men's and women's anger management groups.

It sounds easy. But we often find ourselves at a disadvantage when it comes to times of challenge and controversy. Think back. Contemplate. From whom did you learn to respond to anger, listen with the intent to understand, and appropriately express your emotions? The typical education in the United States does not consist of these fundamental skills, so we must learn from our parents, siblings, extended family, and friends. When I was young, my dad taught me to count to ten before responding when I was angry (to be slow to respond to anger), but I did not learn what to do while I counted to ten. Was I supposed to count to ten and then blow up, or was I to suppress my anger without resolution? Recall Hrand Saxenian's criterion for emotional maturity: "The current level of a person's emotional maturity is indicated by the extent to which one expresses one's own feelings and convictions, balanced with consideration for the thoughts and feelings of others, without being threatened by the expression of feelings, either one's own or others'."

An appropriate response to anger requires emotional maturity: the ability to express one's own feelings and convictions with regard for the feelings and convictions of others. It requires us to be secure in the expression of our feelings without threatening others so that they too are secure in expressing themselves. Thus, the answer becomes apparent: while counting to ten, we need to determine how to be true to our convictions while remaining controlled and considerate.

Perhaps a count to ten will suffice for those who have mastered their techniques, but many of us need more time. Often it is best to remove ourselves from the immediate situation in order to develop an effective response or recall a predetermined plan. It is often helpful to engage the help of family and friends, letting them know that when conflict arises you may signal for a timeout, request all parties go to neutral corners, and agree upon a time that you will get back together to reconcile. Indeed, we need to be slow to respond to our anger and we need others to support this need. Once alone with our thoughts, we need to apply reason to conquer our emotions as we determine a healthy response. To be most effective, we need an anger-response plan. I've used tips from the Mayo Clinic and my experiences to draft an example plan:

1. **Take a time-out, practice relaxation skills, and think before you speak.**

   When your temper flares, counting to ten isn't just for kids; it can help diffuse your emotions. In the heat of the moment, it's easy to say something you'll later regret. Before reacting in a tense situation, take a few moments to breathe deeply, imagine a relaxing scene, or repeat a calming word or phrase, such as, "Be calm, collected, and considerate." Collect your thoughts before speaking and allow others to do the same. If necessary, signal for a time out and take a longer break away from the person or situation, allowing your frustration to subside. Listen to music, write in a journal, or exercise. Do whatever it takes to encourage relaxation. If someone suggests a break is needed, honor that request; it may be more about his or her state of mind than yours. Agree on a time to reconvene.

2. **Once you are calm, seek to reconcile first, and then identify possible solutions.**

As soon as you're thinking clearly, express your frustration in an assertive but nonconfrontational way (with courage). State your concerns and needs clearly and directly, without hurting or attempting to control or manipulate others (displaying consideration). Discuss feelings, behaviors, and their impact without placing blame. Instead of focusing on what triggered your anger, work on reconciliation. Focus first on the relationship. Seek to understand the feelings and emotions of all involved. Restate in your own words each position to the satisfaction of the person you are trying to understand. (Remember that understanding does not mean agreement— only that you grasp the other's meaning and emotion.) Once you and the other party or parties feel understood, two things usually happen: First, emotions are calmed, lowering barriers and creating a safe environment in which to explore potential solutions. Second, with a better understanding of all positions, all are better able to assess the situation and determine if it requires resolution, and thus are better positioned to create a plan of action. In other words, stable emotions are a foundation on which to build trust so that if necessary, you can all work together to resolve the issue.

Remind yourself that inappropriate responses (whether action or inaction) to anger won't fix anything and in fact might only serve to provoke. Stick with "I" statements; avoid "you are" statements. In other words, avoid criticizing or placing blame. Employing "when you" to describe unhealthy behaviors is ok, but should be used sparingly and in conjunction with statements of your feelings. Remember from *VerAegis—Relationships* that it is appropriate, at times, to call upon the FBI (feelings, behaviors and impact). Use "I" statements to describe the problem in terms of your own feelings and the impact of certain behaviors on those feelings. Be respectful and specific. For example, say, "It upsets me [feelings] when you leave the table without helping to clean the dishes [behavior], because I feel unappreciated—taken for granted, and that is not what I expect in our relationship [impact]," instead of "You never help around the house. You are lazy and unappreciative and you always leave messes for me and others to clean. I am not your mother!" By discussing expectations in your relationship, you open the door for your partner to restate your position. He or she may respond, "When I don't help with the chores you expect from me, you feel taken for granted and hurt because that is not what you expected in our relationship. Is there more?" This does not mean the other person agrees, but he or she is seeking to understand. If you do not have more to add, at least you feel understood, and you may respond, "No. I am really just frustrated about having to do the dishes alone every evening. I'm open to discussing barriers and potential solutions."

At this point, your partner may present barriers: perhaps you were unaware that he or she tends to other chores each evening while you are doing dishes, and you decide together that sharing all the chores may make them more enjoyable or that it does make sense to attack them separately but come together for a walk or game afterward. The catch is to create an open atmosphere so that problems can be aired and solutions found.

3. **Use humor to release tension.**

Lightening up can help diffuse tension. When you create scripts with your family and friends, try to agree on "code words" that will lighten the situation. If you tend to use too many words, perhaps those around you can say "pep talk," "time sink," or "air hose" to alert you to the fact that their eyes are rolling back in their heads, and you've lost them. If you feel scolded by a spouse, rather than fighting back, perhaps you can say "Mayday," "wormhole," or "rosebud." The point is to have a plan and to try to keep it light—it is difficult to remain angry while smiling! Don't use sarcasm, as it can be hurtful and make matters worse. Request that your significant other provide you with humorous words that you can use when conflicts arise; when he or she hears those words used with consideration, it will be more difficult to remain angry.

4. **Exercise.**

Physical activity can provide an outlet for emotions, especially if you're about to erupt. If you feel your anger escalating, go for a brisk walk, run, jump rope, lift weights, or work in the garden. Physical activity stimulates various brain chemicals that can leave you feeling happier and more relaxed than you were before you worked out.

5. **Don't hold a grudge.**

Forgiveness is a powerful tool for the forgiver. Storing anger and other negative feelings is like storing toxic waste; it threatens to displace and contaminate positive feelings and drown you in bitterness and a sense of injustice. On the other hand, forgiving those who have angered you often leads to a growing experience. It's not realistic to expect everyone to behave exactly as you desire at all times, so the learning experience may lead to a "reset" of your expectations. Note, forgiving is not forgetting, reconciling, or demanding change, it is a release of resentment previously held in your heart toward someone for a real or perceived offense, flaw or mistake.

6. **Know when to seek help (Mayo).**

   Learning to control (manage) anger appropriately is a challenge for everyone at times. Consider seeking help for anger issues if your anger seems out of control, such as if you damage property, cause physical or emotional pain to those around you, habitually hide your anger, or become convinced that you never become angry (severe suppression). You might explore local community or church-based anger-management counseling, but may need professional help. With professional help, you can accomplish the following:

   - Learn what anger is.
   - Identify what triggers your anger.
   - Recognize indications that you are becoming angry.
   - Learn to respond to frustration and anger in a controlled, healthy way.
   - Explore underlying feelings, such as sadness or depression.
   - Explore the need for antianxiety or antidepressant prescriptions.

   Anger-management counseling can be done on an individual basis, with your partner or other family members, or in a group class. Request a referral from your doctor to a counselor specializing in anger management, or ask family members, friends, or other contacts for recommendations. Your health insurer, Employee Assistance Program (EAP), clergy, or state or local agencies might also offer recommendations.

When drafting an effective anger-management plan, understanding different responses to anger and how they are expressed is a prerequisite. In general, there are five ways people respond to anger, but only two are considered healthy options (Carter). Productive responses to anger are known as "being assertive" or "releasing anger." Unproductive responses to anger are known as "aggressive" (a.k.a. exploding or spewing anger), "suppressive" (a.k.a. burying or stuffing anger), or "passive-aggressive" (a.k.a. leaking or dribbling anger).

Not surprisingly, these anger options map well into a maturity matrix based on Saxenian's criterion for emotional maturity (Figure 10).

It is the mark of an educated mind to be able to entertain a thought without accepting it.

Aristotle

Level of consideration

		Low	High
		Unloving (unkind), disrespectful; prideful and contemptuous	**Loving (kind) and respectful (humble)**
Level of courage High	Confident (open)	**Aggressive**: You firmly and perhaps righteously express your feelings and convictions, but with little concern or consideration for the feelings and convictions of others.	**Assertive**: You express your feelings and convictions with consideration for the feelings and convictions of others. **Release**: You refrain from engaging anger because you believe that a more selfless yet open response will better address the needs of the people around you (e.g., a child or spouse). Release requires forgiveness.
Low	Insecure, fearful (closed)	**Passive-aggressive**: You bury your feelings and convictions without considering the feelings and convictions of others. You may launch covert attacks to avoid open discourse.	**Suppressive**: You bury your feelings and convictions with too much concern for the feelings and convictions of others. **Release**: You refrain from engaging anger because you fear open engagement will not be effective and do not trust the person with whom you are angry. You release your anger so that it will not consume your good spirit. Release requires forgiveness.

Figure 10: Five anger response options as a function of courage versus consideration

Everyone is capable of being assertive or of releasing their anger when necessary. But not everyone has learned how to apply these healthy

196

options in a way that is reproducible. We must first learn what it means to be assertive and how an assertive response differs from our "typical" response. So it is important not only that we clearly understand how to be assertive, but that we identify our weaknesses as well.

1. What are your natural tendencies when angered? If your responses are at times not healthy, then what are they?
   a. Aggressive? Bold, loud, oppressive, and even violent, note—hitting or throwing inanimate objects is threatening and considered violent.
   b. Suppressive? Timid and considerate, but often failing to enforce your boundaries?
   c. Passive-aggressive? Overtly considerate while covertly spiteful, sarcastic and prideful?
2. Many times we respond well to anger, but there exist a few situations or people in our lives that push us over the edge to unhealthy responses to anger.
   a. What are your most sensitive triggers?
   b. Who most often pushes your buttons, and when are they most likely to do so?
3. Other than you, who does your anger negatively impact?
4. Do others feel "safe" when expressing their opinions and convictions openly in your presence? *Safe* means they feel secure that you will respond openly with consideration.
5. Do you feel confident when expressing your opinion and convictions in the presence of your family and friends?

Once you have identified the answers to these questions, you will be better positioned to craft an anger-response plan and gain the confidence necessary to openly share your thoughts and convictions while considerate enough to listen. We simply seek to understand so that our companions feel understood. Upon feeling understood, they will appreciate that you have taken the time to care for them and will more likely take the time to care for you.

In order to identify which is your most frequent unhealthy response to anger, it is important to better understand the five anger responses.

Aggressive Displays of Anger

Recall Aesop's fable depicting the challenge laid forth to the sun by the north wind. The aggressive wind claimed to be the stronger of the two. In order to prove his point, he blew bitterly cold winds in attempts to strip the traveler of his clothing, but the harder the wind blew, the more the traveler clung to his coat. When it was the sun's turn, he took a decidedly more mature approach. He too used his strengths to achieve his goal, but he did so with confidence and consideration. Blanketed in the warmth of the sun's glow, the traveler stripped his garments and bathed in a nearby stream, no doubt later napping under the comfort of a huge oak tree. Influence is better than force!

Why is it sometimes difficult to balance persuasion with courage and consideration? Why do we lean toward control rather than influence? It stands to reason that influence with the possibility of synergy is the preferred approach of the pragmatic optimist. Why then do we often bluster aggressively like the north wind? The answer is a rather simple but often difficult to overcome: we inwardly feel we will not be taken seriously if we don't exaggerate our anger. We often and erroneously believe that being loud and angry is the most effective manner to break down barriers and convince others that we are terribly "serious." In other words, aggressive displays of anger are indicative of a deep pessimism; we pessimistically believe that we will not be taken seriously if we take a fair-minded and respectful approach. We believe that when not taken seriously, we will be taken advantage of and experience missed expectations, and thus, we bristle and bluster to show we will not be victims. But as it did for the north wind, this strategy blows up in our faces, and the respect we strive for is lost in a distasteful and ineffective delivery.

We all have the capacity to be assertive, but at times, we succumb to our weaknesses, and we don't always view those weakness as others do. For example, those who tend toward aggression often consider themselves strong willed and to the point while others see them as opinionated and blunt. Aggressors seek to win and will not be "walked on." When they yield to their pessimism, they become loud and forceful, allowing little room for differences of opinion and stifling all chances for synergy or mutual benefit. Aggressive displays of anger include sniping, bickering, complaining, griping, using foul language, insulting, interrupting, repeating, offering unwanted advice, reacting defensively, and even physically expressing intimidation, such as by throwing things, pounding a hand or fist on a table or wall, pushing, hitting, lunging forward, and entering others' personal space (Carter 1993; Carter 2003; Ingram 2012).

Mutual benefit will not likely be achieved with a person who is actively aggressive. At times, assertive behavior and empathic listening can be used to move a person from aggressiveness to assertiveness (more on this later), but most often, when people act aggressively, they will find themselves mired in a win-lose or lose-lose situation. Recall the interactions between Tom and Toni in *VerAegis—Contribution*. Unfortunately, many aggressive people (with high levels of courage and low levels of consideration) desire win-lose, and for this reason, they love to encounter suppressive people (people who, during conflict, act with low levels of courage and high levels of consideration). The negative suppressive-aggressive encounter starts with the aggressive person believing he or she will not be taken seriously without being boisterous, firm and loud (or believing that a solution can be bullied faster than influenced). Consequently, the aggressor acts with courage but without respect and kindness. The suppressive person becomes withdrawn, acting without openness and mutual respect (kind and respectful to the aggressor but not respectful toward his or her own convictions). The aggressor, sensing weakness, moves in for the kill and perpetuates the win-lose cycle (Figure 11). Aggressors in such cases may feel they have won the battle, but they will often find that they lose the war, especially if the suppressed is someone with whom they desire a lasting relationship. Lasting relationships require mutual benefit; the "I win, you lose" approach will not last, as it violates the golden rule.

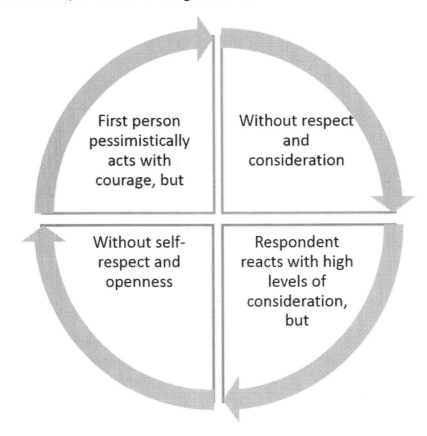

First person pessimistically acts with courage, but

Without respect and consideration

Without self-respect and openness

Respondent reacts with high levels of consideration, but

Figure 11: An aggressive person takes advantage of a suppressive person to achieve a win-lose.

Likewise, mutual benefit will not likely be achieved between two people who are both actively aggressive. When both parties are unwilling to lose, we might like to think that win-win is the only likely outcome, but that is not the case. If both continue to act aggressively, they will find themselves mired in lose-lose situations. The first aggressive person feels that he or she will not be taken seriously (or that a solution can be more quickly bullied than influenced) and acts with courage but without respect and kindness. The second aggressive person, in turn, acts with courage but without respect and consideration, because that person too believes that others are incapable of willingly accepting his or her *considerate* message of self-preservation. The two aggressors will escalate, each attempting to trump the other, force-feed their ideas, and leave no doubt that they will be "heard." If one capitulates, the altercation may end (for the time being), but if neither backs down, a third-party intervention may be required to break the cycle (Figure 12). Another potential outcome is that both parties become passive-aggressive; deciding to no longer fight, they opt to covertly vent their anger and settle for a lose-lose outcome choosing to leak their anger overtime rather than seeking healthy resolution. This pattern of short outbursts followed by long periods of leaking anger is terribly unhealthy (not to mention unproductive): medical research has shown that constant displays of anger and hatred lead to damaged health, potentially shortening one's life-span—definitely not a win for either party.

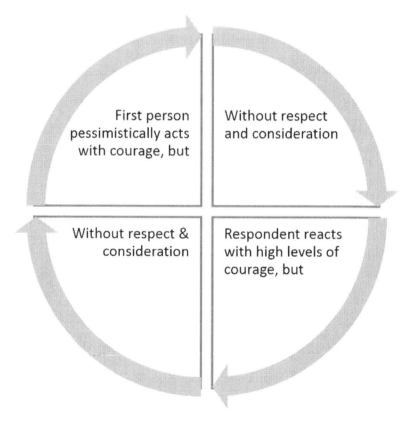

Figure 12: Aggressor meets aggressor, escalating disrespectful and unkind behavior. The cycle will continue until either a third party

intercedes; the aggressors become assertive; or one or both aggressors become passive (covertly angry) to avoid irreparable damage.

There is a possibility of moving to an assertive adult to adult situation, but not while emotions run high. By pausing to refer to their game plan one or both may confidently seek to understand and exit the crazy cycle, moving both parties to the upper right (assertive) quadrant. (seeAssertive Anger Management") Once one party is able to calmly articulate the other's position, there is a possibility of peaceful resolution. The best-case scenario is that each party begins to feel the other has heard his or her message; they each begin to feel understood. If they each have thick skin, they'll "bury the hatchet" and work out a compromise. They may say things like, "At first we didn't see eye to eye, but we each stood our ground. We went toe-to-toe until we understood each other. Yeah, we got a little loud, pounded the table a bit, but what's the problem? We worked it out, came to a solution, and we are both good with it. No harm, no foul!" This may not sound too bad, but these aggressors may have left many "dead bodies" in their wake—that is, there may be others who were scared, unable to contribute, and hurt by the outburst.

> **Peace cannot be achieved through violence; it can only be attained through understanding.**
>
> Ralph Waldo Emerson

Passive-Aggressive

Aesop tells a story of an ass who was not able to deal with problems in an open and considerate manner. Instead, the ass whined and complained even if (he thought) there was no one there to listen. Aesop's point was that we sometimes struggle to handle small problems with the same courage which we handle big problems, and when left unresolved, the little problems tend to grow. Further, we often bury our feelings in the presence of others only to let them leak out when others are not expecting.

The Ass and the Frogs

An Ass [a donkey, not a relative!] carrying a load of wood, passed through a pond. As he was crossing through the water he lost his footing, stumbled and fell, and, not being able to rise on account of his load, groaned heavily. Some Frogs frequenting the pool heard his lamentation, and said, "What would you do if you had to live here always as we do, when you make such a fuss about a mere fall into the water?"

Men often bear little grievances with less courage than they do large misfortunes. (Townsend)

What do you think of when you hear that someone has an anger issue? Most people imagine loud, boisterous, and explosive (aggressive) behavior. Thus, many who are not loud, explosive, or boisterous consider themselves to be free from anger issues or else great at controlling their anger. Giving credit where it is due, it is good that these people do not become openly aggressive. But rather than using high levels of courage and consideration, those who engage in a passive-aggressive approach to anger choose to belittle others through hidden means that leave themselves least exposed—displaying low levels of both courage and consideration: "Knowing that loud or obnoxious expression of anger leaves them vulnerable to the rejection of others, they become passive while still engaging adversarially with the person who is the object of their anger" (Carter).

Passive communication of displeasure minimizes vulnerability. Passive aggressors are deeply pessimistic, believing they cannot openly preserve their self-worth and convictions without being controlled or overpowered—thus, they do not fully disclose the nature of their anger. They often bear common grievances with less courage and openness than they do with big problems. They are not comfortable exposing their feelings and beliefs and are insecure when confronted, often remaining silent when the object of their anger desires to hear from them. Passive-aggressive displays of anger include inventing flimsy excuses to avoid open engagement, agreeing though you are unlikely to follow through on your commitment, doing your own "thing" at your own pace even when you know that it disrupts other's plans, sniping people behind their backs but rarely face-to-face, stating what the other person wants to hear while doing what you want to do, being closed and evasive to avoid exposure and the risk of being controlled, repeatedly using the phrase "I don't know" when being asked to explain your choices, and ultimately becoming passive while face-to-face and then slyly managing conflict by engaging in an adversarial, covert manner (Carter 1993; Carter 2003; Ingram 2012).

> **Hateful to me as the gates of Hades is that man who hides one thing in his heart and speaks another.**
> Homer

Those who succumb to passive aggressive tendencies during moments of conflict believe that if they openly communicate their desired results and fail to achieve those results, they are exposed and vulnerable, like the donkey stuck in the mud. Rather than openly bearing the burden of little grievances, they avoid the exposure, do not state their desired results, and covertly send a message to "leave me alone" as they wallow in the mire of the unresolved situation.

In Western culture, we tend to value argument as a dominant form of communication, especially when searching for a solution to a problem (Bono). An idea is offered, and others counter and banter in search of weakness, often—but not always—with the intent to fortify the idea. But a strong conflict-aversion mechanism motivates the passive-aggressive person to avoid any type of argumentative situation, even those intended to fortify important and even urgent ideas or concepts. They will often close up completely or become agreeable with covert intent when faced with aggressive and sometimes even assertive behavior. When dealing with a passive-aggressive person, one must avoid becoming aggressive and seek to assertively guide the conversation to draw out both the courage and consideration necessary for full engagement (see "Assertive Anger Management").

Suppressive

In another story, Aesop tells a tale of a goatherd who sought to hide injury he caused to one of his master's goats. While reading the fable, consider the broken horn as a representation of our anger—all too often we strive to hide our anger rather than use it for its intended purpose of protecting our convictions and establishing healthy boundaries.

> A Goatherd had sought to bring back a stray goat to his flock. He whistled and sounded his horn in vain; the straggler paid no attention to the summons. At last the Goatherd threw a stone, and breaking its horn, begged the Goat not to tell his master. The Goat replied, "Why, you silly fellow, the horn will speak though I be silent."
>
> Do not attempt to hide things which cannot be hid. (Townsend)

Suppressing anger is like ignoring mold and mildew in a dark, damp basement—like ignoring the "check engine" light as you speed down the highway. Many girls and boys alike are taught that open expression of one's emotions, especially anger, is unbecoming of a lady or gentleman. As a consequence, many attempt to hide or suppress their feelings. Those who seek to suppress anger are often deeply pessimistic, believing that open communication will not lead to peaceful resolution or that it will be emotionally painful. Consequently, the legitimate need to preserve one's values and convictions is buried, replaced by a facade of composure—cool, calm, and considerate but leaving one exposed by failing to establish appropriate behavioral guidelines or boundaries for others to follow.

Behaviors indicative of anger suppression include avoiding or exiting conflict even if unresolved; attempting to hide problems, weaknesses, or needs; and striving to preserve one's image rather than standing for values and convictions. The suppressors' goal is to appear to have it "all together." They often lack the courage to stick to their convictions, second-guessing their own good judgment and attempting to keep the peace just to please others. Because they are often motivated by fun or peace, they tend to make excuses for others' behaviors, hiding resentment and believing that self-expression, especially anger, is not acceptable (Carter 1993; Carter 2003; Ingram 2012).

People who suppress anger falsely believe that hiding pains and frustrations will magically dissolve them into thin air, but as Aesop warned, we should not attempt to hide that which cannot be hidden. Like unseen mold and mildew in a dark, damp basement, your anger will grow and build, until it has silently infiltrated the core of your being and caused the many glass balls you're juggling to drop. You will become a ticking time bomb waiting to explode. Your spirit, health, and relationships will suffer. In fact, Dr. John Burns and his team conducted experiments demonstrating that anger suppression actually increases pain intensity among chronic lower-back pain (CLBP) patients, who ironically felt angrier when the experiments were completed than patients who were encouraged to express their emotions during the experiment (Burns 2008).

By choosing to suppress anger, one risks ill effects to health and well-being. Scientists call the condition caused by anger suppression a distressed personality. When we are angered, our flight-or-fight response is triggered. Our body generates adrenaline (a.k.a. epinephrine) to provide a surge of energy and focus our attention; norepinephrine, which helps redirect our blood flow away from noncrucial organs, such as our skin, to more essential areas, such as muscles, to prepare us for flight or fight; and cortisol (a.k.a. the stress hormone) which serves to maintain fluid balance and pressure while regulating body functions such as reproductive drive, immunity, digestion, and growth. When we suppress our emotions (we stew on rather than address our anger), our body's pituitary gland sends signals to the adrenal gland, which in turn generates more and more cortisol. The increased cortisol level is important for survival during a given stressful incident, but it is just as important that the body deactivates the stress response and activates its relaxation response once the source of stress is removed. When one suppresses anger rather than truly dealing with the issue at hand, the body's relaxation response is not triggered, and the continuous release of cortisol negatively impacts all the body's organs, nervous system, and even the immune system. Thus, suppression of anger can decrease our ability to fight off colds, flus, and other communicable diseases; contribute to heightened levels of back, joint, and muscular pain; lead to elevated blood pressure; and potentially lead to premature death. It is important to note that continuous "explosive" behavior, just as well as sly, covert anger, can likewise inhibit the body's relaxation response, leading to similar health problems (Klein 2013; Stork 2012; Burns 2008). The key is to learn to keep the peace assertively, managing your emotions. Your health and relationships will improve.

Assertive Anger Management

Courage is what it takes to stand up and speak; courage is also what it takes to sit down and listen.
Winston Churchill

Some people are able to communicate their anger clearly, calmly, and deliberately, turning it on and off as needed. Once they have effectively addressed their anger and achieved their desired results, they let it go. A colleague used to say that anger was a man (he had a more colorful name for this man) he carried in his back pocket, whom he took out when needed and put away as quickly as possible. When handled correctly, healthy anger enhances the possibility of mutual benefit, cooperation, and even love. Anger arises from difference, from conflict—conflicting views, conflicting understandings, conflicting interests, and conflicting (misaligned) expectations. Recall from VerAegis—Relationships that when faced with conflict, one needs only to ARM oneself in order to remain courageous, yet considerate.

Acknowledge: Accept your anger. Accept that it is your choice how to respond to your anger. Agree that to be angry is a God-given gift to help each of us preserve our self-worth.

Root Cause: Investigate the cause (or causes) of your anger. Refrain from action until you have identified the root cause...what is the real issue. Anger is like the warning light on the dashboard of our cars, the light is not the problem, it is only an indication of a deeper issue that needs to be addressed, and just like auto-mechanics cannot fix our vehicles by working on the warning light, we cannot adequately respond to anger until we have identified the underlying cause.

- Has someone failed to meet your expectations?
- Was performance below your expectations?
- Did they fail to adhere to your values or rules
- Do they share your values and agree with your rules?
- Do you feel they attacked your self-worth...your self-esteem?
- Did someone fail to meet your needs...?
- Do you understand their convictions...do they understand yours?

In close relations, the root of conflict is often misunderstanding. Thus, it is important to seek understanding without necessarily seeking agreement. When in a conflict, understanding is required to first determine if the conflict is even "real." How many times have you been involved in a major dispute...over something that was petty and unimportant? When you truly seek to understand, you may realize that you are not so far apart. In other words, when both parties are understood to their satisfaction, there may not be a conflict at all...or you may find the issue does not merit the time and energy required to reach resolution.

Manage: *Manage* your response to emotions and anger–don't let your emotions get the best of you! Refer to your plan of action. Conduct yourself with a balance of courage and consideration:

- Courage to stand for your values and convictions.
- Consideration of the values and convictions of whomever has contributed to your angst.

The process of ARMing yourself, as expected, requires that private victories proceed public victories.

- Private victory: You achieve a private victory when you acknowledge and accept your anger as a God-given gift, then commit to defending your principal-aligned-values and convictions.

- Public victory: You achieve a public victory when you manage your anger rather than let your anger manage you; when you act openly with courage and with consideration; when you protect your self-esteem and maintain the self-esteem of those whom are the focus of your anger; when you place the importance of reconciliation over being right.

In the face of legitimate conflict, when the beliefs and convictions of both parties are brought forth and understood, the chances of eliminating the root of the conflict—or at an absolute minimum, arriving at a calm place—are much greater. A few positive outcomes of anger are accessible once courage and consideration are successfully balanced:

- Holding true to beliefs and convictions

- Establishing and respecting personal limits and behavioral boundaries

- Expressing heartfelt concerns over perceived poor choices made by others

- Addressing problems related to irresponsibility or misguided priorities

- Establishing discipline and cohesiveness during situations that require teamwork in order to succeed

According to Dictionary.com, being aggressive is making an all-out effort to win or succeed—in other words, it is being competitive. Similarly assertive is defined as being confidently aggressive or self-assured.

Assertiveness	Aggressiveness
1. Discretion regarding the necessity of anger	1. Anger in response to minor or frivolous issues
2. Calm, even tone of voice, soft eyes	2. Pleading or coercive, furrowed brow, hard eyes
3. Respect consistently maintained.	3. Respect summarily disregarded.
4. Succinct	4. Long-winded, wordy, repetitive
5. Keeping other person's needs in perspective	5. Ignores others' needs as self takes center stage
6. Open-minded (open hearted)	6. Rigid and demanding
7. Win-win oriented; guided by constructive motives	7. Win or win-lose oriented; often destructive in nature
8. Seeking mutual benefit	8. Seeking personal benefit
9. Responding to resistance calmly and firmly, with humility and strength	9. Responding to resistance harshly and contemptuously with excessive pride
10. Balance of consideration and courage	10. Abundance of courage, lack of consideration

Figure 13: Differences between assertiveness and aggressiveness

Given that the word *aggressive* is used in the definition of assertive, it is not difficult to understand how the two modes of anger management can be confused. Whereas aggressive behavior is often absent of common courtesies, being assertive (in a nutshell) is remaining faithful to our convictions and boundaries while simultaneously remaining respectful and considerate of the others' personal boundaries, beliefs, and convictions—even in the face of disagreement. Figure 13 illustrates the differences between assertive and aggressive behavior. Being well versed in assertive anger management improves our confidence and ability to recognize when to pull that man (or woman) we call anger from our back pocket, how to put him or her to effective use returning to the pocket as soon as possible.

Ideally, if one expresses emotions assertively, with respect and decency, others will react in kind. Quite often this is merely a dream, but by focusing inwardly and calling on a higher spirit (for me, that higher spirit is Jesus), the dream can live on! Yet, at times remaining assertive can be difficult. When emotions swell, it is best to have a predetermined plan or script to follow, such as the one below:

1. I have clear objectives for my anger. I will use my anger to
   a. preserve my self-worth and stand up for my values and convictions;
   b. establish increased harmony in my relationships;
   c. preserve my well-being (health and spirit) and the well-being of my friends and loved ones.
2. When angry, I will follow these behavioral guidelines:
   a. I will determine if it is really necessary to respond to this emotion. If yes, then
      i. is it okay to respond immediately; or
      ii. should I remove myself from the situation to think further about the underlying cause of my anger and my response? If yes, I will
         1. take a walk;
         2. meditate, pray;
         3. exercise, and
         4. I will agree to time to reconvene.

b. It is okay to talk about my anger and what has made me angry (FBI).

c. It is not okay to hurt others with the things I say or do.

d. It is not okay to damage property.

e. I will treat others with respect and consideration, attempting to respect boundaries and preserve their self-worth, values, and convictions.

f. I will employ coordinated thought. Recall the section "Framework of Thought," parts one and two from *VerAegis—Relationships*.

3. I will be open, succinct, clear, and direct.

4. I will avoid placing blame. I will avoid "you are" and "you did" statements and present my concerns directly, openly discussing my feelings and behaviors, as well as their impact (FBI).

5. I will not be pessimistic.

a. I do not need to become aggressive. I believe that those with whom I am angry will take me more seriously if I am fair-minded and respectful.

b. I do not need to become passive-aggressive. I will openly disclose the nature of my anger, preserving self-worth and convictions without being controlled or overpowered. I do not require acceptance or approval for my anger; others do not determine my self-worth, and I will not entertain a covert agenda.

c. I do not need to hide my anger. Open, respectful communication will lead to more productive results and stronger relationships. I will address my legitimate needs to preserve values and convictions while remaining cool, calm, and considerate.

6. I will seek to understand the needs and boundaries of others.

a. I will listen empathically, reflecting emotions and the impact of my behaviors.

b. When both parties are calm, I will restate the position of the person with whom I am angry in my own words, until he or she is satisfied that I do indeed understand. I can entertain a thought respectfully without agreeing with that thought.

Early in my career, I worked at an aggressive Silicon Valley start-up. We were driven to develop the world's leading lasers, and we worked hard. Many who worked there were assertive and at times aggressive. We were open and often blunt. Most did not realize how intimidating our behavior was to others who were more timid by nature. We felt that aggressiveness was not only expected but necessary to succeed in our cutting-edge endeavors. The downside was that to those who often suppressed anger or who were passive-aggressive, this open aggressiveness was stifling, eliminating the chance to harvest synergy.

Later I worked in an organization that had a surprisingly large contingency of passive-aggressive or suppressive people, who were not nearly as open in their communication. It was difficult to transition from an extremely open and often aggressive environment to one that was not as open to discussions of potentially "controversial" topics. I found that the most effective tool in these circumstances was to use the six thinking hats to guide conversations (refer to "Framework of Thought, Part II: Put on Your Thinking Cap!" from *VerAegis—Spirit*.) We would invite all to don the green hat when thinking creatively, the yellow when finding all that was good about a topic, and the black when thinking about potential pitfalls and negative outcomes, which was liberating for those who tend to avoid conflict. You see, for those who are conflict avoidant, it is difficult to openly share (or hear, if on the receiving end) the potential shortcomings of an idea. However, it is liberating when all are on the same page, working together to identify potential pitfalls. Even finding shortfalls can be synergistic when coordinated rather than presented in conflict. Someone may say, "Let's think about what can go wrong so that we are not blindsided down the road." Or when an idea comes to mind, one may open with, "Thinking about this critically for a second, we might find..." This type of coordinated thought helps open the lines of communication by creating an environment in which it is safe to share.

Similarly, at home, it often felt that I played the "spoiler" role. Sheri and the kids would get excited about an activity or idea, and I would listen to all the great things they were planning. Then I would join in with the "yeah, buts...safety issues, schedule conflicts and so on"; their spirits would deflate—or perhaps ignite. They were looking for the sunshine, and I showed them the rain. I am still on a learning curve, but I have found that it is a better approach to acknowledge their good suggestions and even offer ideas that would build on the fun before inviting everyone to look at the potential downsides. Once the exciting ideas have been exhausted, I might say, "What are some of the problems we may encounter? What can go wrong?" Once we have discussed the downsides, we are better positioned to determine whether the upsides are worth the risk, and if so, then we can use the green hat to creatively brainstorm solutions to the potential problems.

In addition to coordinating thought using the various thinking caps, one needs to coordinate thoughts using successful paths of communication, most often adult to adult (refer to *VerAegis— Relationships*, Framework of Thought Part I). However, when emotions run high (usually when one or both parties try to take on the parent role or when both assume a childlike role), successful and assertive communication is nearly impossible. Emotions need to be tamed for assertion to take hold. Recall our discussion of Plato's charioteer and his two horses (*VerAegis—Relationships*). The first horse is wild, emotional, and at times unwieldy, and the second well behaved, focused, and driven. The horses represent our emotions and drive to achieve, and the charioteer our ability to reason between alternate inputs and views. To be assertive, we need to quiet our and others unwieldy horses (calm emotions) by drawing upon the staid, focused and determined horses and then relying upon the unemotional logic of the charioteers to guide our responses to emotions. Below is a process that has worked for me:

1. Seek to first understand what the other person is feeling.

   a. When a person is upset and highly emotional, reflect his or her emotions without judgment: "It seems you are feeling [sad, angry, frustrated, isolated, alone, etc.]." They will not become calm until they feel understood.

   b. One time will not magically do the trick; be genuinely concerned about the other's emotional state. Don't expect him or her to calm immediately; prepare to be tested.

2. Once the other person confirms that you have adequately understood his or her emotions, and they have become calm, seek to understand his or her message.

   a. Repeat the message in your own words until he or she is satisfied that you understand.

   b. Warning: Most of what is communicated is contained in facial expressions, intonations, emphasis, and pauses, rather than words; don't be surprised if the person whom you are trying to understand informs you that you are way off base with your first attempt. The first time I tried this approach with my wife, Sheri, she angrily replied that I was trying to put words in her mouth. She did not believe that my understanding could be so far from her desired message! Once she realized that I sincerely misunderstood her, she tried to explain herself differently.

   c. This process is powerful when we invest the time necessary, but it's difficult when you try to hurry. If needed, schedule some time away from other distractions when you can talk without being rushed.

Assertiveness is tricky yet powerful and often the best approach to anger management. But assertiveness is not always feasible; there are circumstances in which it just will not work. For instance, sometimes we need to refrain from engaging in anger (setting aside our needs) because in that situation, a more selfless yet open response will better address the needs of the people with whom we are angry (people who are important to us, such as a child or spouse). For instance, perhaps an acutely ill spouse treats you poorly, taking your help and love for granted. Your anger is kindled, but you realize that the illness is the cause of his or her behavior. You love the person, you let it go, and you move on.

We may also refrain from engaging anger because we realize that it will likely result in physical or emotional injury. For example, perhaps you are in an abusive relationship, but only when your spouse drinks. He or she has been on the wagon for six months, and everything has been going well. You arrive home to find your spouse's car in the driveway—home early. You see through the front window that he or she is sitting at the kitchen table with a drink in hand. Your anger rises, but if you enter and confront your possibly drunk or upset spouse, things may not go well. You decide to wait until he or she is sober and perhaps call an AA sponsor for immediate help.

We release anger so that it will not consume our good spirits. Release requires forgiveness, but it does not require subjecting ourselves to continued abuse. Forgiveness is for the forgiver. Once again, forgiving is not forgetting, reconciling, or demanding change, it is a release of resentment previously held in your heart toward someone for a real or perceived offense, flaw or mistake. It involves extending God's grace and mercy, and it requires God's strength. To successfully release our anger, we need to invoke God's power, compassion, mercy, and grace.

Release

Katie had a broken spirit. Kevin Renner, later to be the author of *In Search of Fatherhood: Stories from Women around the World,* sat across from his childhood sweetheart, listening intently. Only semicoherent, Katie related the sad direction her life had taken since they had parted ways as children. She was a five-time divorcée with three failed suicide attempts, who sought escape in a haze of drugs and alcohol. As she was unable to parent her children, they lived with her father. A couple of years after this meeting, Kevin began recruiting women for his book. He reached out to Katie. She replied, "I am the wrong person for your book. My dad had nothing to do with who I am. Life did. I grew up without a dad. No...I am not pissed off...although it does sound like it with my reply" (Renner 2011).

Katie's life changed direction; she changed her mind. This is how she related her story to Kevin:

> My life was just a party. I didn't want to deal with anything serious. I was like tumbleweed, just blowing in the wind. Wherever it stopped, I would stop and if the wind picked up, I was gone again. And I'd use any chemical that could keep me from thinking too much about what I should have been thinking about and doing to get my head screwed on. (Renner 2011)

Katie's third suicide attempt was in 2001. She suffered cardiac arrest and entered a coma for three days after swallowing a bottle of Tylenol and nearly two bottles of wine. During her coma, Katie's life was changed: she had an out-of-body experience wherein she communed with God.

> That's when everything turned around for me, because I didn't see Him, but I knew there was a presence and I was somewhere I've never been before in this life. It's not of this life. It was something completely different. I just clearly remember feeling or hearing this—it wasn't a voice—it was a very large thought (but it wasn't mine) that said, "You have something very large to do. And you

have to stay around to get it done. You're just not going anywhere."

Katie heard a calling. This spiritual experience altered the course of her life, putting her on a path of redemption with her father, who had abused her as a child. He was born in Michigan and raised on a farm by a "tyrant" whom he resented. At eighteen, he joined the air force and then married Katie's mom.

> He's been a piece of work and was a big thorn in my side all my life...My earliest memory of him was he was a womanizer and an abuser. He abused my mother and he abused his kids.

Katie recalled having to care for her brothers after they were beaten with a belt buckle. She had to clean and bandage open wounds. Her father did not show prejudice when dishing out corporal punishment.

> And he beat me, too. He slapped me around a lot, one time so hard that I hit the corner of a wall and cracked my head open. And he had to take me to the hospital...to get some stitches in my head. When he brought me home, I didn't have a fever, but he insisted on taking my temperature with a rectal thermometer, and having sex with that thermometer in my ass. And my mother had come in the room and said, "What are you doing to her? She doesn't have a fever." I had blood coming out of my anus for a week after that and I never told my mother. I hated him. I really did hate him. Everything he did I just knew was wrong and evil.

During her teen years, Katie sought escape. She repeatedly ran away from home. She drank alcohol and experimented with drugs. She despised how her father treated women as objects, yet she became sexually promiscuous, thinking that sex was her path to love. Drugs and failed relationships led to suicide attempts and the loss of her children. Katie hit rock bottom, but in her coma, she found salvation and spiritual renewal. Once physically recovered from her coma, armed with newfound strength in her spirit, Katie entered a therapy program and one by one, vanquished her demons. Katie was on the path to recovery.

Then Katie received a call from her mother, who was having serious health problems. Katie did not hesitate; she moved to Nevada to live with her parents, where her spiritual recovery continued.

Making the desert road trips, I found big therapy there. I would just get these very strong thoughts...coming from somewhere...It's like every wall in me is gone and I'm really receptive to all these insights. That's where I really grew by leaps and bounds personally. I became more aware of me and what I wanted to do and who I really am, and my parents were seeing that.

From [age] 51 until 53, that's when our relationship was repaired, because I was repaired. I had gotten through all my issues. Well, I realized once I was there, I didn't want to go back to San Diego, so I asked if I could stay. I was helping my father, but I didn't know it. I got him to try to see life sober, to see the beauty in things around him, to get in touch with himself and his feelings and his past, to let go of the anger he had with his own mother and his brother, even though they're dead.

I remember him saying, "What are you doing, because you seem lighter; you seem happier; you seem freer; something's different." I told him it was the road trips into the desert. You go out there and park and listen [*Listen carefully.*] to nothing and you're going to hear something; you're going to hear a lot. You can't run from yourself anymore when there's nowhere to go and you're stuck with no human contact [*Try reaching back.*].

And he saw me working with my art, my painting, my jewelry, the things I made. He got to know how I think and how I feel [*Examine your motives*]. He would hear my phone calls with my kids. We lived together as adults without the bullshit when I was younger [*Write your worries in the sand*]. So we were both really seeing the other person the way we are now.

We both grew in that two and a half years and our relationship benefited from it immensely. I'm not mad at him anymore. I forgive him for all of it. He was a very sick man and he didn't know how to ask for help. So he hurt the ones closest to him. It wasn't until the last two and a half years I lived with him that he finally saw me as me and accepted me and he's blown away by who I am. And so in the last two and a half years I've gotten more pats on the back from him than I did in my whole life.

Kevin felt the authenticity of Katie's words and did not doubt the conviction of her forgiveness, but could not comprehend where she found the grace to forgive her father and let go of the anger that had so damaged her life. Katie responded:

You have to forgive, because if you don't, it [anger] festers inside of you like cancer. You may think you're not thinking about it, but it's always there and it eats at you. I knew in order to get past it, to get to the next level, I had to sincerely forgive my father. And because I have, that opened up so many doors for me. And I'm able to love completely now, holding nothing back, expecting nothing from anybody. I just love so unconditionally. It's freed me.

It took two years for me to realize the man loves me. He always loved me. He just didn't have the right tools to show me and he didn't have the tools to be a good parent, because he had his own issues. Now when we're together, we have a great time. And he's so happy for me and he's so happy how I've turned out. He got to learn a lot about me, what I'd been through, not just my childhood that he's probably forgot, but my relationships. And he learned things that happened to me that he didn't know about. So, it's almost as if he's at peace now and he's let go of his issues and forgiven himself.

He first told Katie he loved her when she was fifty-two. When Kevin asked her what that was like, she said he was crying, and went on to explain:

I about fell over. I actually stopped what I was doing and turned around and said, "What?" He said, "I love you. I think you should know that." And he would say it more and then, I found that I was saying back, "I love you, too," instead of just going, "Oh, okay." He's had regrets and I've told him that I've forgiven him. I'm like, "I accept your apology. I don't want you to spend the last years of your life kicking yourself in the butt for stuff that's happened. Just know I love you and I forgive you for it." I cried with him. It choked me up, because I didn't think he had any sensitivity in him at all. I thought he was just a hard-nosed jerk. But he's a real soft man. I think the years of abuse that he did to himself and the way his mother treated him, he just didn't know how to get off that.

Katie's is a true story of anger release, the fifth alternative to anger management. Release is quite different from suppression, which was Katie's first approach. Her suppressed anger so poisoned her spirit that it rendered her incapable of living an effective life. Ultimately, she was able to find full release by surrendering her pain to God and accepting His strength so that she could move on.

Likewise, release requires each of us to surrender our anger to a higher spiritual entity (God, for those who have a relationship with Him) and continued prayer and forgiveness. No father should subject his daughter to the horrors Katie endured, and no daughter should have to suffer so. Katie had no mentor to teach her how to handle her father's abuse and her subsequent anger. Her response was to suppress her anger and seek refuge in meaningless relationships, drugs and alcohol. She feared her father and could not be open with her mother. But as she found the spiritual strength to forgive, a miracle ensued. Her inner self grew strong, and by focusing on her circle of greatest influence, her inner spirit, she was able to expand her influence and slowly help her father to heal his own wounded spirit.

By choosing to release anger, when practical and safe, we are better positioned to emphasize relationships, engaging in more selfless yet open responses to more effectively address the needs of the people with whom we are angry. By releasing our anger and subsequently elevating the needs of others over our own, we call on high levels of self-restraint, humility, and acceptance. Other fundamentals of release include the following:

- Showing genuine tolerance for others' flaws and weaknesses
- Recognizing when not to press an issue
- Being fair in your expectations of others
- Choosing to set aside a critical spirit, becoming fair-minded
- Giving priority to forgiveness
- Choosing kindness and consideration, even if others have not earned it
- Refraining from fruitless debate
- Allowing others to commit mistakes
- Dropping the requirement that others should live up to your ideal standards
- Converting expectations to desires (Carter 1993; Ingram 2012)

Katie clearly found the strength to forgive and to choose kind humility over prideful spite. She did not forget or demand change; she released the resentment from her heart—she release the hatred of her father for years of offenses, his serious personal flaws and his many major mistakes. By accepting her own and her father's weaknesses, she found an inner strength fueled by a higher spirit, and when allowed to flourish, His strength grew to consume both her and her father's anger. Katie's weakness became a channel for her creator's strength to shine through, and His light not only kindled her spirit but ignited those of her loved ones as well.

Anger Management Summary

Pride goes before destruction, and a haughty spirit before a fall.
Proverbs 16:18 (NKJV)

I believe it is obvious that more strength is required to stand one's ground than to cower angrily in the shadows, but it is perhaps not so obvious that more strength is required to stand firm in humility than to bluster about with courage while devoid of consideration. This kind of strength is not the strength that moves lead weights; it is the kind that moves souls. Inner strength is required to understand that your value comes from a higher spirit, not from the person with whom you are angry. There is nothing anyone (other than you) can do to bolster or weaken your true value and inner strength. Others may influence your moods and desires, but your choices and decisions are yours and yours alone. *Others may trigger emotions* that kindle your anger, but *you choose your response*. Choose to act with courage and consideration, or choose a less noble path. Choose to connect your spirit to an infinite power of good, or choose to confine yourself to worldly ways. In other words, you own the choice of whether to succumb to your natural "weak" response when angered (aggression, suppression, or passive aggression) or elevate to a positive, assertive response or in some special cases, one of full release. Will you choose to act with high levels of courage and consideration? Figure 14 summarizes positive and negative anger response styles. "Assertive" and "release" are the productive methods by which we address anger. We all should strive to be more assertive and release anger when appropriate.

Joni Eareckson Tada is a quadriplegic. In 1967, as a teenager, she broke her neck while diving into the Chesapeake Bay. She had the choice to be bitter and resentful or become a blessing in the lives of others; she chose the latter. During two years of tough rehabilitation, Joni learned to create pictures and paintings, first with a pencil and then with a paintbrush—held in her mouth. She became an author, and a movie was produced chronicling her life. Then she founded an organization called Joni and Friends, which teaches churches and other organizations to minister to people who are physically impaired.

	Low	High
High (open)	**Aggressive:** • Open to communication but often overly assertive or aggressive, damaging a free exchange of ideas • Overtly unkind and inconsiderate • Often hostile • Concerned with self	**Assertive:** • Open to communication • Balances courage and consideration—listening with the intent to understand • Concerned with self and others **Release:** • Forgiving spirit • Believes that a selfless response (due to the nature of the relationship) is more important in some circumstances than demonstrating the power of one's own convictions • Responds openly to better address the needs of others
Low (closed)	**Passive-aggressive** • Closed and uncommunicative, with low regard for others' positions and needs • Often agrees just to end the conversation but then pursues own agenda when not face-to-face • Covertly unkind and inconsiderate due to a covertly hostile attitude • Lack of integrity, misleading • Concerned with self but not open regarding needs and boundaries	**Suppressive** • Closed and uncommunicative • Fails to communicate own position • More regard for others' needs than own • Often comes across as a martyr **Release (quiet courage)** • Chooses to avoid communication of own position due to belief that others are not open to input and that there may be a danger of physical or emotional abuse if the point is pushed • Engages a forgiving spirit, choosing to understand others' flaws and forgive them (which does not mean condoning their behavior)

Level of courage and communication (vertical axis label)

Figure 14: Summary of anger-response styles

In the early 1980s, Joni met Ken Tada, who later became her husband. She is a remarkable person and has had to rely on family friends, Ken, and most of all, God, to get her through each day. Some mornings while waiting for her friend to arrive and get her ready for the day—by giving her a sponge bath and brushing her teeth and hair—Joni prayed: "God, I have no strength for this. I can't face this day. I have no resources for this; I have no smile for this woman. But you do, God.

You have the strength. You have resources. Can I please borrow your smile?" (Tada).

One of life's greatest lessons for Ken and Joni has been that "God's power shows up best in our weakness" (Tada). And it is His strength that helps Joni face each day. It is His strength that helps Ken as he supports Joni. If you are someone who has a tendency to suppress your anger, you are naturally considerate, and to become assertive, you now need to be unnaturally brave. Perhaps if you borrow Joni's prayer, God's strength will surface in your weakness: "My weakness, that is, my quadriplegia, is my greatest asset because it forces me into the arms of Christ every single morning when I get up" (Tada).

To move from aggressive to assertive anger management, we most need to focus on the platinum rule (which is slightly different than the golden rule): "Treat others as they wish to be treated." Doing so requires that we invest time to learn how they wish to be treated. For example, those of us who are aggressive often have what we refer to as "thick skins." In other words, when people are blunt with us, we tend to not take it personally. Consequently, when we treat others in a manner that we are comfortable with, we run the risk of offending those who are not "thick-skinned." Aggressive people are naturally courageous when angered, but to become assertive, we need to become unnaturally considerate. Here we should borrow Joni's prayer to find God's kindness and compassion in our weakness. Learn to be humble. Learn that it is indeed more powerful to stand firm in humility (like the sun) than to bluster about (like the north wind) with courage while devoid of consideration.

To move from suppressive to assertive anger responses, we must no longer attempt to hide that which cannot be hidden. Sooner or later, suppressed anger will surface in a sudden explosion (a ticking time bomb) or damaged health (unaddressed mold and mildew in a dark, damp basement undermining our foundation). Suppressive people are naturally considerate when angered, but to become assertive, we need to become unnaturally courageous. Here we should borrow

Joni's prayer to find God's courage and passion in our weakness. Remain considerate, but learn to be bold setting healthy personal boundaries. We need to find the inner strength and courage necessary to considerately stand up for our needs and convictions rather than bury them to preserve others'.

To move from passive aggression to assertiveness, we need to simultaneously increase both our courage to speak openly and honestly and our ability to act with consideration. We need to find an unnatural strength to refrain from covertly manipulating others through commitments we do not intend to keep and to avoid leaking our anger through sarcasm and gossip. Invoking Joni's prayer in our weakness, we need to find God's strength—the strength of conviction and the courage to act openly and considerately. We need His strength to discuss and protect our boundaries with appropriate regard to others' boundaries.

Recall that there are times when it is appropriate to feel anger, to feel the "emotion of self-preservation." In fact, it is the responsibility of the emotionally mature to preserve personal worth and perceived needs, expectations, and heartfelt convictions, and to do so in a manner that preserves the dignity and worth of others. We must realize that we can control our actions and influence others', but just because we are making progress with our anger issues does not mean that our friends, acquaintances, and loved ones will act in kind. We should stop assuming that others will meet our expectations and hold ourselves accountable instead. Replace pride with the strength of humility. Replace expectations with desires, and align desired results with family, friends, and colleagues.

Nearly two thousand years ago, James, son of Joseph and Mary and half brother of Jesus, penned this message for us:

> Understand this, my dear brothers and sisters: You must all be quick to listen, slow to speak, and slow to get angry. Human anger does not produce the righteousness God desires. So get rid of all

the filth and evil in your lives, and humbly accept the word God has planted in your hearts, for it has the power to save your souls.

But don't just listen to God's word. You must do what it says. Otherwise, you are only fooling yourselves. For if you listen to the word and don't obey, it is like glancing at your face in a mirror. You see yourself, walk away, and forget what you look like. But if you look carefully into the perfect law that sets you free, and if you do what it says and don't forget what you heard, then God will bless you for doing it.

If you claim to be religious but don't control your tongue, you are fooling yourself, and your religion is worthless. Pure and genuine religion in the sight of God the Father means caring for orphans and widows in their distress and refusing to let the world corrupt you. (James 1:19–27 [NLT])

We have learned that our actions often anger God, but James instructs that we as humans have a tendency to respond differently to our anger and that *human anger* does not make you right with God. Human anger does not make you strong in spirit. Human anger makes you ill spirited and strains your relationships. Human anger is aggression, suppression, and passive aggression. They all fall short. Assertiveness, on the other hand, is godly anger. Release is giving our anger to God. Both assertiveness and release require us to channel God's strength, compassion, love and wisdom through our weaknesses. Godly anger is the ability to stand up for principles without trampling the people in our paths. It is being pragmatically optimistic that you will manage anger well despite our and others' flaws, and it is believing that humility and gentleness are strength. Godly anger is acceptance of imperfection in oneself and others; it is being emotionally mature enough to realize that all people will not act with the same level of acceptance and emotional maturity. The emotionally mature emphasize the importance of relationships, responding to anger with courage and consideration and then releasing it to a higher authority. Release is calling upon God's spirit and strength to forgive so that the anger will not build like a time bomb, ready to explode, or a cancer, ready to devour from within. Godly anger is pure, enabling us to be angry without sin.

Will you continue to be bound to the constraints of human anger or accept the gift of godly anger? Will you settle for a weak, prideful and angry spirit or seek a kind, humble and powerful spirit? Is your anger kindled quickly, with little cause, and unleashed with fury, or is it controlled, strong, humble, gracious, and loving—that is, godly? Will you choose to invoke God's power to control anger or continue meekly allowing anger to control you? Will you communicate overtly or covertly? Will you avoid aggressive outbursts and covert conniving, and will you cease attempts to hide that which cannot be hidden? The time to invoke His unnatural power and embrace assertiveness and the true release of anger is now. Be quick to listen. Be slow to speak. Hold your tongue, engage your brain, and invoke your plan—be slow and considered in your response to anger. Act with courage: stand calm yet firm while treating others with humility, kindness, and respect. That is power. That is strength. That is a strong and healthy spirit. Do not permit anger's venom to poison your spirit and your relationships any longer. Be VerAegis.

Your Inner Spirit beyond Anger

Aesop tells a story of a mighty lion who is rudely awakened from his peaceful slumber when a tiny mouse stumbles across the lion's nose. The lion was enraged at the affront and was ready to devour the culprit, but the mouse, who was of rather large spirit, was able to convince the lion that showing mercy might be a win-win solution.

> A Lion was awakened from sleep by a Mouse running over his face. Rising up angrily, he caught him and was about to kill him, when the Mouse piteously entreated, saying: "If you would only spare my life, I would be sure to repay your kindness." The Lion laughed and let him go. It happened shortly after this that the Lion was caught by some hunters, who bound him by strong ropes to the

ground. The Mouse, recognizing his roar, came and gnawed the rope with his teeth, and set him free, exclaiming:

"You ridiculed the idea of my ever being able to help you, not expecting to receive from me any repayment of your favor; now you know that it is possible for even a Mouse to confer benefits on a Lion." (Townsend)

In his book *The 7 Habits of Highly Effective People*, Dr. Stephen Covey describes six paradigms of human interactions (Covey 1989). As illustrated in Figure 15, these paradigms or attitudes align well with the least and most mature responses illustrated in *VerAegis—Relationships* Figure 12 and are likewise based on Saxenian's maturity continuum.

Level of consideration

	Low	High
	Prideful and contemptuous	Humble and respectful
Engaging (High)	**Aggressive engagement (less mature):** • Seeks "I win whether or not you lose" outcomes • Seeks to be understood Covey's win-lose or win and perhaps lose-lose when pushed to extremes	**Assertive engagement (most mature):** • Seeks mutually beneficial outcomes: "I win and you win" • Seeks first to understand, and then to be understood Covey's win-win and win-win or no deal
Avoiding (Low)	**Passive-aggressive avoidance (least mature):** • Ultimately settles for "I lose, you lose" outcomes due to secretive agenda and avoidance • Does not seek to be understood nor to understand Covey's lose-lose	**Suppressive avoidance (less mature):** • May seek to understand but does not work to be understood • Does not stand up for convictions and beliefs; instead seeks to hide rather than address anger Covey's lose-win

(Level of courage — vertical axis, High to Low)

Figure 15: Characteristic responses to anger correlated to Dr. Stephen Covey's six paradigms of human interaction

Win-Win or No Deal

Do nothing from selfishness or empty conceit, but with humility of mind regard one another as more important than yourselves; do not merely look out for your own personal interests, but also for the interests of others.

Philippians 2:3-4

Win-Win or No Deal is the paradigm that is employed most often by pragmatic optimists willing to face the reality of each situation, confident that they will: prevail, put first things first, start with the end in mind, and not set arbitrary goals based on false hopes. Each situation is approached with open hearts and open minds, with conviction that each has something to offer, just as the mouse believed that it was possible for "even a Mouse to confer benefits on a Lion." When seeking solely a win-win outcome, all parties involved seek mutual benefit. But parties committed to win-win or no deal are committed both to attaining mutual benefit and to the idea that if reaching terms of mutual benefit is not impossible, involved parties can disagree in an agreeable manner and settle for no deal. They believe no deal is better than having one of the parties involved settle for a loss.

Abraham Lincoln captured this mature philosophy well when he stated, "I am not bound to win, but I am bound to be true. I am not bound to succeed, but I am bound to live by the light that I have. I must stand with anybody that stands right, and stand with him while he is right, and part with him when he goes wrong."

Bound to truth, relationships, and synergy; standing with those who also seek truth; and discerning when the evils of this world pull one astray, all the while holding true to one's convictions—this is the mission of a person who has the courage to stand for convictions and the consideration to stand with others, but whose loyalty and consideration do not come at the expense of values and principles. Such a person truly seeks win-win or no deal.

Win-Lose or Win

People who only think about winning don't necessarily want others to lose; they just want to win and let others fend for themselves. Whereas Abraham Lincoln said, "I am not bound to win," this person may state, "Winning is not everything—it's the only thing!" This is a common paradigm during negotiations. Rather than searching for a way for both parties to win, each party focuses on preserving its own interests. Often a facilitator can find common ground and reach compromise, and in some cases, synergy.

However, when one party is truly seeking a win for himself or herself, and a loss for others, synergy is not possible. This person aggressively seeks "I win and you lose" outcomes. He or she is often prideful and contemptuous, forcefully seeking to be understood without understanding. This person welcomes (and will take advantage of) a win-lose personality and ride the crazy train to lose-lose when confronted by a like-minded, strong-willed individual.

Lose-Win

Early in my career, my colleague Gerry and I were building a production line to manufacture what we called high-power laser "bars." This was a high-pressure environment. I noticed that Gerry was missing some of his commitments. I began to "document" his commitments more clearly, with due dates and expected outcomes, but to no avail. Gerry was a good friend and never refused to help, but I began to realize that he must be seriously overwhelmed. I felt myself becoming angry, thinking that he was making commitments to me but prioritizing commitments to others. One day, as my anger grew, I walked to Gerry's office ready for a confrontation. On my way there, I bumped into another colleague and friend, Masamichi, who was on his way back from Gerry's office. During our brief conversation, I learned that Masamichi had also requested a lot of Gerry, and Gerry was having difficulty delivering.

I was glad to gain understanding prior to meeting with Gerry. When Gerry and I sat down to discuss the slipping schedule, I was able to maintain my consideration and respect for him. It was clear to me that he wanted to help, but he had gotten himself into a no-win situation: he had too much to do, balancing too many requests from too many colleagues. He was frustrated but appeared to be suppressing his feelings out of a strong desire to maintain our friendship. He did not want to tell me that he could not deal with all the demands that were on his plate. I suggested to him that it would be much better for me to know that he would not meet a commitment rather than for him to overcommit and miss his deadlines. It was truly difficult for Gerry to begin to say, "No, I can't do that right now," but as we progressed in our careers, we both improved in our abilities to interact, multitask, and seek win-win outcomes rather than accept win-lose or lose-win.

Gerry was clearly suppressing frustration and avoiding confrontation. He had been assuming more and more responsibilities, supporting both production of existing products and development of new products. Like so many who make sacrifices with expectations that others will recognize their dedication, Gerry kept accepting more and more until he could no longer meet his commitments. At first, he settled for lose-win, but when he became overwhelmed, it quickly turned to lose-lose. Due to Gerry's high levels of consideration, we were able to work through the issues and eventually hired another engineer to ease his load.

When confronted by those who tend to be more closed in their communication, it is vital to create a safe environment to encourage open discussion—don't kill the messenger! Instead, let them know that it is better to notify you sooner that they cannot meet your requirements than to surprise you with news of delays and missed expectations when it is too late. Only with two-sided, open communication will you be able to achieve win-win. Due to high levels of consideration and a strong desire to avoid conflict, some may seek to understand but withhold information that is crucial to understanding; in other words, they will agree to most anything in order to help you succeed but will not inform you of the requirements for them to succeed. The selfless willingness to help is often seen as a panacea for aggressive people who are out there to win but ultimately leads to failure when a team member becomes overwhelmed and can no longer meet all of his or her commitments. When one member of a team fails, ultimately the team fails.

Lose-Lose

On the surface, it is hard to believe that people actually seek lose-lose outcomes; it does not appear to be grounded in logic and is often indicative of strong underlying emotions. Buried emotions are often accompanied by buried convictions, and unlike those who suppress anger, those seeking lose-lose do not act with consideration and do not seek to understand or acknowledge the feelings and convictions of others.

I remember a time when I was in fifth or sixth grade. My older sister, Dawne, was doing well in school, and for her birthday, my parents decided to take us all to her favorite restaurant as a reward dinner. While going about our afternoon chores, my father said something (aggressively) to Dawne about her "messy" cats. His bluntness hurt her feelings and wounded her pride. They argued briefly, and Dawne ran to her room in tears. Later, when it was time to leave for her favorite restaurant, Dawne refused to budge. She would not go. Dawne was willing to miss out on her favorite food and family time because she knew it would hurt my dad's feelings. This was a lose-lose situation. My dad had acted aggressively, and Dawne had fought briefly (meeting his aggressiveness head-on), but faced with his blustery, overwhelming "authority," she retreated to passive aggression. Both my father and Dawne acted with pride and contempt for each other. They started with open communication, but when overwhelmed by his aggressiveness, Dawne shut down. She had not yet learned how to preserve her self-worth and simultaneously be respectful of my father's demands—a difficult task for most adults and even tougher for a preteen who had yet to learn of win-win, assertiveness, or even lose-lose. Ultimately, my father and sister were able to work things out, and we went to dinner—a bit later than expected, but we made it nonetheless.

I did not understand how Dawne could be so mad that she would punish herself to hurt our dad's feelings. (I could not imagine foregoing food, especially good food, because I was mad.) It was not until many years later, and only after encountering many lose-lose adults, that I began to understand that buried beneath this prideful contempt were struggles for self-preservation in a twisted sort of logic: "If I can't win, neither can you; and if nobody wins, then I am not really a loser—so there!" Understanding the state of mind of those who find themselves stuck in a lose-lose paradigm is paramount when attempting to move them to a win-win outcome. It is a difficult task, and ultimately, one needs to create a safe environment for open communication. People who feel insecure will not be open, and to feel secure, we must believe we will be treated with respect and consideration.

We are all capable of being assertive at times; in those instances, we are able to avoid falling into the traps of our weaknesses. But in order to achieve mutual benefit (or even synergy), we must not only accept but seek to understand and value the differences between ourselves and others. Without difference, there can be no synergy. If in a brainstorming session there is only one idea, then there is need for only one brain and no more. Whether in a relationship or an organization, differences are vital to long-term mutual benefit. However, there are many forces that try to drive out differences and thus stifle creativity and any hope for synergy. Again, many (if not all) of the character traits of individuals and organizations can be organized into the quad charts that we have discussed regarding the maturity continuum. As you might have already guessed, high levels of courage and consideration are necessary to foster synergy (win-win), and low levels of both tend to kill possibilities (lose-lose).

In this analysis, it becomes clear that in order to be effective in a relationship of differences, one must manage thoughts, words, and actions. Ultimately, one must learn to pragmatically deploy high levels of courage and consideration in the face of emotional strain, refraining from reverting to character traits and behaviors that were perhaps learned early in life. We need others to be confident that we will treat them as they desire to be treated—only then will they feel safe. Finally, we need to embrace the fact that, though it may not come to us naturally, we have the strength to be calmly courageous and humbly considerate, in spite of being emotionally vested!

Self-Improvement: Put Up or Shut Up?

Physical fitness is not only one of the most important keys to a healthy body; it is the basis of dynamic and creative intellectual activity.

John F. Kennedy

The first wealth is health.

Ralph Waldo Emerson

Education is what remains after one has forgotten what one has learned in school.

Albert Einstein

I am always ready to learn although I do not always like being taught.

Winston Churchill

Live as if you were to die tomorrow. Learn as if you were to live forever.

Mahatma Gandhi

Even where sleep is concerned, too much is a bad thing.

Homer

I love to learn, but I don't necessarily enjoy the tests! Learning and thinking are to the mind as physical exercise is to the body; without it, our minds would decay. The second law of thermodynamics states that an isolated system naturally tends toward a less ordered state. Simply put, everything decays, and without maintenance, we decay more quickly. It is difficult to envision a world that defies entropy. Imagine we have a box of ordered black and white imagine a marbles, black separated from white in neatly interlaced rows. The only difference between the marbles is color. We close the lid and shake the box vigorously. What do you expect to see when you reopen the box? It now consists of randomly mixed black and white marbles. Replace the lid and shake the box. Will you be able to shake it in such a way that the marbles reorder themselves in neatly separated rows or perhaps a checkered pattern? It is inconceivable that the box of marbles will become more ordered without adding more energy and intelligence than is possible by mindless shaking.

Similarly, it is inconceivable that one can combat entropy in body and mind without intelligently maintaining both. I believe that everyone understands that change is inevitable. We either seek to improve or degrade; we do not remain the same. Do you know anyone who is identical to himself or herself twenty, ten, five, or even one year ago? When on a cross-country road trip, it is clear to most that we have a few choices: we add gas to our tank, change our oil when needed, or simply drive until we can go no farther. In the case of our automobile, the need for fuel and maintenance seems obvious (at least that we need to add fuel). Yet we all struggle with the concept that we need to consistently and intelligently feed and exercise our minds, bodies, and spirits.

> Suppose you come upon a man in the woods feverishly sawing down a tree. "You look exhausted!" you exclaim. "How long have you been at it?"
>
> "Over five hours," he replies, "and I am beat. This is hard."

"Maybe you could take a break for a few minutes and sharpen that saw. Then the work would go faster."

"No time," the man says emphatically. "I'm too busy sawing." (Covey)

Interesting—too busy sawing. Over five hours of sawing perhaps could have been reduced to two hours if he had taken a few minutes to sharpen his saw prior to taking the saw to the tree. Stephen Covey's seventh habit, "sharpen the saw," is based on the concept of balanced self-renewal; you are the saw.

We need to continually invest in our minds, bodies, and spirits. There are many simple activities that will help to combat entropy, but often these elusive self-improvement endeavors not only require self-discipline but also the help of others who we know will hold us accountable:

1. To exercise your mind: read, imagine—dream, plan, write, paint, sculpt, knit, create with wood, metal, or clay, and so on
2. To maintain your body: exercise, ensure proper nutrition, and sleep
3. To sharpen your spirit: commit to helping others, practice empathy, seek spiritual enlightenment, read and study, meditate and pray, seek friendly social interaction, worship with others during church services, and seek fellowship with like-minded friends.

To consistently exercise all these areas, we must first recognize the need to do so and then devote the time. It is all too easy to neglect many of these areas, but like turning away from evil, successful renewal requires us to say no to temptation. Your spirit is called to rise up, join with others, and shine. It cannot do so without continuous renewal—that is, self-improvement. Your body will inevitably give in to the grip of time, and it will do so more quickly without proper exercise, rest, and nutrition. Your mind will ultimately become feeble, disordered, and unreliable if allowed to wither rather than be kept fit by deliberate and regular mental and physical exercise. We are tempted to act as though this were not true, so we must have a plan:

Step 1: Recognize the pattern of temptation.

Step 2: Evaluate the motives behind your desires both to renew and to avoid renewal.

Step 3: Do not be intimidated or feel weak. Commit to renewal.

Step 4: Be prepared to do good in each of the three dimensions of renewal. Schedule time on your calendar and "just do it."

Step 5: Take time to ask God for help. He will often provide an escape route that leads to doing something good. Find an accountability partner for each of your endeavors—be strong for each other.

I met a woman in a management training class who had a plan. She liked to work out early in the morning before going to work, but she also liked her sleep. It was a constant tug-of-war: Work out? Sleep? When asked to share her strategy to consistently work out, she smiled and said, "Mom!" We were surprised, thinking her mom actually woke her up for her workouts. But she went on to explain that MOM stood for "mind over mattress." She called on MOM each morning to routinely keep up with her workouts.

In our society, we are bombarded with messages encouraging us to achieve physical well-being. Businesses and marketers seek to influence by appealing to our vanity. Exercise and nutrition gurus pummel us daily with new and improved programs, diets, and miracle foods. Yet in the face of all these "gimmicks," we are growing increasingly overweight. According to the American Heart Association, the overweight and obesity epidemic among both children and adults worsened by as much as five times from the early 1970s through 2010. Obesity among US adults has increased for men and women from 10.7 percent and 15.7 percent, respectively, during 1960 to 1962, to 34.4

percent and 36.1 percent during 2007 to 2010. A 2014 report released by the Overseas Development Institute concludes the following:

> The over-consumption of food...diets are changing wherever incomes are rising in the developing world, with a marked shift from cereals and tubers to meat, fats and sugar, as well as fruit and vegetables...coupled with lives that are increasingly sedentary, is producing large numbers of people who are overweight and obese—primarily in high-income countries, but also in emerging middle-income countries. Over one third of all adults across the world—1.46 billion people—are obese or overweight. Between 1980 and 2008, the numbers of people affected in the developing world more than tripled, from 250 million to 904 million. In high-income countries the numbers increased by 1.7 times over the same period. (Keats 2014)

Increased consumption combined with decreased physical activity has led to increased weight. Why do we overeat and underexercise? I believe part of the problem is that we too easily give in to temptations, which in turn disrupts our balance. Just as we require balance in relationships, contribution, and spirit, so too do we require balance in body, mind, and spirit. When we allow our minds and spirits to weaken, our resolve to care for our bodies weakens. We start to believe that just one more bite won't hurt, and then soon, it is one more helping and then an entire additional course. We become imbalanced and start to slide down an exceedingly slippery slope. Soon we join the ranks of the overweight or obese. To combat this increasing trend, we need to sharpen our saws on all three fronts (Figure 16).

How do you personally sharpen your saw in each of these important areas? Have you taken the time to manage your diet? Do you exercise regularly? Do you have any creative outlets, such as drawing, painting, writing, or photography? Do you strive to help others? Have you written your problems in the sand? Have you taken time to identify weaknesses that you would like to strengthen? Have you analyzed your motivations? Have you identified strengths that may become weaknesses? Have you investigated places of worship and religion? These questions can guide you to identify opportunities for self-improvement.

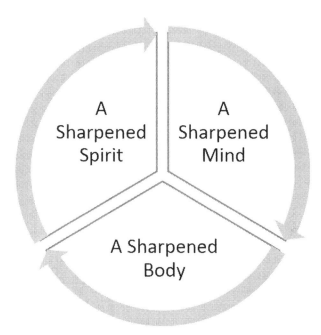

Figure 16: A sharpened spirit is necessary to a sharpened mind, and a sharpened mind is necessary to a sharpened body. The cycle continues.

Three fundamental requirements of successful self-improvement programs are enjoyment, balance, and discipline. Balance brings variety to your improvement activities, which may range from relaxation—vacationing, rest, writing, meditating, and even watching television—to recreation—sports, parties, games, and exercise. Take caution to not allow your routine to become boring. Mix it up to avoid the temptation to quit. When you are tempted, dig deep, pray, or meditate—whatever is necessary to find the strength and self-discipline to continue that which is important but not always fun. Also beware of the trap of "too much." Again, it requires discipline and strength to avoid this trap. Too much of anything is not good and will throw off your balance (Figure 17).

	Fun	Not fun
Important	**Balanced:** • Vacationing • Rest and relaxation • Television • Social interaction, sports, and parties • Games • Mental, physical, and spiritual workouts Varying activities is as key to successful rejuvenation as an accountability partner. Mix up your routine. Invest in body, mind, and spirit.	**Routine:** • Physical workout • Mental workout • Spiritual workout Often our improvement efforts become "routine," losing their appeal. By adding variety, we can move these workouts back to the fun and important quadrant, but at times we need to dig deep to find the self-discipline necessary to do that which is important but not always fun.
Not important	**Too much:** • Vacationing • Rest and relaxation • Television • Social interaction, sports, and parties • Games • Mental, physical, and spiritual workouts Too much of anything is bad. The excess becomes a detriment. When we become obsessed with any one area of our self-improvement, the other areas suffer, and ultimately we pay the price.	**Quid pro quo:** The only reason I find to engage in an improvement activity that is both not important to you and not fun is that the activity is nonetheless important to someone who is important to you. When you participate in an improvement activity with someone you care for, the relationship improves and hopefully the activity will become fun.

Figure 17: To be effective, self-improvement activities require discipline. Balance and variety are required for longevity.

Variety is the spice of life and will improve the likelihood that you enjoy self-improvement activities. It is also beneficial to blend such activities into your everyday life, making them natural rather than special events. For your mind, read a bit each day. Buy a Kindle or other e-reader, or visit your library weekly to find a book or two. Spend time each week, perhaps in the morning before work or in the evenings before bed, doing puzzles and games like crosswords, sudoku, or solitaire—all also available on e-readers. Play board games, such as Pictionary, Cranium, Hedbanz, and many, many more, with family and friends to exercise your mind and spirit through social interaction. Play card games like cribbage, hearts, spades, gin rummy, or tripoli; Hoyle has published several wonderful books with the rules for hundreds of card and dice games, many of which are available at Amazon.com. Engage in hobbies that you find interesting and fun—perhaps activities that you have always wanted to try but never gotten around to. Learn to write, draw, paint, sculpt, work wood, embroider, knit, or play an instrument. Choose a few different hobbies to keep them fresh.

How are you and your family members doing against these standards? According to the CDC, data from a National Health Interview Survey indicates that nearly 40 percent of adults aged twenty-five to fifty-four reported fewer than seven hours of sleep per day, and only 31 percent of high school students reported getting at least eight hours of sleep on a typical school night. This means that nearly 70 percent of teenagers are sleep deprived. Researchers found insufficient sleep amongst teenagers to be associated to a number of unhealthy activities: drinking soda one or more times per day; not participating in sixty minutes of physical activity five or more days per week; using computers three or more hours per day; cigarette, alcohol and/or marijuana use; sexual activity; depression.

The promotion of sound sleep habits needs to be a priority. The data is clear: good sleep is rare. A routine is necessary to increase your chances of sleeping well. Try to go to bed and rise at fairly consistent hours each day. Benjamin Franklin knew the value of doing this well, having stated, "Early to bed and early to rise makes a man healthy, wealthy and wise." Ensure your bedroom is a quiet, dark and relaxing environment. Avoid large meals, alcohol, and caffeine near bedtime.

You should have your last meal or snack two to three hours before your regular bedtime. Avoid nicotine. Employ relaxation and deep-breathing techniques away from bright lights before going to sleep. If you must nap during the day, keep it to no more than twenty minutes. Try reading a relaxing book if you cannot sleep. Avoid computers, televisions, and other backlit electronics, because the light emitted by the screens activates the brain.

Eat right. Maintain a healthy diet. Minimize consumption of highly processed and fast foods. Eat three to five small meals rather than two to three big meals per day. Balance your diet across the food groups and minimize "empty carbs," composed of highly processed flours and starches. Eat plenty of fresh vegetables and fruit. Drink plenty of water. Avoid refined sugar and corn syrup. The per capita consumption of sugar has risen in the United States over the past two hundred years from 10 to 12 pounds in the 1800s to 100 to 150 pounds in the 2000s. According to Mehmet Oz, when slightly overweight people consume sugar, on average 60 percent is metabolized for immediate energy, 5 percent is stored as ready energy, and 35 percent is converted to fat and stored for "long-term" energy (if we ever get to a fat-burning mode). He notes further that 50 percent of the sugar consumed today comes from high-fructose corn syrup in foods like soft drinks, juices, and salad dressings (Oz). According to Gerry Curatola D.D.S., much of the increased sugar consumption has occurred in the past few decades, having increased to around 26 pounds per capita in the 1980s: "Since 1983, sugar consumption has been steadily increasing every year by an average of 28 percent, fueling an epidemic of obesity, dental disease, diabetes and other health problems" (Curatola).

> **Don't you realize that your body is the temple of the Holy Spirit, who lives in you and was given to you by God? You do not belong to yourself, for God bought you with a high price. So you must honor God with your body.**
>
> 1 Corinthians 6:19–20 (NLT)

With adequate sleep and a proper diet, we stand a much better chance to maintain an exercise routine. The benefits of exercise are well known and go far beyond increased aerobic capacity and muscle strength. Exercise certainly can improve physiques, reduce waistlines, and add years to lives, but those are not the benefits that motivate most people to maintain exercise routines. Most people who exercise regularly do so because they have developed a routine that they enjoy and that makes them feel good; they are more energetic during the day, sleep better, and think more clearly. They are in good spirits! Best of all, they achieve these benefits without spending excessive hours pumping weights or running mile after mile. Simply devoting thirty minutes a day (or two fifteen-minute sessions a day) five times a week will ease stress and anxiety, sharpen brainpower, boost your energy, improve your mood, lift your self-esteem and improve your spirit. Exercise releases endorphins and hormones that elevate your spirit by relieving stress and promoting a sense of well-being.

If exercise is new to you, start with short walks through the neighborhood, gradually increasing speed and distance as you feel better. You should be able to carry on a conversation while walking, but perhaps not easily sing a song. If golf is a hobby, try walking the course. Ride bikes—slowly and for short distances at first but gradually increase both speed and distance. I like to use a heart monitor when I work out; this may help some but be a distraction to others. As your energy improves, balance your workouts with a combination of aerobic activities (e.g., calisthenics, running, cycling, and swimming) to strengthen your heart and lungs; strength training (e.g., weight training, push-ups, sit-ups, and resistance exercises) to build muscle and bone mass, improve balance, and combat frailty; and flexibility exercises (e.g., stretching and yoga) to help prevent injury, enhance your range of motion, and reduce strain on joints due to tight and unbalanced muscles. Mixing aerobic with strength and flexibility exercises not only addresses your entire body but also keeps your workouts fresh and enjoyable. Enjoyable workouts lead to a fresh mind. A fresh mind to a happy spirit and an improved commitment to helping others, seeking enlightenment and pursuing knowledge.

Be of Good Spirit: You Are in Good Company

We get older, and we forget that we have to carve a little time out to feel good in your body, in your head, and in your spirit.

Estelle Swaray

Where ever the spirit of Christ is known, there is much of good will, of mutual respect, of love and appreciation and kindness.

Gordon B. Hinckley

Don't follow any advice, no matter how good, until you feel as deeply in your spirit as you think in your mind that the counsel is wise.

Joan Rivers

The spirit and determination of the people to chart their own destiny is the greatest power for good in human affairs.

Matt Blunt

If you be faithful, you will have that honor that comes from God: His Spirit will say in your hearts, "Well done, good and faithful servants."

Adam Clarke

Be of good spirit. We all will enjoy good times and suffer through bad. How we respond to each moment is a reflection of our inner spirit. Like Billy Moore and Eve, we will be tempted to do wrong, and at times, we will give in to that temptation. Like Adam, we may give in to peer pressure and falter when we should be strong enough to steer our loved ones from falling to temptation. But by maintaining a relationship with a higher authority, like Joni Eareckson Tada, we can summon the strength to fight through all trials and tribulations. With His help, we learn to ground our actions in lasting principles rather than fleeting fads and ungrounded social values. By studying His word, we learn to how ensure our values are similarly grounded in unchanging principles.

We will always be tempted. We will face trials and tribulations, but we need not do it alone. We will be confused about what we are meant to do. Like Saul and the prodigal son, we may embark down the wrong path. Like the older brother and Saul's companions on the road to Damascus, pride and the ways of humans may blind us to the true path that is laid before us. Take heart: God will carry us when we are weak. We can each hear our calling and strive to be of service to others, and God will be with us in all that we do. He will lend his supernatural strengths to fortify our weaknesses. He will give us the power to be humble, to love others as we love ourselves, and to practice empathy. He will give us the will to accept our responsibility to choose our response to emotions rather than be controlled by them.

We are called to invoke God's anger and reject human anger. To do so, we must continually sharpen our saws. A healthy diet, proper sleep, and exercise serve to lift our spirits. Devoting our time to read spiritual literature, pray, meditate, and interact with others as they travel along their spiritual paths will increase our spiritual strength and knowledge. Our spirits are the core of our true beings. Relationships and contributions suffer if we allow our spirits to become ill. Contrarily, even in our darkest moments, our spirits are a connection to a source of unending energy that, when drawn upon, enables us to face anything—even the killing fields of Sudan or crippling injury or a near-death experience due to severe physical trauma.

Darkness comes. In the middle of it, the future looks blank. The temptation to quit is huge. Don't. You are in good company…You will argue with yourself that there is no way forward. But with God, nothing is impossible. He has more ropes and ladders and tunnels out of pits than you can conceive. Wait. Pray without ceasing. Hope.

John Piper

Be VerAegis—Live beyond Your Comfort Zone

Touch a Life:

Trust is to human relationships what faith is to gospel living. It is the beginning place, the foundation upon which more can be built. Where trust is, love can flourish.

Barbara Smith

Friendship is unnecessary, like philosophy, like art...It has no survival value; rather it is one of those things that give value to survival.

C. S. Lewis

Inspire a Contribution:

Only those who have learned the power of sincere and selfless contribution experience life's deepest joy: true fulfillment.

Tony Robbins

When you cease to make a contribution, you begin to die.

Eleanor Roosevelt

Ignite a Spirit:

I like your Christ; I do not like your Christians. Your Christians are so unlike your Christ.

Mahatma Gandhi

In everyone's life, at some time, our inner fire goes out. It is then burst into flame by an encounter with another human being. We should all be thankful for those people who rekindle the inner spirit.

Albert Schweitzer

Relationships. Contribution. Spirit. Epiphany: God is interested and involved in all aspects of our lives—our relationships; our contributions, including our chosen "jobs"; and especially our spirits. He cares about how we approach life, and in our approach, He will find the presence or lack of "good works." Our contributions will be evaluated. He knows our hearts. The results of our contributions are directly linked not only to the nature of our tasks but also to the spirit with which we achieve our goals. In turn, the manner by which we accomplish our tasks directly influences our relationships, and our relationships influence our spirits. It is a closed and challenging but potentially beautiful cycle.

I was honored one Monday morning at work by my good friend and colleague, Hailong Zhou. He and his wife, Ann, live in Shanghai, China, but were visiting for work in Vancouver, Washington. They had joined my family and me for dinner over the weekend, and Hailong greeted me cheerily Monday morning: "Jim, you are a Christian? I ask because you are different from other Christians I have met. They tell me, 'Nonbelievers will go to hell when the judgment date comes, but the believers will rise to heaven.' They seem to threaten me, and I don't want anything to do with them. You are kind. Your kids are wonderful. When we were at your home, Teagan and Jimmy showed us around and were kind hosts. Jimmy showed us his presentation about China. He was very respectful. Both Jimmy and Teagan cleared their dishes after dinner! In China, most kids are overly indulged and simply wait for their mom or grandma to serve them. I think I am interested in learning more about your Christianity!"

We should all take care in how we act toward others. If it is with good intent that believers speak of their faith to others, why do so with an ill spirit? Remember the words of Jesus's apostles Paul and Timothy regarding Christians in general and especially church leaders. Paul wrote to members of the Colossian and Thessalonian churches, "Be wise in the way you act toward outsiders; make the most of every opportunity. Let your conversation be always full of grace, seasoned

251

with salt, so that you may know how to answer everyone" (Col. 4:5–6 [NIV]), and "You should mind your own business and work with your hands, just as we told you, so that your daily life may win the respect of outsiders" (Thess. 4:11–12 [NIV]).

Timothy documented also that churchgoers, especially leaders, need to heed their actions: "He must manage his own family well and see that his children obey him, and he must do so in a manner worthy of full respect. (If anyone does not know how to manage his own family, how can he take care of God's church?)...He must also have a good reputation with outsiders, so that he will not fall into disgrace and into the devil's trap" (1 Tim. 3:4-7 [NIV]).

Jesus led by example and commissioned all to live life as role models for others. When he faced crucifixion, he prayed passionately to his Father. His painful display of devotion and faith stands as an example of how we are to submit to God's will rather than cling to our own: "He told them, 'My soul is crushed with grief to the point of death. Stay here and keep watch with me.' He went on a little farther and bowed with his face to the ground, praying, 'My Father! If it is possible, let this cup of suffering be taken away from me. Yet I want your will to be done, not mine'" (Matt. 26:38–39 [NLT]).

During the last supper, Jesus paused and began to clean the feet of his disciples. His message was threefold. The cleansing of feet symbolized that first, his death by crucifixion would cleanse us of our sins; second, leaders are no greater than their followers; and third, we are blessed through our actions, not merely our knowledge: "I have set you an example that you should do as I have done for you. Very truly I tell you, no servant is greater than his master, nor is a messenger greater than the one who sent him. Now that you know these things, you will be blessed if you do them" (John 13:15–17 [NIV]).

After sending Judas away from the supper so Judas could betray Jesus to his persecutors, Jesus turned to the rest of his disciples and told them he would be with them only a little longer, and that where he was going, they could not immediately follow. He left them with a new command: "A new command I give you: Love one another. As I have loved you, so you must love one another. By this everyone will know that you are my disciples, if you love one another" (John 13:34–35 [NIV]).

Jesus expressed his love for us, and as he prepared to fulfill his destiny on the cross, he encouraged us to remain in his love by keeping his commands. By doing so, we will be judged righteous by him, and our joy will be complete. True joy comes from meaning, and meaning comes to us through adherence to his plan.

> As the Father has loved me, so have I loved you. Now remain in my love. If you keep my commands, you will remain in my love, just as I have kept my Father's commands and remain in his love. I have told you this so that my joy may be in you and that your joy may be complete. My command is this: Love each other as I have loved you. Greater love has no one than this: to lay down one's life for one's friends. You are my friends if you do what I command. I no longer call you servants, because a servant does not know his master's business. Instead, I have called you friends, for everything that I learned from my Father I have made known to you. (John 15:9–15 [NIV])

Be of good spirit in all that you do. Even when angered, Jesus did not sin. When your task is difficult, attack it with prayer, vim, vigor, and enthusiasm. Don't be tempted to segregate your life into well-confined compartments. Rather, be whole and consistent in all aspects. Act with integrity, courage, and consideration. With an open heart, commit all that you do to the Lord; He will open your mind to see His plans, which will direct your way. He is pleased when you follow His plans, and in His pleasure, He eases your path. He humbles your spirit, balancing courage with consideration, improving relationships, and blessing contributions. He relieves the burden imposed by others' anger and lifts your spirit. In turn, you grow stronger and recommit to the Lord. Your view of the world thus develops. This wonderful cycle continues, and you are strengthened to stave off future temptations (Figure 18): "Trust in the Lord with all your heart, and lean not on your own understanding; in all your ways acknowledge Him, and He shall direct your paths" (Prov. 3:5–6 [NKJV]).

See

Renew your spirit: Commit to the Lord whatever you do.

Attitude (how you see) shapes how you plan and do.

Plan

In your heart He will establish your plans.

How you plan shapes what you do. Open hearts lead to open minds and creative plans. Creative plans lead to energetic execution.

When you please the Lord with what you do, He makes even your enemies to be at peace with you.

What you get influences your attitude (how you see).

With open hearts, the Lord directs your way. Through Him all things are possible.

How you do influences what you get.

Get

Do

Figure 18: The spiritual renewal cycle

We are called to make a difference; we are not called to do it alone. There may be times when you feel alone, but even if you pull away from God, He will not abandon you. He is pained when you leave, but He will remain loyal and loving. God knows your heart and the person you could be—the person you will be. He is there to help you, and He has designed you to be in relationships, contribute to the world, and grow in spirit. He desires that you help others and that others help you. It need not be more complicated. I enjoy a parable recited by Ravi Zacharias, which I will paraphrase here:

The only son of a rich art collector passed a poor beggar man each day on his way to school. Being a kind young man, he would often stop to share a few words and perhaps a bit of his lunch. The beggar man cherished the companionship and was amazed at the kindness of this young boy. Then one day the boy didn't show, nor the next, and a few more to follow. Finally, the beggar man made his way to the gate of the boy's home and inquired of the boy's well-being to the grounds keeper. The grounds keeper lowered his head and informed the beggar man that the young boy had lost his battle to a sudden and severe illness.

The beggar man was distraught, but he knew that the pain he felt must pale in comparison to that of the boy's father. Using what little he had, the beggar man purchased some paper, colored pencils, and crayons and created from memory a portrait of his young friend. Having completed the portrait, he made his way to the rich art collector's house again. He called to the grounds keeper and presented the portrait, requesting that he give it to the lad's grieving father. The grounds keeper was none too impressed with the drawing, but decided that to pass it along would do no harm.

Years later, news of the rich art collector's passing and the pending auction of his entire art collection reached the beggar man. The beggar man begged and bartered to obtain a bath and suitable clothing to attend the auction. He arrived early to view the artwork, and to his amazement, he found his portrait of the young boy hanging prominently among the priceless works. It was not long before the auctioneer pounded his gavel upon his podium. When the crowd quieted, he welcomed them and announced that the master had left two rules to guide the auction. The first rule was that bidding was to begin with the crayon-and-pencil portrait of his son—and so let the bidding begin. The auctioneer and the beggar man waited. No bids. They continued to wait...no bids. Finally, the beggar man reached into his pocket, counted his change, and bid all he had. The auctioneer shouted, "Going once, twice, three times, sold!" The beggar man was pleased and stepped forward to make payment. The auctioneer smiled and said, "Now for the second rule: whoever claimed the son wins the entirety of the father's collection!"

Simple. Elegant. Embrace the son; gain the father. Do you believe there is a creator? Have you looked at the miracle of life and concluded that it is not a random accident? Or do you cling to the improbable belief that thought, love, imagination, conscience, free will, self-awareness, and life itself have spawned from inanimate material without intelligent guidance? Consider this: to win a state lottery, you have about one chance in ten million (10^7). The odds of winning the state lottery every single week of your life, from age eighteen to age ninety-nine, is 1 in $4.6 \times 10^{29,120}$. The odds of winning the state lottery every week consecutively for eighty years are more likely than those of the spontaneous generation of just the proteins of an amoeba (Eastman)! Stop grasping at lotteries. Abandon the hopeless faith in spontaneous generation of the universe, the earth, and life itself. You are not the descendent of an amoeba or a worm but the descendent of a great and loving god. Jesus has won the lottery for you. Embrace the Son; gain the Father!

Dare to stretch beyond your current comfort zone. Learn to live a balanced, fulfilled life. Escalate desired results. To be VerAegis (Vĕr-ā-jis) represents a way of life that leads to balance in three critical areas: relationships, contribution, and spirit. Ultimately, with balance comes the ability to significantly expand one's comfort zone and masterfully orchestrate one's legacy.

The term *VerAegis* is derived from *veracity* and *aegis*, while invoking the essence of courage. Courage and veracity entail truth, honor, integrity, and adherence to principles such as the golden rule. Aegis relates to our spiritual connection with and protection from a higher authority; and by extension, our ability to shield others by receiving and extending God's mercy.

As for God, His way is perfect;

The word of the LORD is proven;

He is a shield to all who trust in Him.

(2 Sam. 22:31 [NKJV])

…"With men this is impossible,

but with God all things are possible."

(Matt. 19:26 [NKJV])

Veracity: His way is perfect, and His word is proven. Aegis: He is a shield to all who trust Him. Courage: Through Him, all things are possible. In times of stress, heartache, and pain we need to be courageous realizing how we respond (with or without Him) is our choice.

Dare to be VerAegis—courageous yet humble and considerate. Dare to live life to its fullest. Join Him. Hear, understand, and follow His plan to direct your lasting legacy—His path, not yours. It's so simple, yet so difficult. We are here to build relationships, contribute, and grow in spirit through our relationship with Christ.

Relationships: United we are strong; divided we are weak. Just as "iron sharpens iron," relationships are fundamental to realizing our full potential. Embrace the son; gain the father, and choose to live in a manner that touches others. What better way to orchestrate a legacy?

Contribution: Do good things. Our contribution is fundamental to our well-being. By accepting His way (not ours), we can make a difference in a manner that inspires others to emulate us. What better way to forge a legacy? "Jesus looked at them and said to them, 'With men this is impossible, but with God all things are possible'" (Matt. 19:26 [NKJV]).

Spirit: A vibrant spirit is vital to relationships, success, and the lasting value of your contribution. We were made to be a beacon,

257

transmitting the light of Jesus into this world. "Go therefore and make disciples of all the nations, baptizing them in the name of the Father and of the Son and of the Holy Spirit, teaching them to observe all things that I have commanded you; and lo, I am with you always, *even* to the end of the age. Amen." (Matt. 28:19-20 [NKJV]) Will you accept his light and let him kindle your spirit so that you can ignite another? What better way to inspire a legacy?

Balance in life is like the three legs of a stool: to remain sturdy and balanced, each leg must contribute equally. Thus, relationships, contribution, and spirit all need to be firm and strong. Yet how do we hold it all together? Visualize the simple three-legged stool, and remember that there is a fourth component: the seat. The seat holds the legs together; consider it your center. What have you placed in the center of your life? What or who is your idol? Do you worship money, fame and notoriety, and the power of getting things done? Or do you worship peace, intimacy, fun, or perhaps your family? Any of these aspirations may be healthy when appropriately balanced, but when placed at the core of your being, it will not be long before this inner desire warps and grows out of proportion, damaging your spirit, relationships, contribution, or all three. To remain balanced with integrity and fortitude, we need the seat to hold three strong legs together: fulfilling relationships, meaningful contributions, and a healthy spirit. The seat adds balance and stability, dispersing the weight of our lives evenly. There is only one seat that cannot be corrupted—only one that can achieve our desired result. Evil will continually endeavor to convince you otherwise, but He is the only center—the only noble, everlasting desire that cannot be warped by temptation.

Son

Father

Spirit

God

Relationships

Contribution

Spirit

Figure 19: With God as our center we can weather any storm. The Father experienced our fragility through the son who saved us by dying in our place. Together with the Spirit, they help us to forge powerful relationships, to purposefully contribute and to touch the lives of others.

We all live, die, and leave a legacy. Will your lasting legacy be the one you desire? Will you nurture your relationships and follow your calling? Will you approach life as a good-spirited individual? Will you embrace the Son and gain the Father? Will you be VerAegis? Dare—live beyond your comfort zone—orchestrate your legacy!

Afterword

Though one may be overpowered, two can defend themselves. A cord of three strands is not quickly broken.

Ecclesiastes 4:12 (NIV)

Once again, visualize life as a three-legged stool. One leg represents the health of your relationships; the next, the impact of your contributions (negative or positive); and the final, the health of your spirit. We just spent time understanding the importance of our spirit to our overall effectiveness and learning that how we travel through life has a lasting impact on our relationships and our contribution. We learned that by tapping into an infinite source of strength, wisdom, and love, we can kindle our spirit and perhaps ignite the spirits of others, inspiring them to "pay it forward." What better way is there to leave a legacy?

If you have not already read books 1 and 2, we reviewed the value of our relationships and our contribution.

- o Book 1 *VerAegis—Relationships*: Live your life. Touch another.
- o Book 2 *VerAegis—Contribution*: Make a difference. Inspire another.
- o Book 3 *VerAegis—Spirit*: Kindle your spirit. Ignite another.

VerAegis—The Legacy Series illuminates these three strands that are interwoven throughout our lives. We each *will* leave a legacy; and it is within our power and responsibility to leave the legacy we desire. I hope you enjoyed reading *VerAegis—Spirit*. I hope you marked it up and will refer back to it as you strive to balance your spirit with your relationships and your contribution. I also hope that if you have not already read books 1 and 2, you will find them to be every bit as fulfilling. As a rope of three interwoven strands is not easily broken, there is synergy between these three books. Read on. Ignite your destiny.

Acknowledgements

- Sheri, Teagan, and Jimmy
- My dad (may he rest in peace), mom, stepdad, sisters, nieces, nephews, and all my in-laws
- Friends, colleagues, teachers, professors, and mentors

Thank you for your love and support. You have meant so much to me and have taught me more than I can express. Please accept my apologies for all the times I have fallen short of the ideals described in this book! I hope that by writing this book, I will have improved and expanded my comfort zone as I continue my efforts to become more effective and live a more balanced life.

Sheri, Teagan, Dawne, Mom, George, Jimmy, and McKenna, thank you for reading, editing, and suggesting improvements. *VerAegis* is better as a result.

Maria, and Savannah, thank you for great input during the editing process, and much appreciation to the Create Space team for all your help moving VerAegis through the editing and publishing process.

Pastor Bill Heck, thank you for your sage counsel, patience, and passion, and for using your gift of teaching.

Pastors Bill Bucholtz of Family Community Church and Matt Hannon of New Heights Church, thank you for your passion and for using your God-given talents to teach.

Bruce Crawford, of Red Tail Woodworks, thank you for the inlay design of the sun and the photo of the three-legged stool.

Please note, those whom I acknowledge do not necessarily agree with all the concepts contained within *VerAegis*.

Bibliography

Aguilar, Franci J., and Arvind Bhambi. "Johnson and Johnson (A)." Harvard Business School 384–053: 1983.

Allen, David. Getting Things Done: The Art of Stress-Free Productivity. New York, New York: Penguin Books, 2002.

American Heart Association. "Overweight and Obesity (Statistical Fact Sheet, 2013 update)." Heart.org. 2013. Accessed January 2014. http://www.heart.org/idc/groups/heart-public/@wcm/@sop/@smd/documents/downloadable/ucm_319588.pdf.

Andretti, Mario, "Mario Andretti Quotes." Accessed 2015 http://www.brainyquote.com/quotes/quotes/m/marioandre130613.html

Angelou, Maya. "Maya Angelou Quotes." Accessed 2014 http://www.brainyquote.com/quotes/authors/m/maya_angelou.html.

Anthony, Marc. "Marc Anthony Quotes." Accessed 2013 http://www.brainyquote.com/quotes/authors/m/marc_anthony.html.

Aristotle. "Aristotle Qutoes." Accessed November 2013. http://www.brainyquote.com/quotes/authors/a/aristotle.html.

AutCom: Autism National Committee. "How to Think-and How Not to Think-About the Brain." Accessed November 2013. http://www.autcom.org/articles/HowToThink.html.

Bach, Richard. "Richard Bach Quotes." Accessed 2014 http://www.brainyquote.com/quotes/authors/r/richard_bach.html.

Bada, Jeffrey L., and Antonio Lazcano. "Stanley L. Miller 1930–2007; A Biographical Memoir." National Academy of Sciences on Line. 2012. Accessed 2014. http://www.nasonline.org/publications/biographical-memoirs/memoir-pdfs/miller-stanley.pdf.

Barton, Bruce. "Bruce Barton Quotes." Accessed 2014 http://www.brainyquote.com/quotes/authors/b/bruce_barton.html.

Beecher, Henry Ward. "Henry Ward Beecher Quotes." 2001–2013. Accessed October 2013. Henry Ward Beecher.

Bergland, Richard. The Fabric of the Mind. 1985. New York: Viking Penguin.

Berra, Yogi. "Yogi Berra Quotes." Accessed September 2013.
http://www.brainyquote.com/quotes/.

Biblica. New International Version (NIV). Vers. New International Version. Biblica.
Accessed 2013/2014. https://www.biblegateway.com/versions/New-
International-Version-NIV-Bible/.

Bloom, Orlando. "Orlando Bloom Quotes." 2001–2013. Accessed October 2013.
http://www.brainyquote.com/quotes/topics/topic_marriage2.html#cVScf
z361pQlTmkQ.99.

Boa, Kenneth, and Larry Moody. I'm Glad You Asked. Wheaton, IL: Victor Books, SP
Publications, 1982.

Bono, Edward de. "Six Thinking Hats." Accessed 2013
http://www.debonogroup.com/six_thinking_hats.php.

Boorstin, Daniel J. "Daniel J. Boorstin Quotes." 2001–2013. Accessed October 2013.
http://www.brainyquote.com/quotes/quotes/d/danieljbo175243.html.

Bruyere, Jean de la. "Jean de la Bruyere Quote." Accessed 2014
http://www.brainyquote.com/quotes/quotes/j/jeandelabr402511.html.

Burns, John W., Phillip Quartana, Weley Gilliam, Erika Gray, Carla Nappi Justin
Matsuura, Brandy Wolfe, and Kenneth Lofland. "Effects of anger
suppression on pain severity and pain behaviors among chronic pain
patients: Evaluation of an ironic process model." September 27, 2008.
Accessed January 2014. http://psycnet.apa.org/journals/hea/27/5/645/.

Calcaterra, Nicholas Berne. "Transactional Analysis." 1999–2013.
http://www.ericberne.com/transactional-analysis/.

Carnette, Jamal. "Investing Commentary: Here's Why Warren Buffett's Favorite
Stock is Struggling." September 14, 2014.
http://www.fool.com/investing/general/2014/09/14/heres-why-warren-
buffetts-favorite-stock-is-strugg.aspx.

Carter, Dr. Les. The Anger Trap. San Francisco: Jossey-Bass, 2003.

Carter, Dr. Les, and Frank Minirth, M.D. The Anger Workbook. Nashville,
Tennessee: Thomas Nelson, Inc., 1993.

The Case For Christ (Full Documentary). Directed by Lee Strobel, 2007.

CDC Office of the Associate Director for Communication, Digital Media Branch,
Division of Public Affairs. "Insufficient Sleep Is a Public Health Epidemic."
January 13, 2014. Accessed July 2014.
http://www.cdc.gov/features/dssleep/.

Churchill, Winston. "Winston Churchill Quotes." Accessed October 2013.
http://www.brainyquote.com/quotes/authors/w/winston_churchill.html.

"Coca-Cola: Our Company (Mission, Vison and Values)." Accessed 2014
http://www.coca-colacompany.com/our-company/mission-
vision-values.

Collins, James C., and Jerry I. Porras. Built to Last. New York, New York:
HarperCollins Publishers, Inc., 1994.

Collins, Jim. Good to Great. Harper Collins, 2001.

"Confronting the Unsustainable Growth of Welfare Entitlements." June, 2010.
http://www.heritage.org/research/reports/2010/06/confronting-the-
unsustainable-growth-of-welfare-entitlements-principles-of-reform-and-
the-next-steps.

Covey, Steven R. "7 Habits of Highly Effective People Training Material."

———.The Seven Habits of Highly Effective People. New York, NY: Simon and
Schuster, 1989.

Cox, Peter. "The Controversy of the Shack." June 19, 2009. Accessed October 11,
2013. http://www.examiner.com/article/the-controversy-of-the-shack.

Crick, Francis. Life Itself: Its Origin and Nature. London: Future, 1982.

Curatoloa, Gerry. "Carbohydrates." Accessed July 2014.
http://www.sharecare.com/health/carbohydrates/sugar-consume-every-
year

Damasio, Antonio. Descartes' Error: Emotion, Reason and the Human Brain. New
York: Penguin, 1994.

de Bono, Edward. Lateral Thinking (Creativity Step by Step). New York, Philadelphia,
St. Louis, San Francisco, London, Singapore, Sydney, Tokyo, Toronto:
Harper & Row Publishers, 1970.

———. Six Thinking Hats. Boston, New York, London: Little, Brown and Company,
1985.

———. Six Thinking Hats. Boston, New York, London: Little, Bown and Company,
1999.

Derks, Eske M., James J. Hudziak, and Dorret I. Boomsma. "Why More Boys Than
Girls with ADHD Recieve Treatment." Dutch Twin Register. Accessed 2014
http://www.tweelingenregister.org/publicaties/wetenschappelijke-
publicaties/?no_cache=1&tx_sevenpack_pi1%5Bsearch%5D%5Brule%5D=
AND&tx_sevenpack_pi1%5Bsearch%5D%5Bsep%5D=space&tx_sevenpack

_pi1%5Byear%5D=2007&tx_sevenpack_pi1%5Bshow_uid%5D=160&cHash
=79f1eee.

Dictionary.com. "Pharisees." Accessed March 2014.
http://dictionary.reference.com/browse/Pharisees?s=t.

Drucker, Peter. "Peter Drucker Quotes." Accessed 2014
http://www.brainyquote.com/quotes/authors/p/peter_drucker.html.

Eastman, M.D., Mark, and Chuck Missler. "The Origin of Life and the Suppression of
Truth." Accessed 2014. http://the_wordbride.tripod.com/origin.html.

Eastwood, Clint. "Clint Eastwood Quotes." Accessed 2013.
http://www.brainyquote.com/quotes/authors/c/clint_eastwood.html

Edwards, Betty. The New Drawing on the Right Side of the Brain. Penguin Putnam
Inc., 1999.

Eggerichs, Dr. Emerson. "Love and Respect Home Page." Accessed September
2013. http://loveandrespect.com/.

Eggerichs, Dr. Emerson. Love & Respect Small Group Discussion Guide. Grand
Rapids: Love and Respect Ministries 2006.

Eisenhower, Dwight D. "Dwight D. Eisenhower Quotes" Accessed 2015
http://www.brainyquote.com/quotes/quotes/d/dwightdei149102.html

Einstein, Albert. "Albert Einstein Quotes." Accessed 2013.
http://www.brainyquote.com/quotes/authors/a/albert_einstein_2.html.

Emerson, Ralph Waldo. "BrainyQuote." Accessed November 2013.
http://www.brainyquote.com/quotes/authors/r/ralph_waldo_emerson.ht
ml.

"Emeth." Accessed October 2013. http://en.wikipedia.org/wiki/Emeth.

"Ephesians 2:10 (New International Version)." Accessed October 2013.
http://www.biblegateway.com/passage/?search=Ephesians+2:10&version
=NIV.

Epicurus. "Epicurus Quotes." Accessed January 2014.
http://www.brainyquote.com/quotes/authors/e/epicurus.html.

"Face Illusions." Accessed 2013. http://brainden.com/optical-illusions.htm.

Ford, Henry. "Henry Ford Quotes."
http://www.brainyquote.com/quotes/authors/h/henry_ford.html.

Fox News Insider. "Dr. Ben Carson Says Mayme White Miller Poem...Had Lasting
Impact on Him." March 26, 2013. Accessed March 19, 2014.

http://foxnewsinsider.com/2013/03/26/ben-carson-mother-poem-yourself-to-blame.

Franklin, Benjamin. "Benjamin Franklin Quotes." Accessed October 2013. http://www.brainyquote.com/quotes/authors/b/benjamin_franklin.html.

FranklinCovey. "FranklinCovey." Accessed 2014 http://www.franklincovey.com/tc/.

Gallistel, Charles R. The Organization of Learning (Learning, Development, and Conceptual Change). Cambridge: Bradford Books, 1993.

Gandhi, Mahatma. "Mahatma Gandhi Quotes." Accessed January 2014. http://www.brainyquote.com/quotes/authors/m/mahatma_gandhi.html.

"Genesis 2–3 (New International Version)." Accessed October 2013. http://www.biblegateway.com/passage/?search=Genesis%202&version=NIV.

Goethe, Johann Wolfgang von. Accessed January 2014 "Johann Wolfgang von Goethe Quotes." http://www.brainyquote.com/quotes/authors/j/johann_wolfgang_von_goeth.html.

Goleman, Daniel. Accessed January 2014. "Daniel Goleman Quotes." http://www.brainyquote.com/quotes/authors/d/daniel_goleman.html.

Gordon, Authur. A Touch of Wonder. Fleming Revell Co., 1974.

Graham, Billy. "Billy Graham Quotes." Accessed January 2014. http://www.brainyquote.com/quotes/authors/b/billy_graham.html.

Grant, Amy. "Amy Grant Quotes." 2001–2013. Accessed October 2013. http://www.brainyquote.com/quotes/authors/a/amy_grant.html.

Green, Sir Philip. "Philip Green Quotes." Accessed 2014. http://www.brainyquote.com/quotes/authors/p/philip_green.html.

Greenleaf, Simon. "Testimony of the Evangelists." UMKC School of Law. 1846. Accessed June 2014. http://law2.umkc.edu/faculty/projects/ftrials/jesus/greenleaf.html.

Greenspan, Alan. "Alan Greenspan Quotes." Accessed December 2013. http://www.brainyquote.com/quotes/authors/a/alan_greenspan.html.

Hahn, Nhat. "Nhat Hahn Quotes." Accessed January 2014. "Nhat Hahn Quotes." http://www.brainyquote.com/quotes/authors/n/nhat_hanh.html.

Hamel, Gary. "Innovation's New Math Forget strategy sessions. To find one great idea, you must have workers dreaming up thousands." 2001. July 9. http://archive.fortune.com/magazines/fortune/fortune_archive/2001/07/09/306498/index.htm.

Hartman, Dr. Taylor. The People Code (Kindle Edition). New York, London, Toronto, Sydney: Scribner, 2007.

Helpern, Paul. "The Nature of Reality." October 10, 2012. http://www.pbs.org/wgbh/nova/blogs/physics/2012/10/how-large-is-the-observable-universe/.

Henley, Don, Michael Campbell, and John David Souther. "The Heart of The Matter Lyrics." http://www.lyricsfreak.com/d/don+henley/the+heart+of+the+matter_200 42042.html.

Henry, Brad. "Brad Henry Quotes." Accessed December 2013. http://www.brainyquote.com/quotes/authors/b/brad_henry.html.

Hitler, Adolf. "Adolf Hitler Quotes." Accessed October 2013. http://www.brainyquote.com/quotes/authors/a/adolf_hitler.html.

Homer. "Homer Quotes." Accessed 2014. http://www.brainyquote.com/quotes/authors/h/homer.html.

Holzt, Lou. "Lou Holtz Quotes" Accessed 2015 http://www.brainyquote.com/quotes/quotes/l/louholtz450789.html

Houdmann, S. Michael. "Why did blood and water come out of Jesus' side when He was pierced?" Accessed June 2014. http://www.gotquestions.org/blood-water-Jesus.html#ixzz34wZyEuq7.

Hoyle, Sir Frederick. "Hoyle on Evolution." Nature 294 (1981): 105.

Hubbard, Elbert. "Elbert Hubbard Quotes." Accessed January 2014. http://www.brainyquote.com/quotes/authors/e/elbert_hubbard.html.

Ingram, Chip, and Dr. Becca Johnson. Overcoming Emotions That Destroy, ebook edition. Grand Rapids, MI: Baker Books, 2012.

"Innovation at Work." Innovation at Work. Audio Tech Business Book Summaries, 2001.

Jagger, Mick, and Keith Richards. "Rolling Stones Sympathy for the Devil Lyrics." Accessed October 2013. http://www.lyricsfreak.com/r/rolling+stones/sympathy+for+the+devil_20 117881.html.

Jakes, T. D. Instinct: The Power to Unleash Your Inborn Drive. New York, Boston, Nashville: FaithWords, 2014.

James, Erwin. "'Dead Man' Talking." April 22, 2008. Accessed October 25, 2013. http://www.theguardian.com/society/2008/apr/23/prisonsandprobation.

James, William. The Principles of Psychology (Complete Vol. 1-2). 1890. Kindle Edition

Jastrow, Robert. God and the Astronomers. New York/London: W.W. Norton and Company, Inc., 1992.

Jefferson, Thomas. "Declaration of Independence." Accessed October 2013. http://www.archives.gov/exhibits/charters/declaration_transcript.html.

———. "Thomas Jefferson Quotes." Accessed October 2013. http://www.brainyquote.com/quotes/authors/t/thomas_jefferson.html.

Jerajani, H. R., Jaju Bhagyashri, M. M. Phiske, and Nitin Lade. Indian Journal of Dermatology. July–September 2009. http://www.ncbi.nlm.nih.gov/pmc/articles/PMC2810702/.

Johnson, Robert Wood. "Johnson&Johnson: Our Credo Values." 1943. http://www.jnj.com/about-jnj/jnj-credo/.

Jordan, Michael. "Michael Jordan Quotes." Accessed 2014. http://www.brainyquote.com/quotes/authors/m/michael_jordan.html.

Kahn, Jennifer. "Can Emotional Intelligence Be Taught." September 11, 2013. http://www.nytimes.com/2013/09/15/magazine/can-emotional-intelligence-be-taught.html?pagewanted=all&_r=2&.

Keats, Sharada, and Steve Wiggins. "Future Diets: Implications for Agriculutre and Food Prices." ODI.org. January 2014. http://www.odi.org/sites/odi.org.uk/files/odi-assets/publications-opinion-files/8776.pdf.

Keller, Helen. "Helen Keller Quotes." Accessed January 2014. http://www.brainyquote.com/quotes/authors/h/helen_keller.html.

Kelling, George L., and James Q. Willson. Broken Windows. March 1, 1982. Accessed March 19, 2014. http://www.theatlantic.com/magazine/archive/1982/03/broken-windows/304465/.

Kennedy, John F. "John F. Kennedy Quotes." Accessed January 2014. http://www.brainyquote.com/quotes/authors/j/john_f_kennedy.html.

Kiemele, Mark J., Stephen R. Schmidt, and Ronald J. Berdine. Basic Statistics Tools for Continuous Improvement Fourth Edition. Colorado Springs: Air Academy Press, LLC., 2000.

King, Martin Luther, Jr. "Martin Luther King, Jr. Quotes." Accessed December 2013. http://www.brainyquote.com/quotes/authors/m/martin_luther_king_jr.html.

Kipling, Rudyard. "Rudyard Kipling Quotes." Accessed December 2013. http://www.brainyquote.com/quotes/authors/r/rudyard_kipling.html.

Kittisak. "Golden Scales of Justice." Accessed 2014. http://www.freedigitalphotos.net/images/Other_Objects_g271-Golden_Scales_Of_Justice_p85202.html.

Klein, Gary. Sources of Power: How People Make Decisions. Cambridge, Massachusetts and London, England: MIT Press, 1998.

Klein, Sara. "Arenaline, Cortisol, Norepinephrine: The Three Major Stress Hormones, Explained." The Huffington Post. April 19, 2013. http://www.huffingtonpost.com/2013/04/19/adrenaline-cortisol-stress-hormones_n_3112800.html.

Krakovsky, Marina. "How Do We Decide? Inside the 'Frinky' Science of the Mind." Winter 2010–11. Accessed November 2013. http://www.gsb.stanford.edu/news/bmag/sbsm0802/feature-babashiv.html.

Lehrer, Jonah. How We Decide. New York: First Mariner Books, 2009.

Lennox, Annie. "Annie Lennox Quotes." Accessed 2014 http://www.brainyquote.com/quotes/authors/a/annie_lennox.html.

Lewis, C. S. "C.S. Lewis Quotes." Accessed 2014 http://www.brainyquote.com/quotes/authors/c/c_s_lewis.html.

———. The Chronicles of Narnia: The Last Battle Chapter 15. London: Haper Collins, 1956.

———. The Collected Letters of C.S. Lewis, Volume 3. Kindle Edition. Harper Collins, 2009.

———. The Collected letters of C.S. Lewis, Volume III: Narnia. New York: Cambridge and Joy.

Lincoln, Abraham. "Abraham Lincoln Quotes." Accessed October 2013. http://www.brainyquote.com/quotes/authors/a/abraham_lincoln_2.html.

———. "The Gettysburg Address." November 19, 1863. Accessed October 2013.
http://www.abrahamlincolnonline.org/lincoln/speeches/gettysburg.htm.

Lomong, Lopez, and Mark Tabb. Running For My Life. Nashville, Tennessee: Thomas
Nelson, Inc., 2012.

Lowell, James Russell. "James Russell Lowell Quotes." Accessed 2014
http://www.brainyquote.com/quotes/authors/j/james_russell_lowell.htm
l.

Maurois, Andre. "Andre Maurois Quotes." Accessed 2014
http://www.brainyquote.com/quotes/authors/a/andre_maurois.html.

Mayo Clinic Staff. "Adult Health: Anger management: 10 tips to tame your
temper." Accessed 2014 http://www.mayoclinic.com/health/anger-
management/MH00102.

McCall, Ash. "A Timeline of Operation Desert Storm." February 26, 2013. Accessed
November 2013.
http://armylive.dodlive.mil/index.php/2013/02/operation-desert-storm/.

Meeker, Meg, M.D. Strong Fathers, Strong Daughters 10 Secrets Every Father
Should Know. Washington, DC: Regnery Publishing, Inc., 2006.

Moore, Billy. "Billy Moore: People in prison can change." Accessed October 2013.
http://www.nodeathpenalty.org/new_abolitionist/february-2005-issue-
34/billy-moore-people-prison-can-change.

"MSN Money: Bristol-Myers Squibb Com (NYSE:BMY)." September 16, 2014.
http://investing.money.msn.com/investments/charts?symbol=US:BMY#{"
zRange":"10","startDate":"1900-1-1","endDate":"2014-9-
24","chartStyle":"mountain","chartCursor":"1","scaleType":"0","yaxisAlign
":"right","mode":"pan"}.

"MSN Money: Johnson and Johnson (NYSE: JNJ)." September 16, 2014.
http://investing.money.msn.com/investments/charts?symbol=US:JNJ#{"zR
ange":"10","startDate":"1972-6-30","endDate":"2014-9-
15","chartStyle":"mountain","chartCursor":"1","scaleType":"0","yaxisAlign
":"right","mode":"pan"}.

Nicks, Denver. "Study: Obesity Rates Have Surged in the Developming World."
January 03, 2014. Accessed January 2014.
http://healthland.time.com/2014/01/03/study-obesity-rates-have-surged-
in-developing-world/.

Niebuhr, Reinhold. "Reinhold Niebuhr Quotes." Accessed 2014
http://www.brainyquote.com/quotes/authors/r/reinhold_niebuhr.html.

Norton, Roger J. "'s Invitation to Speak at Gettysburg and the Meaning of the Gettysburg Address." Accessed 2013. http://rogerjnorton.com/Lincoln58.html.

Nosowitz, Dan. "The Big Bang May not Have Spawned the Universe After All." September 18, 2013. Accessed April 2014. http://www.popsci.com/science/article/2013-09/big-bang-may-not-have-spawned-universe-after-all.

Orman, Suze. "Suze Orman Quotes." Accessed December 2013. http://www.brainyquote.com/quotes/authors/s/suze_orman.html.

Osteen, Joel. "Joel Osteen Quotes." Accessed 2014 http://www.brainyquote.com/quotes/authors/j/joel_osteen.html.

Oz, Mehmet, MD. "Carbohydrates." Accessed July 2014. http://www.sharecare.com/health/carbohydrates/sugar-consume-every-year.

Peet, J. H. "The Miller-Urey Experiment." Accessed 2014. http://www.truthinscience.org.uk/tis2/index.php/evidence-for-evolution-mainmenu-65/51-the-miller-urey-experiment.html.

Pippert, Rebecca. Hope has its Reasons. Harper, 1990.

"Politics and City Life: Chicago." September 21, 2012. http://www.chicagomag.com/Chicago-Magazine/October-2012/Chicago-Tylenol-Murders-An-Oral-History/.

Reagan, Ronald. "Ronald Reagan Quotes." Accessed October 2013. http://www.brainyquote.com/quotes/authors/r/ronald_reagan.html.

Renner, Kevin. In Search of Fatherhood: Stories from Women Around the World, Kindle Edition. Publish Your Words, 2011.

Reuther, Walter. "Walter Reuther Quotes." Accessed 2014 http://www.brainyquote.com/quotes/authors/w/walter_reuther.html.

Richardson, Renelle. "The 700 Club." Accessed 2014 http://www.cbn.com/700club/features/amazing/billy_moore040209.aspx .

Robbins, Tony. "Tony Robbins Quotes." Accessed 2014 http://www.brainyquote.com/quotes/authors/t/tony_robbins.html.

Rogers, Will. "Will Rogers Quotes." Accessed December 2013. http://www.brainyquote.com/quotes/authors/w/will_rogers.html.

Rohn, Jim. "Jim Rohn Quotes." Accessed 2014
http://www.brainyquote.com/quotes/authors/j/jim_rohn.html.

Roosevelt, Eleanor. "Eleanor Roosevelt Quotes." Accessed 2014
http://www.brainyquote.com/quotes/authors/e/eleanor_roosevelt.html.

Roosevelt, Theodore. "Theodore Roosevelt Quotes." Accessed October 2013.
http://www.brainyquote.com/quotes/authors/t/theodore_roosevelt.html

Rothermel, Richard C. "US Forest Service: Rocky Mountain Research Station."
TreeSearch. May 1993. Accessed November 2013.
http://www.treesearch.fs.fed.us/pubs/viewpub.jsp?index=4613.

Rudner, Rita. "Rita Rudner Quotes.". Accessed October 2013.
http://www.brainyquote.com/quotes/authors/r/rita_rudner.html.

SavannahNow. "Arthur Gordon (1912–2002)." January 5, 2002. Accessed 2014
http://savannahnow.com/stories/010502/LOCgordonobit.shtml.

Saxenain, Hrand. "Maturity in Motion; Design for Leadership." Accessed 2014
http://h2notes.org/maturityinmotion.html.

Schultz, Bob. Boyhood and Beyond, Practical Wisdom for Becoming a Man. Eugene,
OR: Great Expectations Book Company, 2004.

Schweitzer, Albert. "Albert Schweitzer Quotes." Accessed 2014
http://www.brainyquote.com/quotes/authors/a/albert_schweitzer.html.

Scully, Vin. "Vin Scully Quotes." Accessed October 2013.
http://www.brainyquote.com/quotes/authors/v/vin_scully.html.

Seneca, Lucius Annaeus. "Lucius Annaeus Seneca Quotes." Accessed 2013
http://www.brainyquote.com/quotes/authors/l/lucius_annaeus_seneca.h
tml.

Smith, Barbara. "Barbara Smith Quotes." Accessed 2014
http://www.brainyquote.com/quotes/authors/b/barbara_smith.html.

Solzhenitsyn, Aleksandr. "Aleksandr Solzhenitsyn Quotes." Accessed November
2013.
http://www.brainyquote.com/quotes/authors/a/aleksandr_solzhenitsyn.h
tml.

Spool, Jared M. "The KJ-Technique: A Group Process for Establishing Priorities."
May 11, 2004. http://www.uie.com/articles/kj_technique/.

Staff Reports. "Rome News-Tribune." February 19, 2012. Accessed November 2012.
http://cc.bingj.com/cache.aspx?q=ls+Billy+Moore+The+only+confessed+m

urderer+paroled+from+death+row&d=4948688248309041&mkt=en-US&setlang=en-US&w=Z7UHXv3Ox27KZy_Lzw3_JuOYtkcN4B1h.

Stalin, Joseph. "Joseph Stalin Quotes." Accessed October 2013. p://www.brainyquote.com/quotes/authors/j/joseph_stalin.html.

Stanton, Glenn T. "First-Person: The Christian Divorce Rate Myth." February 15, 2011. http://www.bpnews.net/BPnews.asp?ID=34656.

"Steven R. Covey Quotes." Accessed September 7, 2013. http://www.great-quotes.com/quotes/author/Stephen+R./Covey.

Stevenson, Mary. "Footprints in the Sand." Accessed December 2013. http://www.footprints-inthe-sand.com/index.php?page=Poem/Poem.php.

Stork, Dr. Travis. "The Effects of Suppressing Anger." November 9, 2012. Accessed 2014 http://on.aol.com/video/the-effects-of-suppressing-anger-517534016.

Storm, Howard. "Atheist College Professor Dies and Sees Hell and Demons--it changed his life." December 13, 2011. https://www.youtube.com/watch?v=kLimoqZUWgw.

Strickland, Jonathan. "How the Big Bang Theory Works." Accessed 2014. http://science.howstuffworks.com/dictionary/astronomy-terms/big-bang-theory7.htm.

Stump, Mr. B. "Phineas Gage Didactic 2 Part Series." Accessed November 2013. http://www.youtube.com/watch?v=5nr06A3cHQA.

Suzy Platt Congressional Research Service. Respectfully Quoted: A Dictionary of Quotations from the Library of Congress. Edited by Suzy Platt. Washington DC: Congressional Quarterly Inc., 1992.

Tada, Joni Eareckson. "Joni Eareckson Tada Quotes." Accessed February 2014. http://www.brainyquote.com/quotes/authors/j/joni_eareckson_tada.html.

———. "Larry King Show-Joni Eareckson Tada Story." June 06, 2009. http://www.youtube.com/watch?v=Foffh-gneRs.

Tannenbaum Center for Interreligious Understanding. "The Golden Rule." Accessed October 2013. https://www.tanenbaum.org/resources/golden-rule?gclid=CLqG85mbnroCFUFxQgodp0sAkA.

Thatcher, Margaret. "Margaret Thatcher Quotes." Accessed 2014. http://www.brainyquote.com/quotes/authors/m/margaret_thatcher.html
.

The Case for a Creator. Grand Rapids, Michigan: Zondervan, 2004.

The Case for Christ--A Journalist's Personal Investigation of the Evidence for Jesus. Grand Rapids, Michigan: Zonderland Publishing House, 1998.

The Case for Faith. Grand Rapids, Michigan: Zonderan, 2000.

The Case for a Creator: A Six-Session Investigation of the Scientific Evidence that Points Toward God. Directed by Lee Strobel and Garry Poole. 2008.

The Lockman Foundation. "New American Standard Bible (NASB). Vers. New American Standard Bible." Accessed 2013–2014. https://www.biblegateway.com/versions/New-American-Standard-Bible-NASB.

Thomas Nelson, Inc. "New King James Version (NKJV). Vers. New King James Version." Accessed 2013–2014. https://www.biblegateway.com.

Thoreau, Henry David. "Henry David Thoreau Quotes." Accessed November 2013. http://www.brainyquote.com/quotes/authors/h/henry_david_thoreau.html.

Todd, Jody. "Practical Applications for Husbands and Wives." March 22, 2010. Accessed September 2013. http://unraveled1207.wordpress.com/category/online-studies/love-respect-online-study/.

Townsend. Aesop's Fables (Kindle Edition). Amazon Digital Services, Inc.

Tracy, Brian. "Brian Tracy Quotes." Accessed January 2014. http://www.brainyquote.com/quotes/authors/b/brian_tracy.html.

Tung, Mao Tse. "150 Quotes from Mao Tse Tung." Accessed October 2013. http://www.marxists.org/reference/archive/mao/works/red-book/quotes.htm.

———. "Mao Zedong Quotes." Accessed October 2013. http://www.brainyquote.com/quotes/authors/m/mao_zedong.html.

Twain, Mark. "Mark Twain Quotes." Accessed 2013. http://www.brainyquote.com/quotes/authors/m/mark_twain.html.

Tyndale House Foundation. "New Living Translation (NLT)." Accessed 2013. https://www.biblegateway.com/versions/New-Living-Translation-NLT-Bible/.

Varun, Porwal (Bryan Dyson). "30 Second Speech By Bryan Dyson (Former CEO of Coca-Cola)." 2011.

http://inspirationaldaily.wordpress.com/2011/12/22/30-second-speech-by-bryan-dyson-former-ceo-of-coca-cola/.

Viorst, Judith. "Judith Viorst Quotes." Accessed March 2014. http://www.brainyquote.com/quotes/authors/j/judith_viorst.html.

Wadsworth, Walter J. "Goal Setting and Achievement." Bristol Vermont: Velocity Business Publishing, 1997.

Waitley, Denis. "Denis Waitley Quotes." Accessed 2014 http://www.brainyquote.com/quotes/authors/d/denis_waitley.html.

Warren, Rick. The Purpose Driven Life. Grand Rapids: Zondervan, 2002.

Wiggins, Steve; Keats, Sharada. "Future Diets: Implications for agricultural and food prices." ODI.org.uk. January 2014. Accessed January 2014. http://www.odi.org.uk/sites/odi.org.uk/files/odi-assets/publications-opinion-files/8776.pdf.

Wikipedia. "W. Edwards Deming." Accessed October 2013. http://en.wikipedia.org/wiki/W._Edwards_Deming.

Wiley, Josh. "22 Awesome C.S. Lewis Quotes." October 23, 2011. Accessed September 4, 2013. http://www.whatchristianswanttoknow.com/22-awesome-c-s-lewis-quotes/.

Winfrey, Oprah. "Oprah Winfrey Quotes." Accessed March 2014. http://www.brainyquote.com/quotes/authors/o/oprah_winfrey.html.

Young, William P. The Shack. Los Angeles: windblown Media, 2007.

Ziglar, Zig. "Zig Ziglar Quotes." Accessed 2104 http://www.brainyquote.com/quotes/authors/z/zig_ziglar.html.